AMERICAN

PROGRESSIVE

HISTORY

AMERICAN
PROGRESSIVE
HISTORY

☆☆☆

An Experiment in
Modernization

ERNST A. BREISACH

THE UNIVERSITY OF CHICAGO PRESS

Chicago and London

ERNST A. BREISACH is professor of history at
Western Michigan University.

The University of Chicago Press, Chicago 60637
The University of Chicago Press, Ltd., London
© 1993 by The University of Chicago
All rights reserved. Published 1993
Printed in the United States of America

02 01 00 99 98 97 96 95 94 93   5 4 3 2 1

ISBN (cloth): 0-226-07276-2
ISBN (paper): 0-226-07277-0

Library of Congress Cataloging-in-Publication Data

Breisach, Ernst.
    American progressive history : an experiment in modernization /
Ernst A. Breisach.
        p.   cm.
    Includes bibliographical reference (p.   ) and index.
    ISBN 0-226-07276-2. — ISBN 0-226-07277-0 (pbk.)
        1. United States—Historiography.   2. Historiography—United
States.   3. Historians—United States.   I. Title.
    E175.B74   1993
    973'.072—dc20   92-31012
                                                                    CIP

Not in vain the distance beacons.
 Forward, forward let us range,
Let the great world spin for ever
 down the ringing grooves of change.

Alfred Tennyson
Locksley Hall

Contents

Contents

PART 4
THE RELATIVIST EXPERIMENT AND ITS REASSESSMENT
1929–1948

Acknowledgments

During the years of work on this book, I received generous assistance from many persons and institutions, for which I wish to express my sincere gratitude. Professional assistance was given to me by colleagues at various institutions and I am indebted to them for their suggestions and critical remarks. Financial assistance came through a fellowship from the National Endowment for the Humanities, the Burnham-Macmillan Trust Fund of Western Michigan University, and Western Michigan University's Provost and Faculty Research funds. Gracious and expert assistance was rendered by the professionals of the Manuscript Division of the Library of Congress, the Boston Public Library, the Wisconsin Historical Society, the Huntington Library, the Division of Manuscripts and Archives of Cornell University, the American Heritage Center at the University of Wyoming, the Nebraska State Historical Society, and Waldo Library of Western Michigan University. The preparation of the manuscript was facilitated by the painstaking work of my wife and fellow historian, Herma, on the notes and bibliography, and by the patient and untiring typing services of Mrs. Opal Ellis.

Introduction

Scholars who have dealt with late-nineteenth- and early-twentieth-century American historiography have given markedly different meanings to the terms *New History* and *Progressive history*. Under closer scrutiny this apparently minor problem of terminology turns out to be an indicator of important ambiguities in the interpretation of that period's historiography. Thus, despite a considerable body of scholarly writing on Frederick Jackson Turner and the Progressive historians, the positions and roles of these innovators in American historiography still pose puzzling problems. Works on these issues include numerous articles; biographies of Turner, Robinson, Becker, and Beard; monographs on aspects of the works by Turner and the Progressive historians; and informative discussions of Progressive history in books on American historiography by, among others, Robert Allen Skotheim, John Higham, David Noble, Gene Wise, and Peter Novick. Yet, surprisingly, there has not so far been an account of Progressive history as a whole, including a satisfactory explanation of Turner's relationship to it. Cushing Strout dealt with aspects of that history in a critical study of Carl Becker's and Charles Beard's works, *The Pragmatic Revolt in American History* (1958). Despite its alluring title and brilliant analysis, Richard Hofstadter's book *The Progressive Historians* (1968) was not a comprehensive work on Progressive history. The author himself admitted to his book's limitations in the subtitle (*Turner, Beard, Parrington*) and when he spoke frankly about its original limited scope, which was widened as an afterthought. The book does not deal (as claimed) with Progressive historians in general, but with some works by Turner, Beard, and Parrington. And Turner's inclusion is justified only in terms of Hofstadter's overly broad, if not vague, definition of Progressive history. While the inclusion of Beard is certainly proper and that of Parrington understandable, the exclusion of Carl Becker and James Harvey Robinson is regrettable. The work remains a fragment, its "Background" and "Aftermath" sections notwithstanding.

The present work is designed to fill the lacuna. However, those who look for an encyclopedic work will be disappointed. No attempt has been made to deal with or even list all scholars who have been counted among the Progressive historians or have been influenced by them. Neither was it my intention to trace all the channels through which the broad public received Progressive history's message and how it was transformed in the process. The central purpose of this account is the presentation of Progressive history as an important experiment in the theory of history, although no pretense is made that Progressive history was more than a loosely knit school of thought with a tolerably coherent web of explanatory themes. Each of the founding scholars contributed to it according to his interests and inclinations. James Harvey Robinson, Charles Beard, and Carl Becker are in the focus of this book. Next to them Vernon Parrington and Harry Elmer Barnes played subsidiary roles, not quite founders and not yet epigones. Turner is included because he and the Progressive historians were the outstanding American representatives of the contemporary international search for a New History appropriate to the modern age. Because of that kinship, Turner's work offers an especially instructive contrast and parallel to that of the Progressive historians.

This approach departs from the all-too-usual habit of seeing Progressive history as a static assembly of propositions and concepts from which one can select its supposedly decisive characteristics according to the preferences of the day. I would argue that, as an audacious and tolerably systematic attempt to modernize American historiography, Progressive history had a development that mattered. Understanding it fully necessitates an attentiveness to that history's complete story, stretching over the four decades during which it tried to suggest a solution to the problem of how to modernize historiography.

An intent to show Progressive history's full complexity by relating its story prescribes a broadly chronological approach. Mindful of Hofstadter's regrets about having omitted an inquiry into the historiographical situation in which Progressive history originated, I have in part 1 given such an account. Since, from the outset, I have linked Progressive history to the international quest for a New History, the terms *modernity* and *modernization* figure prominently in the text. Unfortunately, their vagueness can be only partially alleviated. They refer not only to trends observable in contemporary life such as the progress of the sciences, industrialization, urbanization, advances in communication, and the increased interdependence of individuals and groups, but also to perceptions of these phenomena that have varied with shifting contexts from decade to decade and from person to person. Indeed, the emergence of Progressive history itself was connected with one such perceptual change from the 1890s to the early 1900s, when views of modernity were colored first by uncertainties about American destiny and tradition in the late Gilded Age, and then by the optimistic overtones of the promise or hope for final mastery of human life in the Progressive Era.

In part 1 of this book the questions and doubts raised by negative perceptions of modernity provide the framework for the beginning of the American quest for a New History. Part 2 presents Progressive history's gestation—its formative Sturm und Drang period, full of enthusiasm for breathing the modern spirit into American historiography, but also full of hedging against the radical doubts about all certainty inherent in modernity. Part 3 reflects Progressive history's brilliant but creatively inferior phase during the 1920s, when it had reached the status of a mature school—fielding without substantial innovations all challenges posed by life and by its own internal contradictions. Part 4 presents first the radical changes in Progressive history's theoretical base during the early 1930s—its brief relativistic phase—and then Beard's and Becker's search for a new stable historiographical foundation that would enable them not only to mount a theoretically sound defense of liberal democracy in the ideological struggles of the later 1930s and early 1940s, but also to respond more affirmatively to the perennial need for a sense of continuity.

So far, most assessments of Progressive history have discussed that history exclusively in its American context. While these interpretations have benefited my work, I have chosen a wider perspective for my attempt to produce for the first time a comprehensive account of Progressive history. It puts Progressive history firmly in the context of the by now century-old quest for a New History—a historiography that in method and substance fits into the modern world. At the core of that quest were attempts to reconcile the universalizing tendencies of scientific culture with different national and cultural contexts. Turner and the Progressive historians are best seen as early participants in that quest. When they attempted to modernize American historiography they undertook to revise the American sense or understanding of history, that as the basic frame of reference—a historical *mentalité*—has supplied to American historiography its possibilities and limitations. Never regimenting American views on history, this understanding has all along allowed a broad range of interpretations or (in more recent terms) *modes* for an American dialogue on history.

The result of collective experience and reflections on it, the American sense of history achieved the reconciliation of change and continuity, so basic to human life, by a unique interpretation of the relationship between the past, the present, and expectations for the future, so basic to historiography. This special understanding of history acknowledged life's incessant change but found the assurance of continuity in timeless rights and values. It even transformed these, by their nature, seemingly static entities into spurs for change when history was perceived as their ever-fuller realization. Change was no longer chaotic but had acquired a clear direction. It aimed at emancipation from the restraints of the past; change was ultimately progress. America's awareness and affirmation of that progress, together with the institutions of the new Republic, were thought to exempt America from the destructive mechanisms of the Old World: they could even make her the catalyst for history's movement toward a new and better universal order. As Progressive historians worked to give this sense of history a modern expression, they would encounter its ambiguities, particularly in the discussion of America's proper role in the modernization of the world and in their attempts to define perennial human problems as only temporary limits to the final mastery of human life.

Progressive history's experiment in translating the American sense of history into historical perceptions befitting the world of science, technology, and cities proved to be a difficult and, in the end, overwhelming task. The proper balance between the American sense of history and the forces of modernity with their universal thrust (particularly science and technology) proved elusive. That very universalizing aspect of a "scientific culture" made advisable sensitivity to the so-far largely unappreciated possibility of illuminating American historiographical developments by highlighting developments in the historiographies of those countries where the modernization process had penetrated deeply into the intellectual world. None of these references has been made in the spirit of seeing in European developments the more truly modern options. In this account, the wider perspective, far from deemphasizing American achievements, yields a fuller appreciation of Progressive history as a uniquely American response to what is frequently called the historiographical crisis in modern Western civilization.

All of these considerations have given this volume its chronological structure. A structure that was not prompted by a longing for a simple narrative but was made necessary by the intent to depict the so-far-neglected development of Progressive history. In this perspective that history's struggle with the problems of historiography emerges as an adventure in ideas, seen not as an intellectual game or as the mere changing of tools for new adjustments, but as the wrestling with basic questions about the human condition, carried out in the midst of life itself.

1

THE PATH TO

PROGRESSIVE HISTORY

1890–1904

Let us think sometimes of the great invisible ship that carries our human destinies upon eternity. Like the vessels of our confined oceans, she has her sails and her ballast. The fear that she may pitch or roll on leaving the roadstead is no reason for increasing the weight of the ballast by stowing the fair, white sails in the depths of the hold.

Maurice Maeterlinck
The Measure of the Hours

1

The American Sense of History and the

Uncertainties of Modernity

On May 1, 1893, the World's Columbian Exposition opened in Chicago with the boom of cannons, the blare of trumpets, the roar of four leased lions, the strains of cheerful band music, and the lofty words of a presidential speech. For five months afterward, the fair demonstrated to millions of visitors the vibrant energy and optimism of Chicago, not quite a quarter of a century after the great fire; proclaimed the American West's ascendancy to equal status with the so-far dominant East; and signaled to all the comforting message that turn-of-the-century Americans were able to master modernity's powerful forces. So well did the "White City's" architecture, grounds, and exhibits blend into a reassuring whole that for a brief summer all talk of perpetual progress and of harmony among classes and nations seemed credible.[1] Even the skeptical Henry Adams praised the "inconceivable scenic display" as a human creation beyond compare on the continent.[2] While a few visitors left the fair unimpressed, among them the future historian Carl Lotus Becker (already, at age eighteen, at a safe distance from enthusiasm), most people went home with their uneasiness about the fundamental changes in their world at least temporarily transmuted into confidence and hope. The changes wrought by science, technology, large cities, ever-expanding industries, and waves of new immigrants would pose no serious challenge to a country where—as George Bancroft had put it for an earlier time—"abounding harvests of scientific discovery have been garnered by numberless inquisitive minds, and the wildest forces of nature have been taught to become the docile helpmates of man."[3]

But the fair displayed the benefits of modernity to a country that harbored much uncertainty about its future. During the last decades of the Gilded Age, that which contemporaries referred to as modernity had shown contradictory effects. On the one hand it had created the world of science, industries, and cities that promised an ever-increasing mastery of human life through rational inquiry, and on the other hand it had called forth conditions that dampened easy hopes for the future. By the

1890s, social conflicts, the problems of cities, especially mass poverty, the suffering in the countryside brought on by agricultural restructuring, and the massive stream of immigrants, combined with the end of territorial expansion on the continent, had caused uncertainties about the course of the American Republic sufficiently severe as to affect the American sense of history. The latter, as a historical *mentalité,* shaped the thoughts of Americans on the universal problems of change and continuity—specifically, on what they could and could not expect from their history. In it, the actual experiences of the national life were inextricably intertwined with the reflections on that life. As an effective, perennial structure for American life and thought, it transcended being a mere myth, a construction by particular interest groups, or an ad hoc invention to solve particular problems. Life contributed the vast space, filled with opportunities, a location at the margin of European power struggles, and the decisive rejection experience, be it the collective rejection of the Old World in the American Revolution or the individual rejection by immigrants of their native traditions. That rejection was made safe by the conviction that in the institutional framework of the new Republic all change, including social and economic conflicts, constituted an emancipation from the past on behalf of a better future. The perennial problems of human existence would find successive resolutions, each of them ushering in a stage of improved harmony. Such an affirmation of change found its reassuring anchor in the view of American history as the ever fuller realization of the individual rights of divine or natural law origins, within the new republican institutional order. This order, perceived as enhancing the constructive and limiting the destructive features in the human condition, would protect America from the old patterns of decadence and corruption. It was potentially universal in application, because progress would tolerate no permanent division of the world into old and new spheres. The uniqueness of America was a temporary matter, and the exemption from the destructive mechanisms of the Old World would eventually be shared by all people in a New World. The only question was whether America was to be the exemplary "city set upon a hill" or an active force for universal change.

This understanding of history makes plausible the acute uncertainties about America's fate in so successful a country as the America of the 1890s. The concerns, reaching into newsrooms, drawing rooms, farmhouses, and halls of politics, arose because, in America more than in any other nation, perceptions of and expectations for the future shaped the sense of history. Since the long past of the Native Americans was not made part of American history, the new nation had a relatively short past. Thus, America depended on the promise of an ever-greater fulfillment of human aspirations in the future for her sense of history and destiny, her dynamism, her sense of historical identity, and even the perfection of her national unity. "Neither race nor tradition, nor yet the actual past binds [the American] to his countryman, but rather the future which together they are building."[4] The American past, too, attained its special weight and value from the promise it held for the future. To those who were concerned, the Republic suddenly seemed no longer immune to the destructive mechanisms of history, as it displayed marks of the old order, such as labor strife, sharper and more widespread inequalities, and the decay of the agricultural way of life.

Doubts were widespread in Chicago's agrarian hinterland, into which the "new America" had penetrated along the visible lines of railroads and communications and the invisible ones of finance. For many in America's heartland the corrosive effects of these penetrations were not the regrettable by-products of a new and better social and economic order but the results of a conspiracy against the good old order of the Republic. Hence the swelling of "the wail of discontent from the masses," until, by the time of the fair, the Populists were riding high.[5] Their pronouncements—while usually concerning demands for specific reforms having to do with currency, land, and railroads—were based on a vaguely defined but powerful vision of history. While some Populists called for the restoration of the old order, most of them wished to reshape the American sense of history so as to point to a new cooperative democracy based on traditional virtues as well as on the masses rather than on classes. Unless this came about, America would repeat ancient Rome's fall or become a variation of the evil European social order.

At the time of the fair, a member of the New England patriciate, with no more sympathy for the newly emerging order than many Populists, formulated a historical interpretation with cultural cycles. In the summer days between his two visits to the Chicago fair, Henry Adams discussed with his brother, Brooks, the latter's draft of *The Law of Civilization and Decay* (1895). While that "melancholy book" (Theodore Roosevelt) did not focus on America, it clearly implied that in the universal and perennial oscillation between barbarism and civilization, American civilization was turning downward. The increasingly centralized modern society, in which leaders came from the commercial class, was dissipating rapidly the pool of creative energy that creative religious, artistic, and military leaders had gathered in the period of the traditional decentralized society. Now, greed replaced awe and reverence as economic competition atrophied the creative minds of the "imaginative people."[6]

The fair itself witnessed to the fundamental tension brought on by modernity's increasingly corrosive intrusion into a world anchored securely in tradition. In its celebrated buildings, exteriors reassuringly patterned after Greek temples, Roman public buildings, Renaissance palaces, and Baroque colonnades incongruously enveloped interiors dominated by the efficiently functional realities of modernity, be they the load-carrying glass and steel structures or the exhibits of engines, machines, turbines, Krupp guns, reapers, and other technological marvels. The brash functionalism of the interiors foretold a future that rejected tradition as the dominant guide in favor of the efficiency of science and technology. Beauty and truth were to be cut loose from ties to the past and linked to the functional needs of the present and the future. A fundamental revolt against the past's hold on the present and future was in the offing.

Henry Adams, never for long enchanted by hope or harmony, sensed the tension and discerned a turning point. To him the fair represented the end of America's period of expansive pioneering, with its scattering of energy in all directions and its imitation of traditional European models. "Chicago asked in 1893 for the first time the question whether the American people knew where they were driving." The fair was "the first expression of American thought as a unity; one must start there."[7] At that time, he left matters at stipulating a turning point without characterizing the quality of the future.

The turning point separated the old phase of American history from the new one. At stake were not just the normal contradictions in human life between the ideal and the real; not that the "White City," the promise of a better future, stood at odd angles to the "Black City," the Chicago of everyday life with its pleasant residences and proud commercial high rises, but also with "the filthy and rotten tenements, the dingy courts and tumble-down sheds, the foul stables and dilapidated outhouses, the broken sewer pipes, the piles of garbage"; and not that the harmony of the "White City" contrasted sharply with the turbulence of contemporary society, where a week after the fair's opening, the first tremors of the severe depression of 1893–96 shook Chicago banks and, in August, evoked a riot by unemployed workers.[8] At stake was the validity of the American sense of history. For example, were those who now protested against the status quo right when they expected resolutions in the course of evolutionary progress? How could one remedy by a new emancipation the dissatisfaction with the delay in the redemption of the radically democratic promise they sensed in modern industrial society? Some reassurance came from the fact that, at the fair, the traditional progressive perspective was still shared by black Americans, who found their functions banned from the exhibition's grounds; by women, who—although for the first time allotted their own building at a world's fair—spoke out forcefully on the equality of rights; and, at a Labor Congress, by prominent critics of contemporary society and many of those who had so far been the "steerage passengers of the ship of state."[9] These protests were optimistic in tone, affirming as they did the still strong traditional American sense of history in Americans, including most of the nearly 6,000 speakers at the 1,283 sessions of the World's Fair Auxiliary (the awkward name for the fair's scientific and artistic conferences).

Some scholarly presentations at the fair started with pronouncements of doubt but ended with reassurances about the nature of the ongoing changes. Thus, the Congress of Evolution, otherwise pervaded by the optimism of Herbert Spencer, heard a gloomy assessment by James A. Skilton, who resurrected the ancient idea that the center of civilization and empire had moved steadily westward from Mesopotamia, making the ascending West always the lively, innovative, and upward-bound area and leaving the East with ordered, well-settled, but stagnant civilizations.[10] The world's course had involved four successive empires, until some had added America as a fifth and last empire.[11] But "just now this westward march of empire and freedom during the ages comes to an abrupt end. The Cherokee strip marks the spot, where, after ages of continuous advance, this movement, during the current month, has dashed itself to pieces." Therefore, Chicago's "Columbian Exposition of 1893 celebrates both the beginning and the end of the Columbian epoch. It also, but not intentionally, celebrates the end of one epoch of characteristic modern Western civilization and the beginning of a new epoch, in which the race is again to be tested as to its capacity to advance toward those higher possibilities from which it has always heretofore recoiled."[12] Skilton, well known for his trust in the constructive power of a new scientific social theory, found reassurance in the expectation of a more harmonious, cooperative world.

Turner's paper on the American frontier, given at the annual meeting of the American Historical Association, held that year in the context of the auxiliary's "World's Congress of Historians and Historical Students," dealt with what had been widely discussed in newspapers and magazines and announced formally in a Census Bureau pamphlet: that the era of free land had ended and America had reached a turning point. But listeners and, later, readers could ignore Turner's somber warning that "now, four centuries from the discovery of America, at the end of a hundred years of life under the Constitution, the frontier has gone, and with its going has closed the first period of American history."[13] Instead they could discern its cheerful, even flattering message, that the frontier was the birthplace of America's uniqueness, where both a new democracy and America's independence from Europe were established. Turner's account of how the shining "city set upon a hill" had been built would impress many, but its hints at the possible dimming of that city's radiance would not.

All the doubts were reminders that Chicago's Universal Exposition addressed a country that, while far from being steeped in turmoil or crisis, was undergoing a severe test of its still sturdy progressive sense of history.[14] Although the contemporary doubts of Americans about it were not unusual, their intensity and wide spread were. While contemporary Germans worried about the new German Empire's social harmony and proper place in the world, and the French were concerned about giving stability and duration to the Third Republic, they both had what Americans had not: those long centuries stretching back into the dusk of time from which nations, in often vague and curious ways, have derived a sense of continuity, stability, and identity. It was not yet clear that modernity would deprive them, too, of much of that comfort. Americans faced a starker prospect. Failure in the modernization of their sense of history would mean that America was not an exception to the coming and going of civilizations and empires, could not fulfill even a secular vision of the "shining city set upon a hill," and could not serve as the trailblazer of universal progress toward liberty and democracy. In a reversal of the American sense of history, the New World would become a part of the Old World, new only in the sense of being different and more recent. The republic of commoners would be reduced from a noble experiment on mankind's behalf to being just an extraordinarily successful republic. And natural rights would be no timeless rationale for an American historical mission, but only the ideals of a people at a given time and place. The American past would then be reflected in a national history, with memories of a triumph over an often hostile land; of a heroic struggle for independence; of a brilliant constitution-based nation building; of the moral drama of a ferocious civil war; and, finally, of a rapid transformation of the country by industrialization and urbanization—all of it evidence to the fact that, since 1776, America had acquired a sufficiently weighty, interesting, even dramatic past, albeit one that would lack the invigorating sense of America's being the main agent in the final chapter of humanity's progress.

In this context there was an urgent need for the reassurance offered by a new version of America's understanding of history, one that conformed to the cool, detached, and functional spirit of modernity without being destroyed by it. In short, historiography had to find a better solution than the fair's architecture had managed by enveloping the manifestations of modernity with the shell of tradition. The doubts that had been present already during the Gilded Age now had reached a great intensity. Scholars of all kinds had attempted to provide solutions. Some wished to turn to European interpretations of society and history. But none of these, not even Marxism, could match the American sense of history's promise and its congruence with America's development. Now was needed a modern Bancroft, whose volumes could stand on bookshelves, ready to reassure and reaffirm. And why not hope? Just then, in the many new history departments at universities and colleges, an ever-increasing number of professionally trained historians were reconstructing the American past according to new rules born of the scientific spirit. Could or would they give guidance toward a modern American understanding of history fit for a "scientific culture"?

2

A Temporary Reassurance:

Scientific History

The new professional historians of the 1890s ignored the presentiments of a dark future. Instead they patiently subjected the vast expanses of the past to the critical scrutiny of their newly acquired modern scholarship, recording their findings in monographs and, from 1895 on, in the *American Historical Review*. These historians showed a sense of excitement and self-assurance, generated partially by their recent victory over the literary historians in the name of modernity, but mostly by their conviction that they were bit by bit creating a true historical science that would eventually deliver a properly modern version of the American understanding of history. In the end, it would show that these Scientific historians underestimated the scope and depth of the modernization crisis. They failed to see that anxieties about America's destiny and their own attempts to modernize their discipline were parts of a phenomenon that extended well beyond America's borders. The claim by the sciences to universal validity, based on the impact of the world transformed by the sciences, made their challenge one to all historical interpretations in Western tradition.

After 1880, historians on both sides of the Atlantic gradually began to grasp how mercilessly destructive of their existing conventions, methods, and body of knowledge science's demands were, and how fundamental, therefore, the changes in the reconciliations of past, present, and expectations for the future would have to be. The technological world, itself shaped by the increasingly triumphant contemporary scientific worldview, tolerated no realm of ideas or theories insulated from its claims to mastery. " 'Machinery begins by altering the day's routine and ends by altering the cosmos.' "[1] In modern parlance, historians on both sides of the Atlantic confronted a fundamental change in their interpretive models, *epistemes,* or paradigms, comparable only to two other previous revolutionary changes in Western historiography: first, the triumph of Christian over ancient historiography, and second, the emergence of the secular philosophies of history, particularly that of progress, as serious rivals to the traditional Christian interpretation of history. Now, the contemporary scientific model of inquiry, with its demands for ceaseless and radical doubt and for verification of a special kind, challenged all areas of historiography—the concept of truth, how to arrive at it, and how valid it was; the perception of the forces that moved human affairs; the aim and purpose of history; the shape of historical accounts; and history's subject matter. Later, historians would discern in that upheaval the beginning of a modern historiographical crisis.

At the epicenter of the quake occurred the destruction of the grand compromise that had temporarily ended the nineteenth-century historical revolution. In the latter, the historical mode of explanation—the understanding of all phenomena through their position in the flux of time—had triumphed over the philosophical mode—the explanation of phenomena by their relation to stable and even timeless values, ideas, or structures. However, since human life both exhibited and required stability and continuity, nineteenth-century historians and philosophers designed interpretations of history that limited the triumph of change over permanence. In the most successful attempt to rein in chaotic change, Leopold von Ranke had created his *Geschichtswissenschaft*, a historical science of systematic critical inquiry that, however, still provided continuity and order through linkages to God and transcendent ideas. France and the English-speaking world remained for a bit longer insulated from the historiographical reappraisal, since their historians were literary people, not yet held to the standards of science. Their accounts conformed to the codes of literary imagination, not in the sense of fiction but in that of plots woven of facts and schemes of order that could still accommodate infinite divine wisdom, beneficent progress, or the forces of liberty or equality. But when the fabric of literary history began to fray, under harsh testing by what the age considered science, most attempted repairs were made with various kinds of Rankean twine.

Now science forced historians to face the ultimate consequences of the revolution they themselves had wrought in the nineteenth century. The contemporary scientific model of truth and truth finding proscribed exactly those transhistorical concepts or forces, be they God, Divine Providence, World Spirit, Reason, Progress, or others, that had enabled nineteenth-century historians to speak, in a world of incessant change, of a stable historical truth, meaning, and continuity. The American sense of history could no longer contain timeless elements, sanctioned by God or natural law. The world of human history had to become, if not identical to that of nature, then at least completely open to scientific inquiry and, implicitly, to human mastery. Humanity was to be "if not its own first cause, at least its own demiurge, and men were determined to discover, if possible, what were the processes by which mankind had formed itself and made its home."[2] Human history no longer had an overall meaning beyond itself, but rather, if it had any at all, one within itself.

With its traditional elements of stability and continuity removed, the nineteenth-century historiographical edifice would collapse. Where formerly all phenomena had had a reference point and all processes a direction, there were now left countless phenomena linked by connections and governed by processes as yet unknown. In William James's terms, where there had been changes within a rather steady climate there was now only "aimless weather." Some historians found all of that an exciting challenge for research, even a promise of an impending clarification of the enigma of human life. Others were simply confident of the prospects for a true historical science. And, again, other historians simply experienced a "malaise" about contemporary historiography, which, as late as 1911, Henri Berr found was "not limited to France and, if anything, was more felt in all countries with an advanced historical thought."[3]

Whence, with all the doubts in the 1890s about America's future and in the midst of the historiographical upheaval, did American historians derive their confidence and sense of positive excitement? Both came from their conviction that they had found historiography's stabilizing and ordering element, properly modern and immune to the corrosion of time: "the" scientific method. In a world of endless flux with as yet unknown structures and forces, that method could endow accounts of the past with certainty without burdening historical interpretation with a priori elements. The scientific method would be the authoritative guide for American history because it guaranteed the universal validity of interpretations.

Like many of their European counterparts, American historians looked for methodological guidance not primarily to the natural sciences but to Ranke's *Geschichtswissenschaft*. The term had long been rendered in English as "historical science," thereby conveniently hiding the great differences between the German *Wissenschaft* (any systematically designed inquiry in the critical spirit) and the English "science" (with its much greater obligation to the natural sciences). It mattered that quite a few of the Scientific historians had studied in Germany with Rankeans (rather than with Ranke) who practiced a *Geschichtswissenschaft* from which Christian and philosophical elements had been purged and which had been reduced to a sturdy positivism of documents. The interposition of consciousness as *Ahnen* (intuitive understanding) between text and interpretation had vanished, leaving the field to a direct apprehension of the past from the text. None of their German teachers had yet any doubts concerning the efficacy of the "factual" approach to capturing the truth about the past. The German anti-positivist revolt by Wilhelm Dilthey, Wilhelm Windelband, and Heinrich Rickert occurred in the philosophy departments from which young American historians stayed away because of their acquired suspicion of the philosophy of history. Thus, most American scholars had returned home untouched by the unfolding revolt against a positivistic understanding of historical truth finding. No doubts disturbed the conviction of turn-of-the-century American historians that their methods of truth finding, patterned after the post-Rankean *Geschichtswissenschaft*, were properly scientific. Yet American Scientific history also bore the marks of other models as it accommodated in a vague way Comtean and Darwinian elements. Auguste Comte's call for a positivist history, based on the natural sciences' methods of investigation and verification and directed toward general laws, found a hearing by way of Henry T. Buckle's *History of Civilization in England* (1857 and 1861). Its positivism, albeit not its penchant for laws, seemed easily fusible with that of the late Rankeans, particularly since Comte's insistence that the investigation must derive verifiable data only from immediate sensory experience had been dropped. The vague combination of modified Rankean and Comtean elements provided the core for what went under the designation of positivism in early twentieth-century American historiography, and for the assurance of being scientific.

Finally, historians did not escape the fascination with Darwin's evolutionary model. "Those of us who read Buckle's first volume when it appeared in 1857, and almost immediately afterwards, in 1859, read the *Origin of Species* and felt the violent impulse which Darwin gave to the study of natural laws, never doubted that historians would follow until they had exhausted every possible hypothesis to create a science of history."[4] From all of that emerged an ill-defined theoretical mix of traditional critical document analysis, genetic or evolutionary interpretation, and positivist faith in data. Isolated from their systematic contexts, the three elements, which when fully integrated into their matrices were seen as theoretically incompatible by German and French historians, for the time being coexisted peacefully, even fruitfully, in the "scientific" method of American Scientific historiography.

By the late 1800s, Scientific history had prevailed over the history written by the literary and amateur historians. Honors were heaped on George Bancroft, but scorn on his historical work. Once the latter had taught reverence for the American past, elucidated the Manifest Destiny, and assured the nation that it was the instrument of Divine Providence for bringing liberty and democracy to all of humanity. Now Bancroft's books, together with the works of Francis Parkman and others, were considered "mere" literature, lacking the reliable access to past reality that only a properly scientific method offered. Scientific historians established their historiography as the American standard for all historical works aspiring to be labeled modern. Their "scientific" method encouraged them to think that they had matched the inductive methods of the natural sciences, with some historians even claiming that the "Baltimore seminaries are laboratories where books are treated like mineralogical specimens, passed from hand to hand, examined, and tested."[5] Just as scientists drew back the veils from nature, so historians would pry open the doors to past reality, one by one.

In the midst of great shifts in Western thought, Scientific history in Europe and America could offer a sense of confidence because it bracketed the issues modern radical doubt was raising about historical interpretation. The proper interpretation would result from many more years of historical analysis by means of "the" scientific method. In the latter, seen as universally valid and immune to all corrosion by time, historiography could find its stabilizing and ordering element. Modernizing history meant above all changing methodology to accord with a scientific standard. Changes in the substance and structures of historical interpretation would follow from it. The suspension of synthesis had the effect of leaving the key elements in the American sense of history without a validation in a modern manner. But it also protected—at least temporarily—such a priori elements in the American understanding of history as the timeless universal rights and their progressive realization from corrosive modern doubts. For the time being the reliance on "the" scientific method was itself shielded from such doubts because nothing in the American intellectual tradition sponsored doubts in that method of the kind the fading idealism activated in Germany and the challenge of sociology brought about in France.

The wait for the new and modern version of the American understanding of history made possible the conservative cast in turn-of-the-century historiography.[6] Neither the historians' social backgrounds nor the intellectual climate in the new profession predisposed them to the radical doubt of traditional views of history or to the engagement in social reform. Ensconced in the new academic departments, isolated to a high degree from those who clamored for a new emancipation, these historians found the wait tolerable. However, the wait clearly could not last indefinitely. A long line of specialized monographs was no substitute for a modern large-scale vision of the American destiny. Yet even when, between 1904 and 1908, Albert Bushnell Hart (on behalf of the American Historical Association) published the multivolume American Nation series, with each volume written by a different and expert scholar, the hope for a true synthesis remained unfulfilled.[7] Where individual Scientific historians tried to "go it alone," the work consumed most of their creative years, and none enthralled the public with a vision of national destiny as Bancroft had done.[8] Partial synthetic accounts concerned mostly the colonial and prerevolutionary periods and were focused on relatively stable institutional structures that favored continuity. The expectation of a future reconciliation between scientific ideals and the traditional American understanding of history could not hide another significant fact: For the first time and for some years to come, American historians and their public had fallen out of step with each other.

A few signs of uncertainty appeared about Scientific history's claim to offer the complete, though postponed, historiographical answer to the complex questions raised by the modern world. Was the reliance on a scientific method a sufficient substitute for revising historiography's substance, and was the unspoken expectation justified that the resulting American history would simply update and not devastate the traditional American understanding of history?

In 1888, the keen British observer of the American scene, James Bryce, doubted that Scientific history itself was intrinsically democratic in nature when he found it hardly "the sort of work which theorists about democracy would have looked for, since it appeals rather to the learned few than to the so-called general reader."[9] In the midst of the profound Western cultural upheaval, could the American Scientific historians and their European counterparts, the German historians of documents and the French *érudits*, really do for democracies and republics what past historians had done for monarchies—endow them with legitimacy, in this case with one rooted in the authority of science rather than that of tradition? In the late 1800s, the question was put anxiously in France, where the Dreyfus affair seemed to endanger the Third Republic, and in Germany, where issues of the new empire's identity and its proper democratic order were raised.

In America, the patience with which the American public and historians waited had its foundation in the optimistic conviction that science, technology, and American democracy were cut of one cloth. That conviction came much more readily to a nation whose sense of history had been confirmed in the years since 1776 by the mastery of the vast continent, the preservation of the nation and its ideals in the Civil War, and the increasing prosperity and power during the Gilded Age, and whose citizens credited the recent advances to the fortuitous combination of democracy, science, and technology. Later on, the publicist Walter Lippmann found hope "in the fact that democracy in politics is the twin-brother of scientific thinking. They had to come together."[10] For the time being, the problem of the right synthesis remained a purely technical one: the patient application of the right method.

Hence, the historians gathered for the 1894 annual meeting of the American Historical Association must have been perplexed not only that their president, Henry Adams, would send them his presidential address from faraway Guadalajara, but even more by the address itself. In it he raised questions of substance rather than of method when he expressed radical doubts about the optimistic premise held by most American historians on the modernization of history. "Hitherto our profession has been encouraged, or, at all events, tolerated by governments and by society as an amusing or instructive and, at any rate, a safe and harmless branch of inquiry. But what will be the attitude of government or of society toward any conceivable science of history?"[11] What if that science presented findings that offended many vested interests or contradicted the nation's traditional sense of destiny? What if it demonstrated the validity of socialism as an alternative prophecy of a harmonious future? Adams had spotted the naïveté in the unspoken assumption that a science of history—cool, detached, and disinterested in any specific nation's tradition and fate—would, by its imagined beneficial nature, bring forth only findings pleasing to the American sense of history: its philosophical foundation, faith in progress, or sense of special destiny. At that point, Adams persuaded few among the public or the historians. Yet a year later, William Sloane, a historian more in the professional mold, felt compelled to quiet doubts about whether democracy could bring forth a history with an imagination comparable to that of aristocratic ages.[12] Sloane was convinced that Scientific history could do so as it was both thoroughly scientific and in accord with the traditional American sense of history. Such expectations would tax the capacities of Scientific history beyond its limits, but not until a few decades later.

3

The Young Turner's Quest for a

New History

During the 1890s, signs appeared that the claim by Scientific historiography, which identified the search for a New History with waiting for results from a patient application of the "scientific" method, would be challenged. One group of European scholars began to deny the claim for Scientific history's positivistically conceived methodology to be the proper path to a truly modern interpretation of historiography. In a fierce German debate about how historical truth finding should relate to that of the natural sciences, Wilhelm Dilthey, Wilhelm Windelband, and Heinrich Rickert were reaching conclusions deeply antagonistic to the positivistic stance. So did, in a less heated but still intense French debate, Alexandre (Alexandru-Dimitrie) Xénopol. Then three scholars in Europe and America voiced criticisms of their national Scientific histories that went beyond epistemology to the substance of history. In 1890, the philosopher-historian Henri Berr issued a still vague call for a New History which, by including many more of life's aspects, could reclaim history's supremacy among the disciplines investigating human life.[1] A decade later, he began publishing the *Revue de synthèse historique* to support the search for a new synthetic interpretation of human phenomena in the manner of a science and not of a traditional philosophy of history. In 1891, the first volume of Karl Lamprecht's *Deutsche Geschichte* began that historian's plea for an empirical cultural history as the modern encompassing new New History and triggered a bitter controversy among German historians.[2] In the same year Frederick Jackson Turner, a young professor at the University of Wisconsin, published an article in which he spelled out his version of a New History in the modern spirit.[3]

As would be typical for turn-of-the-century American historiography, mainstream and innovative alike, Turner paid scant attention to epistemology. In a fleeting reference to that area of historical theory, he quoted from Johann Gustav Droysen's *Historik* the passage on history as the continuous attempt to understand human life. He granted that historiography itself was subject to the incessant flux of time and the understanding that the past must change along with life. But in his brief account of historiography's course through the ages, Turner perceived a constant ascendancy toward the scientific understanding of history rather than a mere sequence of different views on history. On that point he remained firmly within Scientific history's limits.

Turner was more interested in increasing history's usefulness by widening its scope. History must be no less than "the self-consciousness of humanity—humanity's effort to understand itself through the study of its past."[4] Indeed, Turner's address amounted to a call for a life-encompassing history that abandoned the dramatic narratives of past events and instead presented accounts of the common people's life, looked for the grand forces shaping history, gave the economic aspect of life more weight, stressed neverending and pervasive change, and acknowledged world history as the last reference. The justification for such a change was derived not so much from Droysen as from Turner's quasi-Darwinistic conviction that the life of a society was a seamless organic web and thus must be treated in its entirety. All in all, a remarkable program that had not been enunciated so comprehensively by any of Turner's European contemporaries, and for which he would receive remarkably little credit.

Turner's puzzling failure to trigger a debate on historical theory in American historiography similar to that in Europe was not just due—as has been asserted—to his being at a university a long distance away from the Eastern historiographical centers or to the publication of the article in the rather obscure *Wisconsin Journal of Education*.[5] More important was Turner's lifelong reluctance or even inability to delve systematically into problems of theory; in this case, to develop in the wake of his address a sufficiently articulated framework for a New History. Personality accounted for some of that; the different contemporary American historiographical culture—one little responsive to theoretical endeavors—for even more.

Turner and the contemporary European reformers worked in sharply different intellectual worlds. Henri Berr's call for an encompassing synthetic history was inspired by the vitalist philosophy of his teacher, Émile Boutroux, with its emphasis on the whole over separate parts. For his encompassing history of German culture Karl Lamprecht wove together the concept of a collective psyche *(Volksseele)*, derived from German Romanticism and the early empirical psychology of his Leipzig colleague, Wilhelm Wundt, with concepts from the fertile intellectual world of late-nineteenth-century Germany. Turner's conceptual world was the scant theoretical framework of Scientific history, modified by his still strong adherence to the habits and forms of rhetoric. The former contributed the respect for the actual and particular and the latter an intuitive grasp of the grand line. At times they would cooperate to bring forth fascinating results, only to remain for the most part discordant elements. With a genuine interest in and the possibility for a thorough theoretical debate lacking, Turner could not engage in elaborate theoretical discussions on behalf of historiographical reform. These differences between Berr's, Lamprecht's, and Turner's pioneering efforts were early indications that even a New History in the modern spirit would carry the marks of what Berr would call the *différences nationales irréductibles*.[6]

That, and Turner's overriding objective, makes understandable why "The Significance of History" was followed not by another treatise on theory but, in 1892, by a programmatic statement on "The Problems in American History" and, in 1893, by the essay on "The Significance of the Frontier in American History." In them was embedded the continuation of Turner's quest for a New History, and through them he would have to fulfill the substantial requirements for a New History he had set forth in 1891.[7] His quest for a New History would above all aim at updating the American sense of history by introducing a new anchor for continuity: the forces emanating from the geographical space that, measured in terms of human life, were close to timeless (or as Fernand Braudel would put it later, were of *longue durée*). He wished to unlock in a thoroughly modern manner what Lamprecht called "this wonderful and mysterious developmental history of that great American nationality—of how from a multiplicity of ethnic groups and undemocratic backgrounds came a unified nation, dedicated to democracy."[8] Turner remained, for the most part, silent on the relationship of his central provider of continuity—space—to the traditional one in the American sense of history—the timeless human rights. At the least, it could show scientifically how and why America could realize these ideals more fully and create a civilization that was intrinsically democratic. His strongly antimetaphysical attitudes made him often speak of space as the real and only source of continuity in American history.

The choice of space also was in accord with Turner's strong emotional ties to the Midwest. That must caution scholars against connecting Turner's choice of space as the key force of history more than loosely with parallel European explorations of the interrelationships between geographic space and human life.

The German *Anthropogeograph* Friedrich Ratzel, who had toured the United States in 1874–75, had been fascinated by the westward movement. For him, however, it offered one case study from among many large-scale migrations and settlements in history whose only unique feature was the American people's superior "energy in the mastery and utilization of the land" with its sheer endless dimensions.[9] Turner was not aware of Ratzel's work until later, perhaps not until Karl Lamprecht relayed to Turner Ratzel's complimentary remarks about an offprint of the frontier essay.[10] He eventually read one of the editions of Ratzel's *Anthropogeographie*. And, in 1893, he could not have known at all Paul Vidal de la Blache's works on a *géographie humaine*.[11] Actually, the three scholars came to use geographic space as an explanatory principle largely independently of each other, prompted by different national circumstances.[12]

The space Turner chose as his central explanatory concept was America's unique space. From it he hoped to derive an interpretation of American history that would be both scientific and affirmative of America's claims to uniqueness, even exceptionality, as well as a fitting response to his own generally phrased call for a New History in 1891.

In his first attempt at a geographical interpretation, the frontier thesis, Turner gave a new basis to America's identity through a different account of the origin of the unique American nation. The nation-forming was firmly linked to the march of settlers across the continent in accordance with Turner's conviction that the proper American history "needs a connected and unified account of the progress of civilization across this continent, with the attendant results."[13] Without the westward movement American history resembled "the play of *Hamlet* with Hamlet omitted."[14] The so-far prevalent fixation on the eastern part of the United States in most of the accounts of American history was wrong because the frontier experience in the eastern parts had been too limited in space and too close to Europe to have had a transforming impact.

Turner realized that his new American history with space as its center needed to be buttressed scientifically, for which Turner depended heavily on the use of three explanatory models: the adaptation theory in a Darwinian manner; the concept of uniform stages in the economic development of all groups; and the colonization model familiar to historians of the ancient and medieval periods and of human settlements. In a most characteristic and, in the end, decisive manner, Turner accepted in each case the bulk of the interpretation but, constrained by his own version of the traditional American interpretation of history, not the final conclusions. While this rejection could be ascribed to Turner's personal inability to detach himself from his love for nineteenth-century agrarian America, it really was a portent for more general difficulties in reconciling the two demands that a New History must be scientific—that is, universally applicable in its methods and insights—but also fully responsive to historiography's and the historian's real, specific, and diverse contexts of life. For Turner that meant creating his geographic interpretation of history in constant tension with the American sense of history.

Turner drew on the adaptation theory to explain how the American space triumphed over the settlers, when it, like a blast furnace, burned off all that was of the Old World in the pioneers and made them into the "new human beings," the Americans. The New World was not created as an afterthought of the settlers or as a social safety valve, nor was it born of transferred European cultural elements. The New World and the new human beings were created when, at the ever-shifting frontier, land and settlers locked in a harsh struggle that produced the character of the American nation, marked by a rugged individualism, self-reliance, and hostility to direct control. The result was a specific American character.

In a leap of faith Turner transformed what in comparative history were typical and temporary adaptive features in the early stages of all settlement processes into permanent features of America's unique national character and democracy. Since the original ideas and background of the settlers had nothing to do with the uniqueness of Americans, Turner was left with a stark geographical environmentalism, which forced him to credit the unique features of the American land with creating an equally unique American people and democracy. Apart from ignoring the unresolved problems associated with such a causal linkage (which his colleagues pointed out to him frequently), Turner's stipulation of permanent features in American life contradicted not only the logic of the adaptive theory but also his own view of history as continuous change. But such an overemphasis on space's stabilizing influence enhanced the possibility of seeing in geographical space, with its exceedingly slow rhythm of change, a source of permanency—in Turner's case, a scientifically proven anchor for America's uniqueness and democracy.

The explanatory model of a universally valid sequence of stages in economic development derived from the scholars of the German historical school of economics. It led Turner to present the westward movement in terms of a social and economic evolution that led from hunting to food gathering to agriculture to commerce and industry.[15] America offered a unique opportunity to study this law of social development because those "layers" of human existence, which had long been covered in Europe by subsequent "deposits," were still visible there. Hence, Turner agreed with Achille Loria that "America offers the key to the historical enigma which Europe has sought for centuries in vain, and the land which has no history reveals luminously the mystery of universal history."[16] In short, the whole temporal sequence was transformed into a simultaneous spatial order. Yet the claim for America's uniqueness as a scientific showcase for a universal development, though flattering, hardly sufficed as the modern affirmation of America's special position in history. Even worse, the explanatory model contradicted Turner's insistence that it was the West that influenced the East. It also predicted the inevitable dominance of commerce and industry and the doom of the very developmental stage in which Turner had anchored the American character and ideal democracy. In subsequent years, Turner would struggle to remedy that ambivalence toward the industrial and urban America—without much success.

An equally serious problem surfaced when Turner used an explanatory model for expansion and colonization, which historians of migrations and of the ancient and medieval periods had developed and Turner had gotten to know through William Francis Allen and the writings of Achille Loria.[17] Turner celebrated its linkage of vitality and migration in a passage that was vintage Turner in its rhetorical flourish and rare in its comparative spirit. "What the Mediterranean Sea was to the Greeks, breaking the bond of custom, offering new experiences, calling out new institutions and activities, that, and more, the ever retreating frontier has been to the United States directly, and to the nations of Europe more remotely."[18] The passage reflected the thesis, directly spelled out for Turner by Loria, that energetic colonists, migrating from a stagnant mother country, typically established a more vigorous civilization.[19] Yet once more, Turner the champion of a scientific (and hence comparative) New History remained unreconciled with Turner the American from the Midwest, with a strong faith in the westward movement as the birth process of America's enduring uniqueness. He chose to ignore the model's somber message of an inevitable end stage in which all new colonial societies slide into the stagnation of mature countries. Turner hinted at the loss of vigor in the last, increasingly organized stage of frontier territories, but he dealt with it as a troublesome shadow on a brilliant promise rather than as the logical consequence of the model he had used. He was not about to quote Loria's gloomy assessment that "on the other [the American] side of the great ocean there repeats itself and is growing day by day that degradation and squalor that adheres to the old civilization of Europe as to a cadaver."[20] He dealt with societal decline only once, in the case of Rome, but interpreted it not as the mature phase of colonial societies, but as the specific failure of Roman culture. He could not accept the post-1890 period as one of a deterioration of American democracy's vigor.

The same tensions between achievements and limitations marked all other aspects of Turner's attempted New History, such as the inclusion of the common people and the economic aspect of life in history.

Prompted by a passionate populist sense of equality and justice, he had pronounced in the best oratorical fashion that "the focal point of modern interest is the fourth estate, the great mass of the people"; that history must no longer be "the brilliant annals of the few" but also tell "of the degraded tillers of the soil, toiling that others might dream, the slavery that rendered possible the 'glory that was Greece,' the serfdom into which decayed the 'grandeur that was Rome.' "[21] The Turner of the frontier thesis could justly claim that he had partially answered his own call. On the frontier, politicians made only sporadic appearances, not being the focus of important developments (with the exception of Andrew Jackson, who, however, appeared as incarnation of the democratic spirit). They were displaced by hunters, pioneer farmers, traders, Indians, and ever new immigrants; nameless all of them, influencing history in groups and not as individuals. However, Turner did not deal with the actual life of the pioneers—their successes and failures, their daily lives, or the structure of their society. His social history did not try to reveal the multitude of relationships and conditions in American nineteenth-century society but focused narrowly on the establishing of a type of people whose characteristics were those of the American nation.

In line with his 1891 call, he also had enhanced the importance of economic matters in history. Indeed, the frontier thesis relied just about as heavily on economic forces as on space. After all, land hunger directed at "free land" had been the real force that pushed the frontier forward.[22] Hence Beard was right when he credited Turner with being a pioneer of the economic interpretation of history. But in his frontier phase, Turner said nothing of the economic riches besides land that the West offered. But even though the lure of land supplied to settlement histories a plausible and verifiable explanatory force and offered to Turner sufficient opportunities for stressing some unique features of the American frontier, it could vouch neither for a unique American character nor for the incomparability of the westward movement.

When Turner addressed the issue of ideas and their relation to the geographical environment, he attempted to establish a causal link between American space and the democratic experience. He contended that when the American space had transformed the ideas and customs of the settlers by means of the brute need to survive and by the new opportunities and freedoms offered by its vastness, it had created essentially democratic beings and institutions. In a sharp rebuke to those who saw a continuous development of democratic ideas with European origins (such as the historians with a Germanist or Imperial interpretation of America's early history), he stated that "this new democracy . . . came from no theorist's dreams of the German forest. It came, stark and strong and full of life, from the American forest." It was a democracy with "increasing spaciousness of design and power of execution."[23] That Turner did not define that democracy well as to its institutions and endowed it with minimal government would make him the target of much criticism. Also, Turner could only rarely establish a causal link between American space and ideas on government. There was a basic contradiction between his simultaneous assertions of the pioneer's ideal of a minimal government and of the influence of the West on the strengthening of the national government. He demonstrated a more plausible link between space and political ideals when he spoke of the environmental reasons for the different attitudes toward government held by the settlers in the Mississippi basin and those in the Great Plains. His argument became more tentative when he linked soil and slavery in the South. There Turner maintained the superiority of the moral argument over environmental determinacy. The close linking of American democracy and its ideals to America's spatial conditions proved difficult to justify and, in the end, remained unsatisfactory.

The frontier showed its limitations as a basis for a new understanding of American history. Although the westward movement would never again be neglected by historians, space could assure permanency and stability but could not account for or support the dynamic element in America's sense of history, namely, the assurance that all change was emancipation to a better society. In matters of accounting for progress or safeguarding it, Turner was wanting. Unfortunately for Turner, he had not extended the frontier concept to that of a general mobility, which would have had a wider applicability, given more sustaining power to claims for America's uniqueness, and yielded a greater kinship to progress. For a New History with a wider than American validity, the frontier thesis proved to be insufficiently applicable to the general processes involved in settlement histories. Even at this early point, it showed that a satisfactory conciliation in a New History of the transnational demands of a "scientific culture" with the specific ones of national contexts (including their historiographical *mentalités*) would be difficult. In the midst of his growing popularity, Turner himself quietly shifted to the section as a more promising explanatory concept for a New History.

4

The Prelude to Progressive History

Throughout the 1890s, signs appeared of dissatisfaction with Scientific history as the proper route to the modernization of the American understanding of history. However, the mood was one of disaffection rather than of revolt. Not that Scientific history was, as it has often been depicted, a garden of erudition from which all interpretation was banned. The Germanist and Imperial schools of thought on early American history were ventures in interpretations. Neither was Scientific history a harsh mistress for those who remained roughly within its confines. Despite the misgivings many Scientific historians had about Turner's hypothesizing, he coexisted peacefully with Scientific historians. His appointment to Harvard University in 1910 and his prominence in the American Historical Association signaled a high degree of recognition, if not wholehearted acceptance, by the influential Eastern historians; after all, despite his striving for innovation, he "did history" very much in Scientific history's vein. Scientific history also was protected by its innovative reputation. While in Germany and France innovators like Lamprecht and Berr appeared as pioneers of modernity who were undermining an outdated Scientific history, American Scientific history, as the victor over literary history and the key agent in the professionalization of history, could hardly be portrayed as an ancien régime. Despite its limitations it appeared to contemporaries as truly modern.[1] Nevertheless, an uneasiness remained about Scientific history's sufficiency as a historiography for the modern world.

The sense that a modernization which relied too heavily on a method was incomplete produced the temptation to import elements for a new American historiography from Germany, where many Americans still went to study history. Indeed, the phrase *New History* entered American historiography linked to the name of Lamprecht in the title of an 1898 article by Earle Wilbur Dow. Dow praised Lamprecht's methods and interpretation, although, aware of the different American intellectual climate, he trimmed his synopsis accordingly. He spoke little of the *seelische Diapason* (Lamprecht's concept of a collective consciousness), a concept too easily perceived as the product of speculative thinking. Instead, he stressed Lamprecht's critical scholarship to assure readers that "under no circumstances can 'the establishment of facts' be dispensed with, nor the methods of work that have grown up with it."[2] Lamprecht's insistence that the whole governed the parts (that the *Diapason*'s changes governed all aspects of life) Dow transformed into the assertion that material, intellectual, and artistic forces were linked. Besides thus advertising Lamprecht's concept of an encompassing history as scientific and not speculative, Dow pointed out three more attractive features of Lamprecht's historiography for a New History: its usefulness for a "history of the Vaterland which recognized in past centuries conditions and problems like those which attract most attention at the present time"; its quasi-progressive emphasis on evolution with successive sociopsychological stages of an upward development to ever greater complexity and differentiation; and its inductive, even statistical method.[3]

Two years later, the phrase *New History* reappeared in the title of the presidential address to the annual meeting of the American Historical Association. This time, the phrase was not linked to foreign models, but the address itself was a feeble effort by Edward Eggleston.[4] Then in 1903, William E. Dodd, a recent Leipzig graduate, tried to demonstrate the value of Lamprecht's New History to Americans. American historians need not worry about a repetition of the German *Kampf um die Kulturgeschichte*, which had pitted Lamprecht against the traditional German historians, because in America, Dodd asserted, *Kulturgeschichte* had already found wide acceptance. Blithely overstating the prevalence of cultural history and Lamprecht's influence in America, he credited the relatively smooth acceptance of that New History to the "reasonableness of the tenets of the Lamprecht school, the practical cast of mind of American scholars and our comparative freedom from the trammels of tradition and class prejudice."[5] Yet after his summary of Lamprecht's views, Dodd suddenly converted Lamprecht the representative of reasonable reform into Lamprecht the revolutionary against the surfeit of erudition. "One thing is evident, the Rankianer have of late years carried their methods to great extremes, to such extremes that many American students have manifested a disposition to revolt."[6]

Despite Dow's and Dodd's efforts the American New History would not result from a Lamprecht-inspired revolt, perhaps because historians sensed the unclear link between evidence and the vague collective psyche (that is, between Lamprecht's residual positivism and a psychology that mixed Wilhelm Wundt's experimentalism and the German Romantic notion of *Volk*); or because Lamprecht saw in an increasing social complexity not only a sign for greater human mastery, even progress, but also a source of collective neurosis; or because Lamprecht's explanatory model, while yielding useful insights, lacked continuity with the American intellectual tradition, including its sense of history.[7]

The attempt to enhance American historiography's modernization by importing interpretive elements or schemes was already failing when in 1903 Fred Morrow Fling, who had studied in Leipzig and done research in Paris, attempted to interest his American colleagues in the European debates on historical theory. His focus was not on the New History understood as an encompassing cultural history but on the intricate epistemological arguments used by such European scholars as Heinrich Rickert in Germany and Alexandre Xénopol in France, who wished to establish history as a science on its own and not on the natural sciences' terms.[8] Yet these products of the European historiographical crisis remained extraneous to the contemporary American debate on historiography in which intricate epistemological concerns did not figure significantly. New theories on historical truth, carrying assurances that history was indeed a science, though different from the natural sciences, were not needed where no doubts existed concerning the historian's ability to grasp objective truth, given the right attitudes and methods. In the end, not even Fling himself listened much to the voices of doubt.

In those years questions about the nature and role of historical knowledge—and with it the cause of an American New History—moved forward there, in the places where, in a democratic country, theory and life's praxis meet: in the sessions of committees and commissions for the improvement of teaching. At that time the acceptance of history as a full-fledged modern discipline in elementary and high schools was at stake. In these discussions of "the best educational form for history" the questions that historians were slow to confront as theoretical problems appeared as unavoidable questions of pedagogy: What to teach in history classes? How to select the material? How to organize and synthesize it? How to use history? And how to answer those questions in a manner relevant to Americans living at the turn of the century? Answers were needed promptly and had to be in accord with the attitudes of turn-of-the-century America; one could not wait for long scholarly searches to be concluded.

It was fitting that in that debate one of the main figures of the future Progressive view of history, James Harvey Robinson, figured prominently. Judging from his committee work and addresses to teachers, a transformation was well under way in him that would be decisive for the emergence of Progressive history. Graduate studies with Hermann von Holst in Freiburg, Germany, had taught him a historicist approach to American constitutional history. In the 1890s, Robinson developed further his fascination with the interdependence of all aspects of life and of the sciences, foretold by an interest in biology and reinforced by the teaching of William James on the unity of life. At the University of Pennsylvania he established contacts with colleagues in other disciplines—the economist Simon Patten, the biologist E. G. Conklin, and the pioneering social historian John Bach McMaster—and, later, at Columbia University, with a whole group of reform-minded scholars.[9] To the American pedagogical reforms Robinson contributed ideas on a New History without ever downgrading exacting historical scholarship. Although not yet clear about any ultimate objective, he criticized it that the drama of politics by far overshadowed the story of great human achievements in other fields of life, and that the undue emphasis on persons and events obscured the more decisive forces that worked slowly through the habits of the masses. As a yet ill-defined replacement of that drama Robinson offered a wider-flung history that still oscillated between aiming at simply understanding all past achievements in terms of their own contexts (in the vein of German historicism) and viewing them primarily as stepping-stones to the present (progress). Clearer signs of his later progressive interpretation of the past showed when he equated scientific development with the gradual human emancipation from error, leading him to replace martial heroes with scientific ones. Eventually even his views on critical thinking foreshadowed those of Progressive history when he argued that, in the interest of reforming the present, historical students should use their critical spirit not only for analyzing texts but also for attacking the orthodoxies of their society.

By 1902, Robinson felt confident enough about his new grasp of the past to publish his *Introduction to the History of Western Europe*. In a period of few major historiographical innovations the volumes appeared refreshingly modern and gave Robinson one of his finest hours. For his deliberate inclusion of intellectual and artistic achievements and some elements of economic matters as well as his attempts to avoid the anecdotal in favor of the overall story of civilization, he was hailed as a pioneer and rewarded by large sales. While the work's internal inconsistencies did not detract from his success, they told of the need for a few more years of gestation before a New History would appear in a clear form.

In 1904, at the Congress of Arts and Science of the St. Louis World's Fair, American historians had a splendid opportunity to show what their discipline had to say to an America whose mood had returned to one of full confidence in the American sense of history. The doubters of the 1890s had had their years of prominence, but no hour of victory. While Brooks Adams had achieved a publishing success, his message of recurring cycles had lost out to deeply ingrained convictions of progress. The Populist fears for America's future faded in the measure to which Populist ideas were merged into or replaced by Progressive views and at least partially incorporated into plans for reforms.

Yet the early Progressive Era's confident mood highlighted even more the tension in Scientific history between the promise of a thoroughly modern version of the American understanding of history and the actuality of a discipline that stressed the gradual and cautious construction of such a version. The lag would eventually be felt as intolerable in an era when a growing group of intellectuals saw in all scholarly endeavors a means not only for explaining the world but also for mastering all its problems promptly. The World's Congress Auxiliary caught that spirit of mastering the future when it chose as the theme for the lectures of its week-long Congress of Arts and Science "The Progress of Man since the Louisiana Purchase" and wished to make clear that its "chief aim was to serve the progress of knowledge and thus to stimulate interests." That is, "to bring into sharp relief the factors which serve to-day the practical welfare and the achievements of human society." The planners wished for knowledge to serve action. That preference, already elevated to a philosophical principle by William James and, later, by John Dewey, demanded that all contributors should keep in mind the question: " 'What does your science contribute to the practical progress of mankind?' " [10] In such a setting most disciplines, even once rather contemplative endeavors, wished to be viewed as sciences bent on the improvement of the human existence. The historians, who at Chicago still had met in sessions labeled Historical Literature, now gathered in sessions under the heading Historical Science. Yet history's use for practical ends was closely connected with its unresolved problem: the formulation of a modern interpretive synthesis within the context of the American sense of history, including its philosophical foundation (the timeless rights and values) and its dynamics (change as a sequence of emancipations). The congress would illustrate the problems connected with that link and show indications for solutions, but bring no fulfillment of the quest.

The opening address for the sessions in Division B (Historical Science) by the then president of Princeton University, Woodrow Wilson, began with a note of optimism about the profound changes already made and yet to be accomplished in American historiography: "We have seen the dawn and the early morning hours of a new age in the writing of history, and the morning is now broadening about us into day." [11] Despite its poetic tone the sentence had substance. Since Turner's call, 1891, for an encompassing New History, history had become more "broadly and intimately human" as it was gradually widening its scope beyond politics to other aspects of human life such as religion, literature, and language. Yet Wilson perceived a disarray in historiography. Some historians looked for facts, and others were enamored of grander interpretations; some focused on political aspects, and others wished to widen history's subject matter to encompass all departments of life; some concentrated on elites of power, and others placed "the people" into the center of things; and some spoke of events, and others searched for "the silent forces" that moved them. Despite the lack of consensus beyond methodology, the concept of a more encompassing New History had begun to pervade American historiography. Using a more recent terminology, one sees in what seemed to Wilson mere confusion the developing contest between historians with a preference for narration, primarily of political events, and historians of a more structural and generalizing bent so central to the quest for a New History.

Wilson himself offered no clarification on the issue at the core of the American quest for a New History—a new synthesis of the many findings on the past produced by a method that was thought to assure their scientific character. He rejected the Scientific historians' contention that cooperative works by specialists (in the manner of natural scientists) would be the appropriate modern road to a synthesis. Even Lord Acton's much admired *Cambridge Modern History,* for which Wilson had written a volume, did not change his judgment that "no sort of cunning joinery could fit their several pieces of workmanship together into a single and consistent whole."[12] He mused whether the now highlighted concept of society might be the looked-for unifying concept for the future historical synthesis. Most of all, he relied on a combination of facts and literary imagination to supply the future grand synthesis.[13]

Those attending the history sessions could observe the groping for the synthesis. The broadening of history's scope seemed no longer to be an issue, when even a scholar of ancient Roman history conceded some value to linguistic and anthropological studies, and the medievalist George Burton Adams had some kind words to say about the usefulness of sociology, although he would change his mind soon. In a conciliatory spirit it was even suggested that traditional history, based on text criticism, served well for a history of events and individuals, although new methods would be needed to study the life of the masses. Yet broadening the scope of history provided the basis but not the structural framework for the modern understanding of American history.

William Sloane grasped some of the dimensions of the task, but could do little more than exhort American historians to accomplish what a French critic had praised about Arnold Heeren, namely, "that he avoided every pitfall into which cumbrous thoroughness throws its German votaries, and escaped every trap which over-confident logic sets for its acrobatic French disciples."[14] Two foreign visitors offered their advice on a synthesis appropriate to a New History.

Karl Lamprecht, whose work as well as connections with American historians—including Dow, Dodd, J. Franklin Jameson, and Turner—had earned him an invitation, warned the audience not to ignore that "we are at the turn of the stream, the parting of the ways in historical science," and then renewed his call for a New History whose explanatory key was the national collective psyche with its power to shape all human phenomena.[15] On the next day, John B. Bury issued an appeal for synthesis that eventually would elicit a much more affirmative American response because it justified the view of history as progress technically and substantially. Technically, because sources on modern history were abundant, "it is the field in which we may hope to charm from human history the secret of its rational movement, detect its logic, and win a glimpse of a fragment of the pattern on a carpet, of which probably much the greater part is still unwoven." Substantially, because Bury discerned an evolution with the modern age as its advanced stage. "The problem then is, having grasped the movement of the ideas and spiritual forces which have revealed themselves in the modern period, to trace, regressively, the processes out of which they evolved, with the help of our records."[16] Thus, a unified interpretation of history could be achieved based on empirical evidence rather than on the so-far-used a priori elements. Therefore speculative attempts, like that of Hegel "to screw history into his [Procrustes'] iron bed," could be avoided.[17]

Turner, the American pioneer of a New History, had a marvelous opportunity to strengthen his eminent position by presenting a more specific suggestion on a modern synthesis of American history. He chose, however, to read a paper, hastily finished just thirty minutes before the beginning of the session, that contained mainly ideas well-known from his previous essays on the frontier and other problems in American history, although it displayed a moderation of claims for the frontier and a shift of the accent onto geographical sections.[18] After delivering his paper on September 25, 1904, Turner met Lamprecht and Bury for lunch. Whether these three historians, who together with Berr had ventured farthest on behalf of a synthesis, had a serious discussion on the New History, we do not know.[19] It is doubtful. If they did, it would have highlighted three radically different intellectual worlds with at best incomplete communications; one more signal that even a New History conceived in the universal spirit of science would be tied, more than expected, to national traditions.

Only Robinson, who spoke on the conception and methods of history, presented themes that linked the congress more fully and directly to a New History, if not Progressive history: history's needed separation from its old ally, literature; an emphasis on the law of continuity over dramatic events; a greater role for psychology in historiography; the overcoming of overspecialization; and a linkage with the social sciences. As for a synthesis, however, he did little more than suggest a history of "inner man" in a faint semblance to Lamprecht's striving for a unity of history on the basis of a collective psyche. What, in retrospect, remains perplexing was Robinson's failure to introduce in any way the concept of progress into his program of innovation, although the progress of civilization had already become a major concern in his teaching at Columbia University.

Thus, when the congress ended, the issue of how the quest for a New History related to the modernization of the American understanding of history was left unresolved. By then it was obvious that neither the German nor the French contemporary innovators would have much influence on the eventual American New History. Lamprecht, although becoming an honorary doctor of Columbia University and an honorary member of the American Historical Association, never saw his *Deutsche Geschichte* translated into English, and his influence in America would soon wane. His home country proved even less receptive to his ideas than America. There, historicism, in the sense of understanding each period on its own and with the text-critical methodology providing the only universal element, triumphed over his views as well as over Marxist and non-Marxist attempts at a generalizing historiography. French historiographical innovators, who had been strikingly unrepresented at St. Louis, were only slowly becoming more prominent in their own country. Since 1900, contributors to Berr's *Revue de synthèse historique* had been exploring the possibilities and substance of an encompassing history. For French innovators, the properly modern historiographical theory, including a synthesis, would have to be empirical in nature and satisfy the quest for generalizations, in order to prevent Durkheim's sociology from monopolizing the scientific approach to human studies. Indeed, the changes Turner had suggested in 1891—but not his work since then—would have fit comfortably into the statement of purpose of the *Revue*. In turn, Berr was in line with the American wish for a synthesis when he insisted that the synthesis of historical knowledge, derived from "patient analytical work," was the true aim of historiography and not, as had been charged, the result of a mere yielding to a mistaken "craving for synthesis."[20] Berr and the American historians also shared a still substantial reliance on positivism.

The most successful challenge to Scientific history's claim to be the properly modern American understanding of history came from historians who acted in the spirit of Columbia University—a university set upon a hill to radiate the cause of the intellect and of reform to American culture.[21]

There, in 1904, Robinson had just begun to offer his long-running and immensely popular course on the intellectual history of Western Europe that pleaded the cause of a modern progressive interpretation of history. In Robinson's seminar Carl Becker had earlier acquired much of his knowledge of and enthusiasm for the French Enlightenment and, with it, for a philosophical approach to history. At that point, this experience still fed an enthusiasm for progress and modernity. Only his already well-formed skeptical disposition hinted at his later role as the voice of modernity's radical doubt within the new historiographical endeavor. By the time the third key figure, Charles A. Beard, came to Columbia in 1902, Becker, after brief teaching tenures at Pennsylvania State University and Dartmouth College, was just about to remove himself to the University of Kansas, a great distance from Columbia University and its reform enthusiasm. Yet the impact of Columbia, exerted by Robinson, Herbert Levi Osgood, and, to a lesser extent, James W. Burgess, remained with Becker, joining the formative influence of his Wisconsin professors Turner, Charles Homer Haskins, and Robert T. Ely.

Charles A. Beard had set out from DePauw University for graduate school in Oxford, England, in 1898, when the concept of a New History had just begun to excite some American historians. For the next four years he had studied English history in the traditional manner with Frederick York Powell, a study from which the complexities of the modern world were absent. But spurred by a sense of social justice, derived from his Quaker background and his studies at DePauw University, he had devoted at least as much time to the less-than-orthodox cause of Ruskin Hall. The latter aimed at being "of service to those individuals or societies struggling for the moral, physical, and intellectual improvement of mankind"—particularly to members of the working class so as to prepare them for participation in the imminent coming of a cooperative democracy.[22] As a student and then faculty member at Columbia, Beard characteristically absorbed most keenly the influence of Edwin R. A. Seligman and Frank J. Goodnow; one man extolling the economic interpretation of history and the other politics as a process, but neither one quite the person to help vanquish Beard the social prophet from Beard the scholar. It mattered much that both Beard and Becker shared an enthusiasm for Robinson and his drive for innovations in historiography.

The pioneers of what was to become Progressive history, but which in its early stages could have been called the Columbia University school of historiography, came from that "philistine" heartland, the Midwest. Robinson's, Beard's, and Becker's ardent, sometimes bitter, revolt against the rural or small-town world of their youth fueled their desire to accomplish the modernization of America. From it derived a fierce dislike of continuity seen in terms of stability and an unconditional advocacy of perennial change. Hence, what seemed at first glance ironic, followed a logic of reaction: those who experienced the heaviest weight of orthodoxy revolted most strongly against it. Their opposition to the status quo found its special target in Protestantism, although the three historians' views on history would carry the marks of Protestantism's dualism of good and evil and its hope for a final vanquishing of evil. As middle-class members of a new professional group they led a historiographical revolt on behalf of the "scientific culture" of the future and against the dominant ideas and institutions maintained by tradition. The revolt would produce Progressive history; an experiment in modernization that aimed to outdate Scientific history and, for good measure, also Turner.

So comfortable would be that history's fit with the reformist spirit of the Progressive Era that contemporaries as well as later scholars could easily fail to see that Progressive history was not just a feature of that era but part of the wider transformation of historiography in Western civilization. In the early 1900s, such an incomplete understanding was fostered by the state of communications in Western civilization, which increasingly facilitated cross-influences between national cultures, but in which America also still enjoyed a considerable degree of protective isolation. Yet we know now that the quest for a New History was an international one, although it would follow in all countries routes that conformed to the features of the national intellectual landscapes. It would always transform but not obliterate national historiographical traditions. Progressive history's success would depend on whether it could convince Americans—the public and the scholars alike—that its view of American history adjusted the American sense of history to the new realities of American life in what contemporaries understood to be a modern manner. In other words, that the narrowing of the gap between the "is" and the "ought," in the American sense always a question of *when* and not *whether* it was possible, could be done much more efficiently. Doubts about success were far from the minds of those who were ready to answer a challenge issued to scholars by a speaker at the St. Louis fair: "'What have you to offer of similar import?' All your thinking and speaking and writing, are they merely words on words, or do you also turn the wheels of this gigantic civilization?"[23] The future Progressive historians were ready for the turning of the wheels.

2

THE MAKING OF

PROGRESSIVE HISTORY

1904–1917

Let us reject all the counsels of the past that
do not turn us toward the future.

Maurice Maeterlinck
The Measure of the Hours

5

Putting a Progressive Accent on

Encompassing History

Three years after the St. Louis congress, there appeared the first of a series of publications that helped shape Progressive history: Robinson and Beard's much praised *Development of Modern Europe*.[1] As a textbook on European history, the work was not easily perceived as the beginning of an American New History, but it provided important indicators for the future shape of Progressive history. It showed that, at the outset of their experiment in modernization, Progressive historians were part of a broad consensus among American, German, and French scholars that a New History in the modern spirit, encompassing all of life, was needed. The agreement across national borders had more to do with the universal challenge of modernity than with the direct influence of scholar upon scholar. In the turn-of-the-century intellectual climate, the ideal of an encompassing history obligated historians to create a synthesis that was empirical in nature and at least as potent in explanation as those past histories that had relied on metaphysical entities, absolutes, or traditional patterns for grasping the totality of human life. Additional pressure for being inclusive came from the social and political ascendancy of so far powerless groups, who demanded that attention be given to the past of the masses and their routine lives. The task of casting the New History's net of comprehension and explanation ever wider was an exhilarating as well as staggeringly difficult endeavor in which every new answer triggered new questions. Undaunted, many contemporary historians set out to rediscover the strain of historiography that, ever since Herodotus, had emphasized the richness of human life beyond politics. The calls for a New History became calls for a historiography variously characterized as cultural, social, encompassing, total, integrated, or synthetic. Thus, when Progressive historians began their definition of an encompassing history, they did not initiate the search for it—as historians of Progressive history have often claimed—but put their special stamp on it.

In the readiness with and ways in which these calls were answered there showed, as they had before, what Henri Berr called the *différences nationales irréductibles* in the historiographies of countries with the most active debates: Germany, France, and the United States.[2] Progressive history would become the dominant American answer in which American traditions clearly prevailed. After 1904, the Lamprechtian model for an encompassing New History remained no more than a general inspiration. The memories of Lamprecht's visit and the impact of his published lectures on historical theory were fading, not compensated for by an exchange of personnel between Columbia University and Lamprecht's new *Institut für Kultur- und Universalgeschichte* from 1909 to 1914.[3] The French influence suffered from the lack of connections between innovative French scholars and American historians. The widely read *Revue historique* published little about the ongoing fervent discussions on the nature of history, and Henri Berr's *Revue de synthèse historique,* which, since 1900, had done just that, was less well known in America.[4] Indeed, in matters of an encompassing history, the European innovations in historiography were not even successful in their own countries, where in the class-ridden societies the attempts at a widening of historical understanding found fierce resistance for political reasons. While American historians would have their disagreements on an encompassing history, they encountered no fundamental obstacle blocking its creation.

The increasingly dense and complex interdependence of modern societies fostered an encompassing history, since only the consideration of the whole range of social phenomena seemed capable of yielding the desired insights. In 1891, Darwin's view of life as an interlocked system provided the model for Turner's view that "society is an organism, ever growing," and, hence, "history is the biography of society in all its departments." That unity also pointed to the continuity of human life in time. The histories of periods and countries were so interwoven that "each is needed to explain the others."[5] Thirteen years later, at the St. Louis congress, Wilson observed that history writing now fit the temper of the time, one "social rather than political."[6] In 1907, Edwin R. A. Seligman thought it to be conceded by everyone "that the history of mankind is the history of man in society, and therefore social history in its broadest sense."[7] By then, declarations that history must be comprehensive had long become ritual incantations. Even the editor of the American Nation series, written mainly by traditional Scientific historians, agreed that history could no longer simply refer to political or constitutional history but "must include the social life of the people, their religion, their literature, and their schools. It must include their economic life, occupations, labor systems, and organizations of capital."[8]

Progressive historians would gradually depart from that consensus with their attempt to modernize the traditional American understanding of history. The different accents they set on encompassing history first became visible when they joined the campaign against history perceived too narrowly in political terms. Although Robinson and Beard's early and pace-setting book *The Development of Modern Europe* included "the economic conditions and intellectual interests" in its narrative, the authors did not abandon political history; indeed, they gave it considerable coverage. The still strong political component did not result from a failure to accomplish a set goal, but from the internal logic of Progressive history. The Progressive historians were not bent on modernizing the American understanding of history primarily to bring historical scholarship up to date but to persuade American citizens to reform their republic. The nation was their central concern and, therefore, politics remained pivotal. Hence, like Turner before them, Robinson and Beard refused to go along with the elevation of the concept of society to a status "above" the state, making the state just another social form among many others. Only in this modified sense was Robinson and Beard's work a remarkable sign for the ascendancy of an encompassing history over any predominantly political history. Although Progressive historians moved within the mainstream of criticism of Scientific history (by then too readily identified with a purely political history), their presence in it was conditional.

On the argument that political history did not sufficiently reflect actual life, Progressive historians agreed with other critics. Beard, as much a political scientist as a historian, criticized contemporary political history as far too narrow. "Man as a political animal acting upon political, as distinguished from more vital and powerful motives, is the most unsubstantial of all abstractions."[9] In his widely acclaimed *New History*, Robinson, who had frequently spoken out against the history of names and anecdotes, poured all the polemic acid he could muster on the already fading purely dynastic and military history, calling it "a sadly inadequate misleading review of the past," an "unedifying conception of the true scope and intent of historical study," a temptation "to catalogue mere names of persons and places"—all in all a sheer exercise for a mechanical memory.[10] However, in 1912, disdain for such a history was already so broadly shared that a reviewer of *The New History* wondered about reiterating so old a contention, about which "it is hardly worth while now to write a book to maintain it."[11] Indeed, some

years before that, a staunch proponent of Scientific history had described the situation even more concisely. "The classic conception that
was controlling in Thucydides and Tacitus, in Grote and Macaulay, that
the course of political and military events with full attention to the great
personalities involved in them, and an occasional digression on the religious, literary, artistic, and social conditions, constituted the normal
field of the historian" had been losing its hold for some time by then.[12]

Progressive historians seemed also to concur with the second objec-
tion against traditional political history—that it was too much concerned with leading individuals and elites to fit the new democratic
spirit. Turner had understood the new social history's democratic implications, namely that the call for a total history of life must by necessity
wake the masses from their long historiographical slumber. The reality
of the contemporary European and American societies dictated that
conclusion. Indeed, when Robinson asked for shifting the focus away
from kings and aristocrats, he used the industrial life's very structure as
a justification. Industrialization brought much suffering for the common people, but also their emancipation.[13] In life and in historiography
the masses moved now from background to foreground, no longer content to do—in Lucien Febvre's terms—the "donkey-work of history" in
obscurity. In a total history their lives were to be brought out of the
shadows, investigated, and portrayed at the cost of less prominence for
past elites. That feature cast suspicion on social and economic history as
destabilizers of the status quo.

In Germany the reaction would be fiercest. Although German historians in the medieval and early modern fields had for decades gone beyond traditional political history by writing social and economic
history without encountering any opposition, contemporary social
tensions made the encompassing history's extension beyond the early
modern period a turbulent affair. In Germany and France, attempts at
including all people and their lives in modern history would long be denied fulfillment, since the spectre of Marx would taint even Lamprecht's
new *Kulturgeschichte* with suspicions of socialist tendencies. In late-
nineteenth-century America the reaction would be not too different, although at the very core of the traditional sense of history were the people
and their future. In the long shadows of the threat to the Union by the
Civil War, contemporary historiography, still dominated by gentleman-
historians of means, accentuated stability, unity, and continuity. The
abundant conflicts in the emerging urban and industrial society even enhanced that tendency to the point where these conflicts found no mirror
in the dominant American historiography. The new Scientific history,
though by its logic bound to be encompassing, did not change the situa-

tion much. The professional historians, although no longer primarily patricians of lineage or money, still followed a long American tradition and shunned contemporary history. The inclusion of the people into accounts of the less immediate past could be accomplished by historians like John Bach McMaster without much reference to current problems. In their later works, Beard and Robinson would show how radically different an encompassing history Progressive history would be—one which accentuated conflicts. While, in 1907, such innovations were not yet visible, the separation of Progressive history from the broad consensus on an encompassing history could be seen. With the reform of the American Republic as the dominating aspiration of Progressive historians, the logic of a New History inspired by scientific considerations would yield to the logic of a New History perceived as a blueprint for reform.

Alert readers of *The Development of Modern Europe* could already observe the authors' hesitancy to join fully in the encomiums for the masses and the unqualified criticism of traditional historiography's accent on leading individuals and elites. For many centuries, individuals had been considered to be the decisive agents of history, and the event- and document-oriented Scientific historians still gave central place to the individual. In this matter, a paradox emerged. The turn-of-the-century enthusiasm for the human mastery promised by modern science and technology also brought forth views of the cultural world as dominated by vast anonymous forces that facilitated scientific explanations but seemed to limit the capacity of individuals to shape that cultural world. Indeed, interpretations that diminished the status of individuals as rational and decisive actors in history emerged in significant numbers. Guarded by the strong individualism of the American sense of history, no American New Historians joined in such a radical diminution of the individual. Instead, they took mediating positions.

When Turner made the individual yield its formerly prominent role to the "deep-seated" forces of evolution and the geographical environment, he only meant the individual seen as an entity insulated from these forces. He refused to submerge the individual totally into any great force when he rejected the geographical determinism of Friedrich Ratzel and the more radical one of Ratzel's enthusiastic American follower, Ellen Churchill Semple—at considerable cost to his claims for the role of space in history.

The Progressive historians had to mute their attack on the individual's role in history, because they needed the rational, activist individual as the agent of progress. Woodrow Wilson had already warned that, when historians rejected literary history in favor of a history moved by large forces, they had exchanged a history which had spurred people to action by the exemplary actions of individuals in the past for one in which exhortation to activism was out of place. The Progressive historians avoided the dilemma by maintaining that their basic force—progress—did not determine individual actions but relied on them for realization. As stewards of progress, individuals could be at the same time agents and integral parts of the process.

The ambiguity of such a position showed when Progressive historians spoke about the "great men theory of history." The young Beard, more eager to preserve the individual's role in social reform than to affirm the great forces, hailed the outstanding figures of history. "Greater than all man's victories over nature, greater than the works he has wrought in the material elements, greater than all moulded iron, polished steel, and burnished brass are the world's strong, just, and wise men, whose lives gleam along the line of ages as warning and guiding lights burn along a dark and stormy coast."[14] They could be safely praised, he would argue, because, rather than being Hegel's docile agents of the Absolute Spirit, prominent individuals were products of the verifiable ascent of the human race who were keenly aware of history's mandate. Forever the reforming activist historian, Beard would not revise this early pronouncement even in the days when he resided in close proximity to economic determinism.

Robinson, more consistent in theory and more insistent on the abstract scheme of rationality's broad progress, tried harder to curtail the role of the "great men," particularly those of politics and war. Nevertheless, in his early books he celebrated his own heroes, the rational-minded innovators, who defied the great odds posed by the overwhelming forces of superstition and ignorance. Later, Robinson tried to soften such adulation for individuals by calling on historians to keep before them always "the attitude of mind and range of knowledge of the intellectual class at large, rather than that of special investigators and scholars."[15] Hence the title "History of the Intellectual Class in Western Europe" for his intellectual history course at Columbia University. The new heroes were no longer isolated innovators, but contributors to a process that in the present shaped the mental world of the future.

These attitudes make understandable why in *The Development of Modern Europe* the masses remained in the shadows of scientists, inventors, philosophers, and even captains of commerce and industry. Robinson spoke of the brave struggles of Roger Bacon, Francis Bacon, Isaac Newton, and others against the superstition and obscurantism to which the masses stubbornly adhered. Beard praised James Watt, Richard Arkwright, and a slew of social reformers, who for him were the true pioneers of modernity. Heroes, even an elite, they were, but of the right kind, and thus mostly neglected by a strictly political history. Progress relied on them rather than on the largely inert masses. There were also political innovators of the right kind: Peter the Great, the "rude, half-savage giant," who wished to break Russia's still "Asiatic" mold; Frederick William, the Great Elector, who created an efficient army and government; and Robespierre and Saint-Just, who deserved credit for their "over-earnest efforts" to establish a pure republic, although using regrettable terror.[16] All of that foreshadowed the Progressive historians' praise of the modern elite of enlightened intellectuals and social reformers and their ambivalence toward the masses.

The third contemporary argument, which condemned political history for remaining on the surface of things, met with a sympathetic response in the Progressive Era with its suspicion of the easily visible and its preference for the hidden "real." The argument raised the issue of large-scale anonymous forces. At St. Louis, Woodrow Wilson had discerned the widening gap between the "superficial" political history of events and the New History of life's grand forces. In a statement that sketched the developing conflict between narrative and structural historiographies, he saw in contemporary history writing

those who write history . . . only for the sake of the story. Their study is of plot, their narrative goes by ordered sequence and seeks the dramatic order of events; . . . there is the unity and the epic progress of *The Decline and Fall*, or the crowded but always ordered composition of one of Macaulay's canvases. . . . This is history embodied in "events," centering in the large transactions of epochs or of peoples. . . . History in the other kind devotes itself to analysis, to interpretation, to the illumination of the transactions of which it treats by lights let in from every side. . . . His [the historian's] interest centers, not so much in what happened as in what underlay the happening; not so much in the tides as in the silent forces that lifted them.[17]

At the same congress Robinson had declared that compared with deep-running currents which shaped all ideas—particularly those manifested in the habits of the common people—political events were ephemeral; event histories, even those of literary merit, offered only entertainment. Traditional political history had been, so Robinson and other critics charged, exactly such a tale about "surface" matters, lacking insight into the "real" structure of things. As early as 1894, in an article on the Tennis Court Oath, then in his St. Louis address, and later in his *New History* (well before the structuralists and Fernand Braudel), Robinson discussed the difference of event histories and structural histories in terms of the different rhythms of political and social history, using the French Revolution as the example. "Underlying the dramatic episodes of the Revolution, and obscured by them, is a story of fundamental social and political reform which . . . casts much light . . . upon the progress of liberal institutions in Europe at large."[18] To a historian four hundred years hence, the French Revolution's "romantic episodes will so far have sunk into the background that its real contributions to European institutions will be apparent."[19] Such condemnations of event history would have cheered Henri Berr, with his disdain for *l'histoire historisante*, or the young Lucien Febvre, who just then was embarking on a career dedicated to persuading French historians to abandon *l'histoire événementielle*. Yet elevating structures over events constituted not only a severe blow to traditional political history; it also would cause equally severe problems for Progressive history. The slow rhythms of change of the "deep-seated" forces would prove hard to reconcile with the reliance on activist individuals on behalf of the cause of progress. Once more, the Progressive historians proved to be allies with second thoughts in the struggle against political history.

In the discussions of the proper substance of history, the issue of the methodological problems posed by a New History was neglected. At one time, Robinson touched briefly on one such problem, that of sources. "Unfortunately no amount of research is likely to make our knowledge very clear or certain regarding the condition of the people at large during the five or six centuries following the barbarian invasions. It rarely occurred to a mediaeval chronicler to describe the familiar things about him, such as the way in which the peasant lived and tilled his land."[20] The writing of social history would suffer from the incomplete records of the past much more than would political history, with its relatively abundant sources. But as this crucial question lay outside the range of Progressive history's concerns, Robinson and others gave it scant attention. Progressive history's social history would focus on the general dynamics of American society and deal with the multitude of structures and processes strictly in reference to it.

In their *Development of Modern Europe*, Beard and Robinson did show awareness for the dilemmas posed by the quest for a New History. The phrase *all of life* evoked the enthusiasm of historians, but also well-nigh crushed them under the weight of its obligation to find, explain, order, and relate a myriad of phenomena. With the traditional guarantors of continuity and meaning declared to be illegitimate in a scientific age, with the narrative political history of events and persons found to be inappropriate, and the mass of data multiplying rapidly, the task of synthesis became exceedingly complex. The danger of becoming encyclopedic was ever present. At the same time, the pressure on historians increased to redeem their promise of a scientific history with clear principles of unity and continuity as well as universally valid findings. A mass of disjointed elements could not be the final state of any New History that aimed to reflect the dynamics of modern life. After all, even the Scientific historians promised more than that in due time.

On this point, the Progressive historians had a substantial advantage because they claimed to have found the synthetic principle of the New History: Progress provided the direction for human history, or more accurately, for the history of Western civilization. Now the structures and processes of life in the industrial and urbanized Western civilization demanded a New History that understood and actively supported history's trend. In providing one, the Progressive historians distanced themselves from the Scientific historians, who still insisted that scientific historiography meant to interpret gradually and narrowly, always guided by the sufficiency of facts. They also separated themselves from Turner. And they leaped over the epistemological problematics of the German historiographical debate, and did not choose the forever experimental approach toward an encompassing history of the later French New History, which was just becoming visible in its outlines.

Progressive history would become a composite interpretation of history in which elements affirming the transnational tendencies of science, technology, and industry with their impact on human life were intertwined with those stressing the uniqueness in the American understanding of history. The attuning to each other of a general New History and the specific American New History would be the subject of the grand experiment. For it Progressive historians would have to perform a series of complex tasks: give progress a modern justification; find the proper relationship of the present to the past; locate history properly in the now wider universe of inquirers into human life (including the new social sciences); sort out the grand forces that contributed to progress; and finally, describe more specifically the future as the goal of history.

6

The Redefinition of History's

Truth and Usefulness

Much has been said about Progressive history being a part of the pragmatic revolt (Cushing Strout) or the revolt against formalism (Morton White), which proclaimed the dominance of change over continuity in a world perceived as an open process. Therefore, the Progressive historians should have triggered a fundamental and fierce theoretical debate on the new ways needed for truth finding, if not on all of the theory of history. Yet Robinson and Beard's *Development of Modern Europe* gave a good indication of what actually happened, when the authors remained mostly silent on epistemology or, to put it less technically, on how historians arrived at conclusions of sufficient certainty. The ensuing debate would focus on the role of facts in historical truth-finding but have a severely limited scope.

The Progressive historians had no basic quarrel with the Scientific historians' affirmation of correctly ascertained "solid" facts—that is, small-scale exact reflections of past reality, conceived as discrete entities constituted by life itself and not by the historians' judgments. Although Scientific historians readily conceded that in historiographical practice they fell short of a complete match of past reality and account, they experienced none of the doubts about their methods which could be found even in such orthodox contemporary European handbooks of historical scholarship as *Introduction aux études historiques* (1898) by Charles Victor Langlois and Charles Seignobos and *Lehrbuch der historischen Methode* (1889) by Ernst Bernheim. Up to a certain point, even Progressive historians agreed with Dunning that "the absorbing and relentless pursuit of the objective fact—of the thing that actually happened in exactly the form and manner of its happening, is, I take it, thus, the typical function of the modern devotee of history."[1] However, they would stress that this was a preliminary function only. Consequently, the proponents of an American New History, first Turner and then the Progressive historians, did not mount an all-out assault on the concept of "solid" facts.

In 1891, Turner had raised briefly Droysen-inspired doubts about timelessly valid, fact-based histories, and then, not willing to forego the emphasis on facts or to engage in intricate theoretical debates, he had left it at that. Throughout his career he would maintain only that facts alone did not suffice, implying the possibility of establishing facts free of interpretive elements.

Beard, who after 1908 gradually abandoned the concept of isolated facts and of historical accounts as automatic derivatives of facts, but not that of positivist fact finding, made only sporadic and peripheral comments on the matter. Thus, against William Sloane's well-intentioned but incautious remark that historians "must have minds subtle, conscientious, and accurate—minds with a power and aptitude for minutiae, with a patience and endurance which know no bounds, honest minds incapable of even self-deception" stood Beard's contempt for history conceived as an adding machine.[2] He could have argued more persuasively and pointedly—in the manner of the contemporary French scholar Paul Lacombe—that a surfeit of facts tended to destroy certainty rather than establish it, as those who set out to "build" factual total histories were finding out.[3]

Robinson, who between 1904 and 1912 dealt much with historical theory, also touched only intermittently upon the central issue of the relationship between the historians' facts and the reality of the past. In 1904, he found it painful that history's claim to be a science would never be fulfilled, since historical accounts "must forever rest upon scattered and unreliable data, the truth of which we too often have no means of testing."[4] No further epistemological inquiry followed that insight. Instead, in his book bearing the programmatic title *The New History* (1912), Robinson preferred to wage a fierce polemic against historical works written in the "factual manner," in which he spelled out the central position of Progressive historians on matters of historical facts. It was not how facts were established that needed discussion, but how they were weighed and arranged, and at which point they sufficed to yield the proper synthesis. When Robinson found sensationalism, dramatic effects, partisanship, and chronology insufficient principles of order, he refocused the contemporary historiographical debate about facts on a specific question: What was the proper principle of order for the truly modern historical synthesis?

Robinson pointed here to the basic disagreement between Scientific and Progressive historians. At issue was not whether facts could be established independent of interpretation or whether these facts governed interpretation, but when fact-gathering could yield its dominance to the process of synthesis without endangering history's scientific status. The Progressive historians' criticism of the Scientific historians' reluctance to proceed to a synthesis was not, as has often been claimed, a pioneering act. Even Scientific historians had charged that many of their colleagues were oblivious of synthesis, and content with the mere collection of facts; "Augustuluses" bent on reigning over minute subject matter areas; and people who "have diligently spent their intensive labor upon a few acres of ground, . . . and have displayed, the while, very naively, the provincial spirit of small farmers."[5] William Sloane accused them of remaining content with history as "a mosaic of details, without design or outline, like some cathedral windows in England," and of being mere "missionaries of chaos."[6] Already in 1885, one of the pioneers of Scientific history had emphasized in Buckle's manner that only "a philosophical synthesis" of human affairs could endow special investigations and discoveries with value.[7] The fervent debates between the partisans of the Germanist and Imperial schools over the proper interpretation of American colonial history also witnessed to a concern with synthesis.

However, Scientific historians, following the logic of their epistemology, insisted that a true synthesis can come only at that distant point where data would be plentiful enough for historians to form an accurate picture of the past with an absolute minimum of interpretive interference. In the meantime, the collection of facts would have to furnish "an all-engrossing occupation for many who might otherwise have tried their hands, and the patience of their readers, in the hopeless task of synthesizing."[8] It was all a matter of patience. In 1909, in the face of increasing pressure from social scientists and Progressive historians on behalf of a prompt synthesis, George Burton Adams reiterated that "at the very beginning of all conquest of the unknown lies the fact, established and classified to the fullest extent possible at the moment."[9] The building of the body of facts had to surpass in importance all speculation for a long time to come. The task constituted the mark of professionalism for the young discipline of history.

Progressive historians joined reformers in other countries in declaring such a wait to be intolerable. In France, Berr pushed for a synthesis, as did Paul Lacombe, who pleaded that "without erudition, no history; but without history as the final product, erudition resembles an uncompleted edifice, which lacks that which justifies it, the possibility of being habitable."[10] And Progressive historians would agree with Lamprecht's confession that for him " 'the greatest sin of the historian of to-day is the piling up of facts based on poorly digested materials. Of such works we have enough and to spare; indeed we are about buried beneath these uncritical productions. To bring out of the chaos of evidence and the heaps of books a simple, straightforward account of the historical phenomena of our time has been my steadfast purpose.' "[11]

However, the Progressive historians differed decisively not only from the Scientific historians but also from the European New Historians when they suggested that the wait could end because the pattern of progress was already discernible with certainty from the available facts. Progressive historians could do so because they made a crucial compromise on the issue of facts and their relation to synthesis. Except for Becker, they did not contest that facts could be established that were reasonably free from interpretive elements—that is, not decisively affected by the historians' experience and context. In a decisive turn, the Progressive historians maintained that from the available body of facts it could be concluded definitively that human history followed the path of progress. Since the pattern of progress derived its authority from facts, and these in turn depended on progress for their meaning, Progressive history had established a seamless unity between the facts and interpretation. At that point, the actual past and the image of it coincided. This certainty gave Progressive history its firm theoretical base and persuasive power for over two decades. Epistemological debates or a revolt against positivism became superfluous, even self-destructive, when interpretation had a stable basis in the facts-guided conclusion that history was progress; a progress that was no mere interpretive construct by historians but the ordering principle embedded in reality itself; one that fit to the world of constant flux. The perennial issue of the congruence between the past as reality and the past as perception had been settled conclusively. Progressive historians considered their foundation for progress to be empirical, even scientific, and hence free of any metaphysical or a priori elements. All of that held out the promise for a successful and frictionless modernization of the traditional American understanding of history. On the other hand, it was also true that the theoretical foundation of Progressive history resulted from a historiographical coup d'état rather than a genuine revolution.

In a foreshadowing of his peculiar role as the resident radical modernist in Progressive history, Becker threatened the key compromise when he doubted the status of facts as mirrors of past reality. Distrustful of certainties since his break with the Methodism of his youth, but not yet resigned to the unattainability of truth, Carl Becker dug deeper than his colleagues. The doubts he cast on the certainty of even critically ascertained facts resembled those voiced by European scholars, although, at that point, he knew little of them. When the University of Kansas professor extended his and modernity's habit of radical doubt to facts, he discovered in them an element of "imagination." He criticized the view that "the historical reality, the 'fact,' is a thing purely objective, that does not change; a thing, therefore, that can be established once for all beyond any peradventure." Instead, "the historical fact is a thing wonderfully elusive after all, very difficult to fix, almost impossible to distinguish from 'theory,' to which it is commonly supposed to be so completely antithetical."[12] Thus, he concluded that "the reality of history has forever disappeared, and the 'facts' of history, whatever they once were, are only mental images or pictures which the historian makes in order to comprehend it."[13] Becker left it at that, declining Fling's earlier suggestions to join German scholars (such as Dilthey, Rickert, and Windelband) in their attempts to find a new coexistence of the subjective and the objective. And, despite his affinity for French thought, Becker seemingly had not followed Fling's advice to study Paul Lacombe's and Alexandre Xénopol's thoughts on historiography.[14] He also showed no awareness of the more traditional French critical remarks about a pure empiricism of facts, such as Charles Seignobos's insistence that since the document was only a remainder of past reality—an isolated trace of it—the usable fact was constructed from it by the imagination of the historian. This was an argument identical with Becker's, whose doubts proceeded along contemporary European lines, although in his case the doubts were prompted less by conclusions reached in the context of a systematic historical theory than by philosophical doubts of a personal origin. That made it easier for Becker to keep his doubts a private element, separate from some of his other assertions that contradicted them, and live for some more years in the community of Scientific and Progressive historians as a regular and nondisruptive member.

Becker's provocative article sparked no open debate. A few Scientific historians responded in letters to Becker, making points many others silently affirmed. Charles Haskins conceded that the historian's detachment was flawed, but pleaded that there was "no reason why, in most kinds of works, the greatest possible amount of detachment should not be striven for." Fling, too, criticized Becker's all-or-nothing proposition. In its stead he suggested that where facts were "numerous enough to make a causal series possible, *trained scientists* will hardly differ in opinion *as to what took place,* no matter what their opinion may be as to the good or evil involved in the event" (emphasis in original).[15] Most significant is that both Robinson and Beard let silence reflect their lack of concern about the matter.

There was in all of that a contradiction. On the one hand, Progressive historians claimed for themselves in matters of historical truth what W. B. Yeats granted to the poet—that he "can know the ancient records and be like some mystic courtier who has stolen the keys from the girdle of Time, and can wander where it please him amid the splendours of ancient Courts."[16] On the other hand, they felt as full-fledged participants in the pragmatic revolt, with its enthusiasm for change and its hostility to fixity of all kinds. That revolt was part of a crucial development in Western thought, which, in the absence of any reality transcending the empirical range of life, immersed all truth finding into life. When historians on both sides of the Atlantic had to cope with this situation, the Progressive historians turned to pragmatism. One pragmatic philosopher, John Dewey, rendered considerable help at that point. Robinson, Beard, and, in part, Becker, although enamored by William James's open universe and view of human actions as responses to life and not theory, always remained closer to John Dewey's pragmatism (instrumentalism), which spoke of scholarly work as a relentlessly experimental and forever open inquiry that changed life in the process. Yet it was instrumentalism's basic presupposition, occasionally illuminated but never justified systematically, that in the end the inquiry would produce only progress toward a more fully developed, cooperative democratic society. In Dewey's pragmatism the affinity between science and democracy was a "given." His acceptance of this fixed basic truth into his world of ceaseless change was the reassuring philosophical counterpart to the Progressive historians' compromise with a positivist certainty. Hence, the immersion of the historian and of historical reason into the flow of life produced in Progressive history a truth that represented more than the ad hoc adaptations envisioned by William James, and none of the problems it produced for some of the European innovators.

These innovators attempted to save the trustworthiness of historical truth in the new intellectual situation in which the void, created by the absence of the traditional structures of meaning, was being increasingly filled by views of the world as a well-nigh unfathomable manifestation of an onrushing force, vaguely referred to as Life. For Henri Bergson it was the *élan vitale;* for Émile Boutroux a spiritual, creative force; for Sigmund Freud the pan-erotic impulse of the "id"; and for Wilhelm Dilthey, *Leben.* Historical accounts became glimpses at Life by observers, who themselves were immersed in and swept along by Life's current. The historian's consciousness and the "outside" became intertwined, leading to an intense and on the whole inconclusive debate on historical theory in the German and, to a lesser degree, in the French search for New History's appropriately modern epistemology.

German scholars, who already with Hegel had started the submersion of person and mind into a vast cosmic flux, encountered the greatest difficulties and hence plumbed the issue most deeply. So far, there had been the assurance that the human consciousness was linked to an objective spirit as the constitutive force of all reality. That link had made possible an authoritative historical knowledge in the midst of constant flux. With the stabilizing objective spirit gone, German scholars in the field of human studies were set adrift. Wilhelm Dilthey, convinced that the historian as an integral part of life had available the special facility of "understanding," searched fervently for permanently valid categories and concepts of historical thought, only to voice in his old age despair about the "anarchy of opinions." Max Weber had recourse to the ideal types (*Idealtypen*) as temporary elements of order, constructed to shed the light of rational inquiry on segments of the world now perceived as intrinsically irrational. In contrast to the optimistic process philosophy of Dewey, Dilthey mirrored a more resigned mood when he offered the consoling message that the realization and acceptance of "the finitude of all historical phenomena, of every human and social situation, and the relativity of every kind of belief is the ultimate step toward the liberation of the human being." Until the 1920s, such a view of historiography (historicism) had nothing to offer to Progressive history, still confident that it possessed the truth, one that fit the world seen as relentless process, but it would eventually exert a decisive influence on Beard and Becker.[17]

Progressive historians could have felt more kinship with the innovative French historians, such as Henri Berr, and, later, Lucien Febvre, who, inspired by the vitalist philosophies of Henri Bergson and Émile Boutroux, would try to match the vast and dynamic unity of life with a total or synthetic history. They defused the threat to historical truth, posed by the irrationalism inherent in vitalism, when they kept intact a residual positivism with a clear separation of subject and object; Berr would still speak of *la bonne méthode*. And, goaded by the threat to history from Émile Durkheim's sociology, the French innovators asserted the existence of social structures that persisted through all but long-range changes. Rational, even objective, explanations were indeed possible. Yet even if the voice of Berr's reform attempts, the *Revue de synthèse historique,* had been read by more American scholars than it was, few of them would have found the theoretical discussions in it especially convincing. There was simply no great desire for sophisticated epistemological arguments or an empirical historicism as long as progressive answers within the perimeter of the American sense of history were still available.[18] When Progressive history became the dominant American New History, it in effect provided another shield to American historiography against the increasing tendency in modern thought to deny positivism's strict separation of the consciousness of the inquiring scholar from the "outside" world.

Progressive historians gleaned a supplementary scientific support for progress from the concept of evolution. Just as Scientific historians and Turner had done for their purposes, they fell back on that concept when they wished to recast the meaning of progress in more modern terms. In the early 1900s, the concept of progress still carried many features impressed on it by the eighteenth-century philosophy of reason and by Bancroft's providential view. The use of the term evolution resulted less from a clear conceptual analysis than from the dictates of convenience and of conformity to the contemporary enthusiasm for Darwinism. Historians, too, were still under the spell of the "first day of October, 1859, [when] the Mosaic cosmogony finally gave place to the Darwinian theory of evolution." Making history the story of evolution gave history a scientific quality, as it could cease "to be a mere narrative, made up of disconnected episodes having little or no bearing on each other."[19] Even Henry Adams maintained that scholarly immortality would come to the person who succeeded in demonstrating that the human past was governed by laws of evolution.[20]

Reformers among historians, who were impressed by the much more intense interdependence of all aspects of life in the new industrial and urban society, found the concept of evolution useful. It gave order to a mass of phenomena, seemingly had a beneficial aim, appeared to be empirical, and could be left sufficiently vague to serve various purposes. In his summons to a New History, Turner had spoken of society as an organism and of history as evolution. And Dow could assert that "the new history—and herein lies its really fundamental feature—holds to the principle of describing the human past from the point of view of rational evolution."[21] The Progressive historians followed common usage and expectations when they treated evolution as a synonym for a development "upward" or progress. They could plead that their view of history as relentless change without fixed points avoided the contradiction between the Scientific historians' simultaneous affirmation of evolution with its developmental scheme and the basically mechanistic model of physics with its repetitive characteristics, which remained a still strong second theoretical basis for Scientific historians. In contrast to other post-Darwinists, Progressive historians also ignored such Darwinistic concepts as the struggle for existence, the survival of the fittest, and a pure environmentalism, which could not be accommodated into their view of a progress based on the collective increase of rationality and on rational efforts at reform. But evolution offered the necessary sanction of science for a progressive development if one stressed the continuous emergence of the complex from the simple and then declared the complex to be "better." In this modified form, evolution also fit tolerably well to the Enlightenment's views on progress so deeply embedded in the American sense of history.

With progress established as the objective order on a presumably empirical basis, Progressive historians could proceed with the reconstruction in the modern spirit of those elements in Scientific history that were seen as impediments to a dynamic historiography: the traditional views on objectivity and the past's hold on the present and future.

Objectivity, as conceived by historians from Thucydides to the Rankeans, had always meant to grasp the reality of the past by using reflective reason, which, with much effort, had been detached to the highest degree possible from the historian's situation in life. Historians were exhorted to create historical truth in a sort of "internal forum" where the historian's reason, deliberately detached from the passions, preferences, and concerns of daily life and guided by strict rules, would discover timelessly true facts and construct from them statements about the past.[22] While for Bancroft the quest for objective truth was still a sacred duty because "the submission of reason to prejudice would have a deeper criminality; for he [the historian] cannot neglect to be impartial without at once falsifying nature and denying providence," that moral, even metaphysical, obligation changed for Scientific historians into the duty to avoid error for the sake of a pure science of history.[23] In their "internal forum," rigorous procedures of investigation, considered to be scientific, now assisted the historian's intention to be unbiased.

Prior to the late 1920s, the feasibility of objectivity as such was not at issue between Progressive and Scientific historians. First, Scientific historians themselves knew full well that the "internal forum" was not foolproof because technical flaws in the process (a missing source here, a remnant of life's passions there) made the results imperfect and, hence, corrective changes in what was accepted as historical "truth" were inevitable. Even for them, full objectivity was a "noble dream," but one that inspired rigorous research, continuously corrected in a scholarly community. Second, the pioneers of Progressive history had themselves been educated to respect the traditional rules of investigation and evidence, including objectivity. They had no desire to be methodological iconoclasts, and not much opportunity to be, since, in their mature years, they produced mainly works of an interpretive nature, based on little original research. Third, given their compromise on facts, a rejection of objectivity as unfeasible would have been even then as destructive an experience for Progressive history as it would later on prove to be. Becker would demonstrate that point as early as 1926.

At issue was the Progressive historians' new understanding of objectivity, which reflected their compromise on facts. They conceded to traditional objectivity a determining role in establishing that body of facts which sufficed to reveal progress as the structure and force of history. However, once progress had been recognized as the objective context of all of human history, objectivity was defined as writing history in the context of the known all-pervasive process—progress—which assigned each fact its logical place. That obligated historians not, as hitherto, to be uncommitted so as to avoid any bias, but to align their thought and actions with history's known course. Reason need no longer be sheltered from the historian's context in order to find the general truth. To the contrary, it was to be an instrument for the demonstration, affirmation, and realization of the already visible truth. Once more, objectivity had acquired a moral dimension, as all history must be written on behalf of progress. Activist affirmation took the place of scholarly asceticism. This solution to the objectivity problem makes it obvious that, until the late 1920s, the label "relativist" did not fit Progressive history—not if one uses the term in its prevailing sense to imply that a historical truth changes from period to period, person to person, cultural context to cultural context without common reference point or standard. Progressive historians knew an absolute standard in the reality of a clearly defined progress.

Carl Becker, the keenest analytical mind among the Progressive historians, lashed out at the Scientific historians for maintaining that to be scientific meant "to assume, in respect to historical events, the objective and detached attitude of mind with which the scientist regarded natural phenomena."[24] Such an ideal demanded that histories should be prepared "'with as much supreme indifference as if they were written in another planet,'" and later he would call the traditional concept of objectivity the rigor mortis of historical research.[25] Like Robinson and Beard, Becker was not disturbed by the prospect of relativism after the "internal forum" had been rejected. Characteristically, his tranquillity resulted not from the assurance derived from progress as anchor of truth but from his denial that stable truth had ever resulted from any method. When "historians, with justifiable pride in their achievements, have sometimes supposed that a method of studying history has at last been discovered which owes nothing to time or place," they had harbored an illusion.[26] Denying, as all Progressive historians would, any distinction between a deliberately reflective reason and an engaged instrumental reason—the one striving to transcend all specific contexts and the other to serve life residing in them—he could say that "even the will to be purely objective is itself a purpose, becoming not infrequently a passion," and that "complete detachment would produce few histories and none worth while; for the really detached mind is a dead mind."[27] At the time, Becker's faith in progress was still sufficiently strong to prevent him from realizing or spelling out the message in a truly instrumental historiography that progress, too, was not a force inherent in the world but the result of an act of will in interpretation. Therefore, if the traditional objectivity were abandoned, historians must face up to no objectivity at all, not just a modified version of it. Once again, Becker did not press his points, and his colleagues were not eager to do so.

The second element in the prevailing historical theory that Progressive history wished to see revised was the traditional view of the usefulness of history—or, as they put it, how much the present should be guided by the past. Historians had so far spoken of such usefulness in terms of the lessons derived from the past, relying on similar structures and recurrent patterns in the human condition throughout the ages. Scientific historians were neither discouraged by how little the lessons of history had accomplished nor led by their own strict rules of evidence into a splendid uselessness. They were willing to teach lessons before the last fact was in, because although historians could wait, the nation could not. In the creation of national unity out of a growing ethnic diversity, the academic historians and the various commissions for the reform of the study of history in public schools saw a useful civic role for history. Thus, they viewed a course in American history "as the best preparation for civic duties and for the comprehension of the meaning of American society."[28]

Progressive historians rejected such a definition of usefulness in terms of the traditional "lessons-from-history" approach because it assumed those timeless structures in human life that were anathema to them. Asking for these lessons to be heeded encouraged citizens to adapt to circumstances of long-vanished eras. Even worse, such lessons escalated the temporary limits encountered by human actions in past periods into permanent human limitations. Perhaps the immigrant children should not have been encouraged to conform to the given structures of American life that mirrored the past, but should have been encouraged to shape that very life anew.

Accordingly, Progressive historians never tired of condemning as obstacles to progress's course all lessons based on "Platonic ideas, Aristotelian essences, the Christian dogma of special creation, and 'eternal verities' in general," as well as the tenets of the English classical economists.[29] A static and repetitive world contradicted the identification of history's course as evolutionary progress, in which the never-ending creation of the genuinely new made timeless features a fiction and the present and the future the masters of the past. The modern period especially differed too radically from what had gone before it to draw valid lessons for it from the past. "Our situation is so novel that it would seem as if political and military precedents of even a century ago could have no possible value."[30] Few readers of the works of the Progressive historians realized what a radical transformation that would mean for the traditional American understanding of history. As for the Progressive historians, they deduced from it that historians not only had to avoid giving people lessons gleaned from the past, but also needed to alter radically their views and attitudes toward the past. The adjustment of the past, present, and future to each other—the historian's response to life's demand for a balance between change and continuity—must no longer be accomplished on terms giving overwhelming weight to the past, lest the millennia of the past immobilize life under an "arch of permanency."

Such exhortations fit the zeitgeist of the early 1900s, when many harbored the conviction that a totally new age was emerging. The years between 1900 and 1917 spawned exuberant hopes, as shown in the profusion of new-age expectations—"New Freedom," "New Democracy," "New Federalism," and "New Nationalism." Accordingly, Progressive historians found much resonance, even in the public, with their message that the emancipation of the rational human being was at hand, sponsored by basic forces that inhered in history. Historiography had to be present-minded and future-oriented, and reject the centuries-old habit of giving the past the key to continuity. They found much support for their contention in the early works of H. G. Wells, the English prophet of progress, who had become well known to many Americans through the addresses he delivered on his American tour in 1906–7. He distinguished two types of mind: The dominant and outdated one "interprets the things of the present, and gives value to this and denies it to that, entirely with relation to the past"; the other and proper one does so "in relation to things designed or foreseen." Hence, he maintained "that the deliberate direction of historical study, and of economic and social study towards the future, and an increasing reference, a deliberate and courageous reference to the future in moral and religious discussions, would be enormously stimulating and enormously profitable to our intellectual life."[31] In that spirit Progressive historians assured all historians that they no longer needed to trouble themselves with capturing the past in complete accounts in order to inform the present or to make the present conform to the structures of the past. Those who knew about history's progressive pattern understood that the dominance of the present, as the age in which the entirely new future was being shaped, over the past had become a necessity. The historian had a mandate to help shape the proper future in William James's "decision time," the present. Therefore, in historiography recent periods must get priority over earlier ones, not just for the technical reason that the sources for them were more abundant and reliable, but because progress allotted them the attribute "better."

In their *Development of Modern Europe* Robinson and Beard stated proudly and defiantly that "the writers have consistently subordinated the past to the present. It has been their ever-conscious aim to enable the reader to catch up with his own times; to read intelligently the foreign news in the morning paper; to know what was the attitude of Leo XIII toward the social democrats even if he has forgotten that of Innocent III toward the Albigenses."[32] The attitudes would please a multitude of reformers in a period in which a well-known publicist pronounced the present to be most important and maintained that "the past has been used to throttle the present. Why should we not turn around and use it for a different purpose? We have sunk under the weight of its gloomy sanctity."[33] And Robinson put it just as bluntly when he said that "the present has hitherto been the willing victim of the past; the time has now come when it should turn on the past and exploit it in the interest of advance."[34] Any other view of the relationship between past and present would be not only false, but also immoral, because a wrong historiography led to wrong actions, thus impeding progress.[35] These pronouncements attuned Progressive history to the Progressive Era, in which dominant thoughts and institutions fell easily under the suspicion of being the results of outdated orthodoxies, kept in place by self-interests of groups and individuals.

The logic was impeccable. In a world without perennially repeated patterns and timeless values or structures, where there was a ceaseless creation of the uniquely "new," the past had to lose its former preeminence. John Dewey said as much when he maintained that the nineteenth century had discovered *past* history while the twentieth century had to discover *future* history.[36] Just as other historians did, Progressive historians knew that the past's hold on the present diminished automatically as more and more of the past world vanished with the passage of time. But they were not content to let time's slow erosion of the past do its work. Too many of the past's elements had survived and, since they did not "fit" into the present, exerted a drag on the progress of history toward its goal. Let historians, then, find the obstacles to progress, the historical counterparts to the "useless buttons upon a man's coat sleeve," and destroy them in the interest of efficient progress.[37]

The call for historians to be activists increased a tendency latent in the progressive philosophy of history, using progress as the criterion, to see most problems in history in terms of a grand moral struggle between the forces of good (the future) and evil (the past). This simplification was helped by the suspicion—quite prevalent in the Progressive Era—that many ill-fitting elements of the past survived into the present not only through inertia but through the efforts of people who profited from the status quo and therefore wished to delay progress. Hence, the formulation and social application of Progressive history would be a battle and the scholar's study an armory, not a refuge for contemplation. The historian as activist must first demonstrate how, in the past, reason has destroyed many obstacles in the path of true progress, and then must assist in their destruction in the present. As Becker put it later, we study the past "for our own sake and not for its sake."[38]

American Progressive historians offered Americans a new type of historian, no patient solver of historical jigsaw puzzles, but a co-worker in creation; no static restorer of the past, but a designer of an action program who looked at the past with the interest of the future uppermost in mind. American society offered these historians ample opportunities to infuse their ideas into the minds of many through books that appealed to educated readers, textbooks for schools and colleges, and addresses to professional and general associations—opportunities that were lacking in Europe, where academic historians did not usually write books of broad appeal, government bureaucracies controlled textbooks, and historians found few professional forums and had no wish to address the broad public. In a good turn of fortune, all of the American pioneers of a New History loved the public forum.

Turner, in his moderate way, already had wedded the New History to activism. Although the wish to augment a meager salary supplied a motive, it was primarily the missionary spirit of the innovator that made him write for a broad public, enthusiastically "ride the circuit" of the University of Wisconsin's extension service, keep up a bone-wearing schedule of addresses to teachers, and sit on state committees on behalf of a history that promised to be more useful to society and to bring greater credit to the discipline. However, once more, Turner's attempts at a New History fell well behind. He had shifted the relationship between past and present only slightly when he observed that "the antiquarian strives to bring back the past for the sake of the past; the historian strives to show the present to itself by revealing its origins from the past. The goal of the antiquarian is the dead past; the goal of the historian is the living present."[39] While evolutionary, that perspective lacked the now advocated absolute deference of the past to the present and future. Turner considered history as "minister of conservative reform" rather than as instrument of radical reform.[40]

Activism on behalf of progress through decisive social reforms came more easily to Beard, who as early as 1897—while an undergraduate at DePauw University—had spoken out against any search after truth for truth's sake, and had acquired there the debater's skills with which he not so much persuaded but crushed his opponents. Beard's activism had gained its focus at Oxford's Ruskin Hall. As the hall's cofounder he addressed, up to five times a week, audiences in the English black towns in order to train "those who are oblivious to the large issues of life; but also to help train the conscious members of society, so that they . . . may render truly rational service in this great conflict with social and natural forces limiting the development of man's highest nature."[41] The English experience, particularly the reform programs of Sidney and Beatrice Webb and of Annie Besant, based on the conviction of an evolutionary progress in history, would color Beard's work well into the 1930s. At Columbia University he found a soul mate in his erstwhile teacher and then colleague, James Harvey Robinson, who had come more hesitantly to a sense of mission on behalf of progress, seen by him as the advance of rationality. Between 1907 and 1917, Robinson and Beard produced a stream of lectures, articles, and books—all designed to push Americans toward the right future by teaching them the proper perspective on history.

Even Becker spoke with enthusiasm of those who had fought "the enemies of the Republic" and showed how "historical thinking is part of this [reformist] intellectual activity, and like philosophy and science, literature and theology, it is a social instrument, helpful in getting the world's work more effectively done."[42] However, residing in Lawrence, Kansas, he did little more than write a few articles and book reviews in the affirmative spirit; whether he would have done more had he lived nearer to New York City can be doubted. Becker, who wrote with irony and wit, harbored a fascinating irony in his own personality. Distrustful of passions, even emotions, this critic of the historian as detached observer never vanquished his own tendency to be a cool and distant observer of things. Becker's reluctance to join in the fervent activism of other Progressive historians originated not in a wish to protect tradition as the force of continuity and stability, but in his already insufficient faith in a future radically different from the past.

Scientific historians and, later, the American public had reasons to feel ambivalent about the new view of history. If, as has often been asserted, basic American attitudes were indeed pragmatic in the widest sense, Progressive history's views on historical truth and usefulness should have appealed to them as properly modern. Yet at the core of the traditional American sense of history were the timeless values and rights whose ever fuller realization made for progress. They had no place in

Progressive history. Americans would have to learn to think of history not in terms of the increasing fulfillment of timeless and abstract ideals of Liberty, Equality, and Truth, but as the constant creation of liberty, equality, and truth in ever better forms in the changing contexts of American life. While that preserved the view of history as the gradual prevailing of the good in a still flawed world, the element of stability and continuity was no longer given by timeless structures. Now, that assurance came from reliance on the intrinsic benevolence of history as an open and creative process and on modernity's new means "with which to control its [mankind's] social destiny for noble ends."[43]

7

The Fragile Alliance between Progressive

History and the Social Sciences

The formative phase of Progressive history occurred in the midst of the realignments in the field of human studies brought about by new disciplines that often claimed to be more in tune with modernity than the established disciplines. Such claims grated much less on Progressive historians than on others because they sensed a kinship with the new social sciences. Also, the new complex interdependence of modern life seemed to provide ample tasks for all kinds of inquirers.[1] Progressive historians hoped not only for new, useful insights but even for an alliance of modern-minded forces so as to give strength to the group of scholars intent on reform. In a parallel development, the importance of old associates of history, such as philosophy and theology, was diminishing together with that of literature. Philosophy, which never had played a significant role in American historiography, now was distrusted as the origin of speculative philosophies of history. Protestant theology was combatted as the foremost source of outdated ideas, while at the same time its redemptive features were secularized. In the case of the campaign against history's linkage to literature, the Progressive historians once more joined in a battle past its decision point. As early as 1896, Turner had advised his student Becker that "the old union between history and literature is now broken in all the growing colleges."[2] Literary historiography with its narratives had become an outcast from serious historiography, unfit for the scientific age. Scientific historians insisted that empirical findings about objective reality, not the constructs of language, must structure historical accounts. In these accounts, language must play a purely passive role so as not to intrude into the distortion-free reflection of "real" connections and forces in past reality. Only after a scientific synthesis of substance had been achieved could a linguistic form be draped like a beautiful and enticing cloth over empirical findings. "Till that time comes the work of the man who writes history as literature will be more ephemeral than that of the man who records his scientific work upon the facts of the past, even though the latter's monography be forgotten and his name perish."[3]

In 1904, Robinson condemned literary history because the structure of its works consisted of "those stylistic expedients which belong to fiction and poetry, oratory and the drama, without which these [accounts] would collapse and fall away into dust and ashes."[4] In order for the structure of reality to govern historical accounts, he thought to assure history's independence from literature through the development of a special scientific language for history. In the future "the historian will more and more boldly appeal to his own fellow scholars, as do the representatives of other sciences; and so freed from the restraints imposed by the tastes of the public and their want of special knowledge, history will develop a technical literature, the prerequisite of progress."[5] Such a new scientific language would carry its price, as it called for works that were carefully documented and constructed, that were aimed at and written for like-minded historians, and that offered that hallmark of all true sciences, the cumulative building of knowledge; in short, the triumph of the monograph over all writing with popular appeal. That actually reflected what most American and European Scientific historians were doing, although without a consciously constructed technical language. They all would have agreed with Henri Berr's view that substance mattered and language was, at best, helpful, because language was not seen as being an active force in historical interpretation. Yet the activist imperative kept all Progressive historians from following Robinson's brave declaration, because doing so would have been to the detriment of history's public role. Instead of long rows of monographs, Beard, Becker, and Robinson produced well-written works that stood on bookshelves in the place of Bancroft's volumes, silently contradicting Robinson's radical iconoclasm of the early 1900s. In their defense these historians could argue that literary ambitions, forms, and constructions could not harm a historical account already in accord with reality, namely, being scientifically structured by progress. As for Becker, he was reluctant to condemn literary history because his works resided in close proximity to literature—a fact that earned him a warning in William Dunning's response to Becker's article on Kansas. "If you are not careful you will make a reputation as an epigrammist," a reputation Dunning considered of doubtful value for a historian, but highly desirable "for a producer of literature and perhaps that category is what you are seeking to qualify for."[6] Henry Adams found the paper "charming" but warned that "if I were he, I should be a little afraid of indulging so freely my fancy for humor." However, Adams admired Becker's remaining "always in good taste."[7]

Progressive historians, however—much like such contemporary French scholars as Henri Berr, Paul Lacombe, and François Simiand—understood the link between narrative (or literary) history and a strong accent on individuals whose decisions and actions produce events. *L'histoire événementielle* preferred the literary form; analytical history did not. A history as Robinson described it at the 1904 congress, concentrating on the important slowly moving forces, had no use for literary artifice or elegance. Progressive historians soon found that the key aspect of their history saved them from making a difficult choice. Their known central force did not, like other glacially and impersonally moving forces, lack congeniality to narration. Progress needed the individual's effort and cooperation, and its accounts would know of heroes and antiheroes in the grand struggle for the future. In fact, Progressive history could produce works of greater narrative power than Scientific history, with its suspended synthesis.

Progressive historians could move on to another, more urgent issue: defining history's relationship to the new scholarly endeavors that had joined history in the scientific exploration and explanation of human life. The wish to master human life in the modern spirit had created new disciplines—sociology, anthropology, and social psychology—and had revised existing ones, especially economics. They were akin to Progressive history in their aim to bring rational analysis to bear on the problems of the day within the overall American sense of history. They also shared in the Progressive historians' dilemma of how to satisfy both the universal ambitions of science to see matters in terms of universal structures and processes and the specific demands of the American intellectual context with its unique sense of dynamics and affirmation of liberal institutions.[8]

With some exceptions, the social scientists of the first and second decades also found the solution to their interpretive dilemma in an evolutionary progress. It connected the natural and cultural realms in a manner that allowed for scientific explanations that seemed to support the hope for social reforms. Hence, the Progressive historians had no reservations about the expectation by most social scientists that "the searchlight of social science . . . would dispel much of the haze which surrounds these problems [of the American political and economic order], especially when they are treated with the thought-apparatus of a hundred years ago."[9]

With their social criticism made more acceptable by its evolutionary and, so it was thought, progressive spirit, American social scientists moved into academe with relative ease when compared with the difficulties their European counterparts met. By the turn of the century, the professionalization of the study of social phenomena had been largely accomplished. The old American Social Science Association (1865) faded in importance as the American Historical Association (1884), the American Economic Association (1885), the American Sociological Society (1905), and the American Political Science Association (1903) ascended to prominence.[10] At Columbia University, Progressive historians enjoyed especially fruitful ties with the social scientists. Elsewhere, relationships between historians and social scientists ranged from benign neglect to the perception of a hostile challenge by the young disciplines. The most contentious issue proved to be the claim by the social scientists that their proper concern was the establishment of generalizations, while that of historians was the study of individual events and phenomena; by implication, theirs was a modern endeavor, hence superior to that of history. This reflected an attitude toward Scientific history that Becker, as a student, described as "a noticeable fact that most ethnologists, anthropologists, philologists and professors of kindred sciences and even many philosophers consider the science of history as little above contempt."[11] On that point conflicts soon arose. In 1904, George Burton Adams, still sympathetic to sociologists, expected them to shed light on "the difficulties of medieval history" through comparative studies with primitive societies. In a division of labor they "will assist us [the historians] less in determining what the fact was—that is primarily our work—than in the understanding it when known."[12] However, only a few years later, he considered the social sciences unnecessary, since they were "concerned with the same facts of the past which it is our business to study."[13] Far from being benevolent allies, they reduced history to the status of supplier of critically sifted material for generalizations. Worse, these disciplines were not empirical enterprises interested in facts, but inquired after "the ultimate explanation of history, or, more modestly, what are the forces which determine human events and according to what laws do they act," and hence they were no better than the a priori philosophies of history of old.[14]

The Progressive historians' attitude toward the social sciences was both more affirmative and more complex than that of the Scientific historians and Turner. The latter had hailed "the economist, the political scientist, the psychologist, the sociologist, the geographer, the students of literature, of art, of religion" as "the allied laborers in the study of society." They all "have contributions to make to the equipment of the historian."[15] In practice he used a few of their findings and left it at that. The bonds of Progressive historians to the new disciplines were more substantial and threefold: a positivist epistemological core, faith in progress, and eagerness to accomplish social reform. Such agreement made impossible a general attack by social scientists on history as intrinsically unfit for the modern age in the manner of Émile Durkheim, who had built French sociology into the synthesizer of all knowledge—a sort of encompassing history. He deprecated contemporary Scientific history because after the accumulation of a large mass of isolated facts "it then decays into mere erudition. It may well interest a small circle of *érudits,* but it no longer yields useful and vibrant work."[16] Only a decade later did Henri Berr's synthetic history defuse much of Durkheim's criticism. In America, Progressive historians had already sensed the period's prejudice in theoretical matters for the general and the collective and could claim to have satisfied it when they had discovered the *idée directrice*—progress—that shaped history into a meaningful whole.

Thus, for some years, Progressive historians and the social scientists, equally intent on modernizing American thought and society, existed in a largely unreflected-upon collaboration. Only Robinson dealt with aspects of the relationship in an analytical manner, while Beard and Becker, who both shared his views and sympathies, were not outspoken on the issue. Beard, never patient enough for intense theoretical considerations, simply practiced cooperation by being at the same time a political scientist and a historian. He treated the two fields as one, since each could isolate itself from the other only at the cost of impoverishing itself. Becker, upon the invitation of Albion Small, once formally addressed the relationship between history and the social sciences. In a rare failure for Becker he said little of significance on it; not so much because of a lack of insight, but because of the absence of an ardent conviction.[17]

For Robinson, evolutionary intellectual history necessitated an alliance between history and the social sciences. The progress of rationality had led to the continuous emergence of new disciplines and the concomitant changes in the status of existing ones, albeit not in proper synchronization. Robinson discerned a particularly disturbing gap between the actual and the needed development of the sciences dealing with human affairs. In the past "the biological and physical sciences were entering upon the settlement of a new continent, while history was undertaking the reorganization of an old commonwealth."[18] At fault was the egregious influence of outdated thought, especially of Aristotle's writings on ethics and politics. Once the "human sciences" were liberated from traditional obfuscation, they too could follow an unobstructed path of modernization.

Robinson warned that the lag was aggravated by what he considered the historians' repudiation of the new social sciences, which threatened to widen the gap. What marked the new disciplines as truly modern was their thoroughly evolutionary and hence historically minded attitude.

Robinson put his criticism of historians who opposed an alliance with the new sciences into the form of an appeal. "Above all, let the historical student become unreservedly historical-minded, avail himself of the genetic explanation of human experience, and free himself from the suspicion that, in spite of his name and assumptions, he is as yet the least historical, in his attitude and methods, of all those who to-day are so eagerly attempting to explain mankind."[19] Historians were mistaken in putting on "the armor of the Lord to defend the lawful frontiers of history against invaders."[20] Instead, historians should learn from all evolutionary-minded scholars: from biologists about the link of humans to primates; from geologists about the ever-changing physical environment through the "language of the earth"; from archaeologists about the true length of human history, as opposed to the Protestant Bible-oriented early history; from social psychologists about the social nature of human existence and the strong animal behavior base of even modern people; and from comparative religion about the relativity of Christianity.[21] Four decades later, Lucien Febvre would exhort historians, in his *Combats pour l'histoire* (1953), to be geographers, psychologists, jurists, and sociologists. But in the 1920s, he and Marc Bloch were only laying the foundation for such a broad alliance, while working at the University of Strasbourg. Berr was already transforming it into reality.

Characteristically, Robinson found no lesson to be learned from economics, which, increasingly relying on marginalist theory, perceived a sequence of equilibriums between needs and gratifications. One could only hope that it had a progressive direction. Nevertheless, Robinson's optimism relied on the condition, still sufficiently met at that time, that the social sciences shared with the Progressive historians the evolutionary outlook. At that point, it was easy to overlook features of the social sciences that would gradually deemphasize the evolutionary matrix— be it Franz Boas's nonprogressive cultural anthropology or the increasing predilection for detailed empirical studies with a small interpretive range.

Robinson relentlessly preached to historians that "the progress of history as a science must depend largely in the future as in the past upon the development of cognate sciences,—politics, comparative jurisprudence, political economy, anthropology, sociology, perhaps above all psychology. It is these sciences which have modified most fundamentally the content of history, freed it from the trammels of literature, and supplied scientific canons for the study of mankind. They are the auxiliary sciences of history in a far deeper sense than are paleography, diplomatics, or even philology."[22] Those who opposed the alliance overlooked that history "is bound to alter its ideals and aims with the general progress of society and of the social sciences." After the change it would "ultimately play an infinitely more important role in our intellectual life than it has hitherto done."[23]

None of the Progressive historians shared the fear of a good many American and European historians that they would end up as mere fact gatherers for others. Robinson's vision of history as the integrating discipline of all knowledge about human life matched Henri Berr's confidence in history as the future *maîtresse directrice* in the face of Durkheim's and François Simiand's call for sociology to annex history and reduce it to the status of a mere supplier of facts. Independently of each other, Robinson and Berr saw in a New History, constructed of its own insights and those of the social sciences, the best hope for creating the needed unity of knowledge in the studies of human life. Robinson, of course, knew of the promise of unity through progress that could console those who worried about the increasing specialization in scholarship, made so much worse by the rise of the social sciences.

Robinson mentioned only indirectly another powerful tie between Progressive historians and social scientists—the wish to redefine and reform American society. Like many American social scientists, Robinson, Beard, and Becker as well as some of their followers had translated their originally Protestant moral and social ideals into secular reform programs. Like Comte earlier and Durkheim later, they wished for a civic religion that combined a secularized Christian ethics with scientific knowledge. Even in Europe the distance of the public purpose from the social sciences and social history was short. Durkheim's intent to stabilize the Third Republic by insights from his sociology and Gustav Schmoller's attempts to lessen the social tensions in the new German empire through the work of the *Verein für Socialpolitik* were cases in point. In America the connection took its own form. What Mrs. Potter Palmer, a prominent speaker at the 1893 world's fair, had proclaimed to be true of charities, Progressive scholars wished to make true for every aspect of American social reform. " 'We are now entering upon a new era of charitable work. We are now considering the administration of charities in a scientific way.' We are not attempting so much to alleviate existing conditions as we are to prevent their existence."[24] Progressive historians and social scientists were convinced that the next American step in the emancipation from the past would come through an activism informed by scientific knowledge. The certainty that progress was the true structure of history provided the ethical component. Not only poverty but all other social ills (including the capital versus labor issue) had become technical problems rather than tenacious parts of the human condition. When Albion Small and Thorstein Veblen, both critics of the status quo, spoke of the need for more scientific analysis before concrete remedies could be prescribed to restore social harmony, they questioned only the timing of the reform effort, not its basic soundness.

The drive to reform society benefited greatly from the manner in which Progressive historians understood the structure and dynamics of societies. In the American tradition, they relied not on creating new social structures and processes, but on reforming the existing ones through actions by individuals. Hence, studying social phenomena meant always to study relationships between individuals. The so-called social structures were no more than multitudes of relationships frozen at a certain point; snapshots of social actions, so to speak. That augured ill for any borrowing of Marxist concepts of social change or any expectation that Progressive historians would strive to find laws governing social behavior. Above all, the individualistic approach made for the use of psychology as a favored auxiliary discipline.

In 1898, Dow had predicted that psychology would become the key discipline for the humanities, comparable to the position of mathematics in the area of the natural sciences. Although the prophecy proved somewhat exaggerated, it appreciated the new status of psychology in modern thought in which that discipline provided the substitute for philosophy. When ideas, like all other phenomena in the realm of thought, became purely instruments of adaptation to life and therefore lost most of their autonomy, psychology provided the fitting key to obtain access to the mechanisms of human life. The change also appeared to fit well with the pragmatism of the Progressive historians. Only for a brief moment, in 1904, Robinson seemed to catch a glimpse of the looming epistemological problems that a psychological approach posed for the hermeneutics of texts and sources. But far from pursuing the matter, he considered psychology simply a helper in sorting out "the relation between the sources and the objective facts they purport to record."[25] Robinson expected from psychology reaffirmation and support for the evolutionary progress through new theories on the interactions between people and their environment. He found it in the insights of William James, Edward Lee Thorndike, and John Dewey.

The stipulation of a forever-emerging new world negated attempts to find some kind of permanent human nature; this time, one shaped not by philosophical ideas but by fixed psychological traits or some sort of stable collective psyche. Hence the lack of receptiveness for some French and German experiments that derived general structures from psychology, such as Lacombe's omnipresent *homme général,* who was the common basis for "the proper object of the historical science, the human being of one epoch, one place, the time-bound human being . . . the historical one."[26] Karl Lamprecht, who at first glance appeared to be a closer soul mate with his insistence that "history in itself is nothing but applied psychology," no less than the "mechanics of the mental science [Geisteswissenschaften], in particular of the science of history," proved not to be that.[27] He spoke of the evolution of the collective psyche of a people, a concept not favored in American social psychology with its emphasis on the constitutive role of the individual. American social scientists and Progressive historians preferred psychologies that saw society as the aggregate of socialized individuals and, therefore, offered opportunities for reforming society. Hence, Robinson appreciated Gabriel Tarde's imitation theory, but even more the work of his Columbia colleague Edward Thorndike. Thorndike's "law of effect" defined socially accepted behavior as the one tested in a process of trial and error and proven successful in obtaining the proper adaptation. Since the "law" lacked a ready affinity to his evolutionary view, Robinson simply assumed that all changes in adaptation brought about by the "law" were either progressive in nature or could be made to be so by human intelligence. Resistance to such experimentalism accounted for the persistence of attitudes and habits (called "simian" or apelike) that had once been successful means of adaptation but now were fossilized obstacles to change. Robinson readily identified these old attitudes and social forms with those advocated by traditionalists and conservatives.

In the end, social psychology was hailed for its clarification of the dynamics between individuals and society as much as its serious study was neglected, even by Robinson. Becker, rightfully considered to be among the Progressive historians the most sophisticated user of psychology as an analytical tool, worked with a self-taught psychology that was anchored in the keen sensitivity of a gifted literary man. One need only read in his student diaries the skillful psychological portraits of people he had observed to grasp how fundamental psychological explanations were to Becker even then.[28] Their importance increased in inverse proportion to Becker's loss first of his religious and then of his philosophical faith. Psychology, although not as a systematic but an ad hoc source of answers, offered to him a substitute approach to the explanation of human life.

As long as the "law of evolution" was the only law requiring assent, Progressive historians and social scientists coexisted in relative harmony. Yet at the turn of the century, evolution provided not the only scientific explanatory model. Physics depicted a mechanistic universe with repetitive and nonteleological patterns. Some social scientists were not averse to that structural model, since it held great promise for the predictability of phenomena, and hence for the mastery of human life. They, among them Albion Small, wished to see the structure of society, including its lawlike regularities, scientifically ascertained before social reforms were undertaken. Quietly they assumed that such laws would be supportive of progress. Nevertheless, Progressive historians could not reconcile themselves to laws governing human life because they saw them as "static"—that is, nonprogressive—elements in the human world. On that issue Progressive historians joined rather than opposed those Scientific historians who, since the 1850s, had been skeptical of the idea that laws were a sign of a mature science. In his *History of Civilization in England,* Henry T. Buckle had attempted to wed science to history by envisioning a scientific history with laws that would "accomplish for the history of man something equivalent, or at all events analogous, to what has been effected by other inquirers for the different branches of natural science." All there remained to do, it seemed, was to imitate those scholars who "have studied natural events with the view of discovering their regularity; and if human events were subjected to a similar treatment, we have every right to expect similar results."[29] By the turn of the century, however, all the affirmations and proclamations notwithstanding, little progress had been made toward Buckle's goal.

All Progressive and most Scientific historians refused to link the scientific status of history to the discovery of laws, but they put forth different objections to the stipulation of laws in history. Scientific historians either wished to postpone raising the question of such laws until many more objective facts had been gathered, or they rejected the search for laws in principle because a science of history must not aim at generalizations but deal with "the lives and deeds of individuals—individual men, individual peoples, individual states, individual civilizations."[30] On their part, Progressive historians found the search for laws misguided because it pointed historians in the wrong direction, toward a static world and away from the explanatory principle of the genuine dynamic quality already ascertained in progress. Even many social scientists defused the impact of the lawlike "natural" forces they found by affirming an evolutionary tendency toward a cooperative harmonious society. Thus, Franklin Gidding's "consciousness of kind" increased over time, and even the economist John B. Clark's marginalism (built on the law of diminishing returns) could be seen as tending to establish and reestablish equilibriums on higher and higher levels of social and economic comfort. With the exception of William G. Sumner's social theory, the opportunities for human intelligent action were given, and the ethical dimensions as well as the element of progress in the American sense of history preserved. While Scientific historians considered a scientific methodology as a sufficient guarantor of history's scientific standing, Progressive historians found their guarantor in the one grand law of general progress.

Nevertheless, during their early careers, Beard and Robinson still had voiced some sympathies for laws. In his famous lecture "Politics" (1908), Beard sounded, at points, like an orthodox Bucklean. Impressed by strict causality, he opined that "a treatise on causation in politics would be the most welcome contribution which a scholar of scientific training and temper could make."[31] However, for Beard an alliance with the social sciences did not mean the affirmation of laws. First, he did not wish to wait with his work as a reformer until sufficient "laws in history" were established to guide him, and second, laws perceived as determinant structures contradicted his view of an open cosmos in which efficacious, rational human action was possible. For Beard the activist historian, the science part of the social sciences, particularly the search for an affirmation of laws, always remained less important than the social part of the phrase, understood as a spur to activism. When he eventually settled on a history in terms of economic interests, he would be much plagued by his ill-defined attitudes on laws and determinism.

Robinson kept a safe distance from laws of history patterned after those of physics because early on in his studies of intellectual history he had proclaimed that the Newtonian model of science with its laws of mechanics had lost out to the Darwinian one. Evolution with its greater leeway for innovative human action offered a history-friendly scientific model. Robinson's rather skeptical remarks on Buckle reflected this attitude. "It was inevitable that attempts would be made to reduce history to a science by seeking for it laws and by reconstructing it upon the lines suggested by the natural sciences."[32] In objecting, Robinson did not repeat the contentions of European and American Scientific historians that "history deals only with phenomena individualized by time, that is to say, those that are produced but once in the course of the ages."[33] Laws were out of the historian's reach because, compared with the natural sciences, history would always be an inexact and fragmentary body of knowledge. He ascribed this not only to the fact that history concerns itself with human beings and their "devious ways and wandering desires which can never all be brought within the compass of clearly defined laws," but also to the fact that it "must forever rest upon scattered and unreliable data, the truth of which we too often have no means of testing."[34] The law of evolutionary progress, of course, was not seen to be affected by such skepticism.

As for Becker, he never did put much stock in a history governed by laws, an attitude easily derived from his increasing skepticism concerning any objective order in the universe and his view of the human mind's insufficiency for grasping such an order, if it existed. He questioned whether the human freedom to act purposefully could be preserved even in a cosmos structured by the law of evolution, which was perceived as intrinsically benevolent.[35]

8

Sorting Out History's Grand Forces

Progressive historians had the advantage of knowing the very structure and course of history: It was progress. Yet they also wished to know which forces propelled human events along that path of progress, not just to gaze at the truth, but to guide history along its proper course. This intent required the abandonment of the traditional philosophical or metaphysical forces that had been seen to guide the world from "above." The search was directed toward the silent, powerful forces "behind" or "below" the surface of institutions and events, but fully accessible to human understanding. As Turner put it, "behind institutions, behind constitutional forms and modifications, lie the vital forces that call these organs into life and shape them to meet changing conditions."[1] Such a search attuned Progressive history perfectly to the general temper of the Progressive Era, with its craving for realism in the arts, literature, and politics. The quest for "realistic" historical interpretations represented history's counterpart to the ashcan school, the realism of Theodore Dreiser's novels, and the political muckrakers—all of them viewing themselves as destroyers of harmful illusions, rooted in naïveté or corruption, and as pioneers of a new, sound order.

The forces that mattered could also only be few in numbers. While all innovators agreed that, as Turner put it, no New History could accept a world of sheer accidents, fortuitous circumstances, or a welter of "surface" phenomena, a maze of forces would prove no more useful. Historians needed to single out a few forces, preferably even only one, that through their dominance would configure the historical world much as the application of a magnetic force gave structure to what before had been an amorphous pile of iron filings. Therefore, the Progressive historians, who already knew the basic order of history to be progress, sifted all empirically ascertainable forces for those that had an inherently progressive thrust or at least could be channeled into a progressive direction. The latter was crucial since it alone permitted a nexus that logic seemed to exclude: the simultaneous affirmation of an overall teleological structure of history and of rational ordering activities by individuals that really mattered. In the course of their work Progressive

historians assessed such previously identified forces as race, geographical space, ideas, and economic motivations.

Progressive historians never considered race a history-shaping force.
In the early phase of Progressive history the race-centered theory of
Anglo-Saxon dominance had in its historiographical form been already
fatally weakened. Turner rejected the Germanist thesis according to
which American democracy constituted the maturation of the ancient
Germanic idea of liberty. He ignored claims that English world dominance and American ascendancy to great-power status could be taken
as verification for the concept of Anglo-Saxon racial superiority. For
Turner, who aimed to divorce America's history from that of Europe,
American democracy had no racial origin because it "was not carried in
the *Sarah Constant* to Virginia, nor in the *Mayflower* to Plymouth. It
came out of the American forest, and gained new strength each time it
touched a new frontier."[2] Writing after the vanquishing of the Germanist thesis, Robinson and Beard did little more than make sarcastic
comments on it.[3]

An obvious opportunity to deal with race as it pertained to American
history had offered itself all along in the all-too-visible problems experienced by blacks and Native Americans. Still, despite the large-scale
northward emigration of black Americans and vivid memories of the
"Indian wars," the race problem was largely absent from the works of
the American pioneers of a New History, be it Turner or the Progressive
historians. In contemporary historiography the issue of the role and position of black Americans in the American past and present was transmuted into a regional problem, dealt with mostly in histories with a
focus on the South. Typical were those by William A. Dunning and
Ulrich B. Phillips, with their strong accent on racial superiority and infe-
riority. But the New Historians slighted the race problem because in
their interpretations of history race did not represent a primary force.

Turner deemphasized the problem of black Americans and slavery
when he severely criticized Hermann von Holst for putting it and not the
westward movement into the center of American history.[4] In 1910, he
again asked that geographical viewpoints be adopted, because "if this is
done, it will be seen that the progress of the struggle between North and
South over slavery and the freed negro, which held the principal place in
American interest in the two decades after 1850, was, after all, only one
of the interests of the time."[5] While slavery was a most important feature
of American history, the central shaping force had been the settling of
the West.[6] The important issue of the relationship with Native Americans appeared only infrequently as the "Indian problem." On occasion,

Turner would hold forth on ethnic issues, particularly on his misgivings about the nature of the contemporary wave of immigrants from eastern and southern Europe, but even there his worries about the assimilability of the newcomers in the now limited space overshadowed his concerns over any "wrong" ethnicity.

Robinson expected race problems to disappear once human relations assumed a sufficiently rational character, and Beard did not see race as a source of problems in the cooperative society of the future. Race problems would be solved automatically in the course of progressive developments. Such a resolution was not merely a hope but a certainty, because racial differences were manifestations of the evolutionary differences between less and more fully developed peoples; the race problem, like many others, resulted from a time lag, not from biological differences. Thus the young Beard could call American Indians savages and speak in favor of entrusting development projects in colonial territories only to white supervisors, and still, as the eighteenth-century *philosophes* had done, claim to love all humanity as well as not contradict the spirit of his Quaker background. More profound were his concerns that Anglo-Saxons understand the limits to dominating other people, lest these people eventually avenge themselves on their masters, and his insistence that an acceptable imperialism was not one that planted the flag in new lands for commercial exploitation, but one that planted "a new colony of rationally organized white men" to create a new world.[7] The mature Beard pointed out to black Americans the logic of his economic interpretations: First they would gain economic power and then achieve equality. In the properly ordered society, race would be an insignificant factor. Racial explanations of history wrongly relied on a biologically fixed category that in turn led to intolerably static explanations. The whole issue lost its centrality if one exchanged—as the Progressive historians did when dealing with the issue of race—the "timeless" and unbending features of nature for the controllable and constructed features of culture. That made the issue one that could be mastered technically and that would be so mastered in the future reformed American society. Full emancipation was a matter of time, not a question or a problem.

The question of geographical space as a history-shaping force was for Progressive historians identical with the vexatious Turner problem. They had respected Turner for his attempts to modernize American history. However, they had found in the frontier thesis not much to approve and much to reject. Would that change when, in 1907, Turner presented in his *Rise of the New West, 1819–1829* a more sophisticated geographical interpretation of American history, based on the concept of the section? Essentially it came down to whether space—that solidly stable point of reference for all changes—could in the sectional American history enhance a progressive destiny more plausibly than it had done in the frontier interpretation.

When Turner set out on his venture without a clear definition of the concept of a "section," he did not only continue a bad habit but already revealed the crucial problem of his sectionalism: an unresolved connection between geographical and cultural phenomena. As a theoretical problem it mattered little to Progressive historians; its impact on the issue of modernizing the American sense of history, however, did matter.

In order to give space the dominant position in the forming of the American destiny, Turner needed to perceive the section as primarily a region prescribed by physiography. Thus, he would endow a whole region with a special character defined by its geographical location (New England was provincial; the middle states mediating and transitional; and the West radically democratic). Or, in a parallel to his earlier dictum that the Americans "were pouring their plastic pioneer life into geographical moulds," he maintained that the region of Kentucky brought forth the typical Kentuckian as that of Virginia produced the Virginian.[8] However, Turner soon understood the complexities involved in causally connecting the determinants—soil, climate, and topography—with specific features of American culture. He came to give an influential yet not a dominant role to physiography. He had conceded that when, early on, he just about adopted Josiah Royce's stipulation of a section as a "part of a national domain which is, geographically and socially, sufficiently unified to have a true consciousness of its own unity, to feel a pride in its own ideals and customs, and to possess a sense of its distinction from other parts of the country."[9] With that, sections came to be regions shaped by physiography and culture, making it more feasible to connect sections, progress, and the American sense of history.

In the end, progress could not be shown to have resulted from the impact of sectionalism. There it was significant that in the sectionalist history the drama of the settlement and its nation-forming forces was not prominent—a fact that reduced not only the popularity of Turner's historiography with the public but also its dynamic possibilities for the modernization of American history on spatial terms. Sections modified the nation-forming process, but did not originate or enhance it. To the contrary, their interests tended toward particularism. National political parties, the demands of commerce and industry, communications, labor, and the established political institutions—all of them cultural forces—provided the dynamics toward national unity that moraines, rivers, valleys, and salt springs could not offer.

Such a tension between the whole and the parts was systemic to re-

gional approaches; only the solutions differed. Ratzel had seen in regions with their people's consciousness formed by distinct historical
developments a detriment to national unity. However, Vidal de la Blache
had celebrated the historical regions based on geographical characteristics *(régions naturelles)* over the artificial and nongeographically determined *départements (régions politiques)*. Moved by his central concern,
the growth of the American nation, Turner sided with that supreme
"artificial" and political unit, the nation. Turner then fell back on America's uniqueness in order to resolve the tension between the particular
geographical sections and the primarily cultural concept of the nation,
which Ratzel and Vidal de la Blache had appraised so differently. The
tensions between the unifying forces, including the federal government
and most economic realities, and the by-their-nature separatist sections
were resolved in American history by a unique mechanism: recurrent
compromises between sections—an American continental "foreign
policy" that prevented a European-type system of states. That persistent
preference for the nation as the ultimate reference should have brought
Turner closer to Progressive views, but actually did not. The sequence of
ever new equilibriums between sections had no clearly progressive direction. Even the rise of the new West to prominence represented no
more than the creation of a new equilibrium, although it "was the most
significant fact in American history in the years immediately following
the War of 1812," and the whole union would "be influenced by the
ideals of democratic rule which were springing up in the Mississippi
Valley."[10] Progress was not essential to the process of intersectional adjustments, and therefore represented no central concern of Turner's
sectional American history. On one occasion, Turner hinted at progress
when he stated that "just as the pioneer, widening the ring-wall of his
clearing in the midst of the stumps and marshes of the wilderness, had a
vision of the lofty buildings and crowded streets of a future city, so the
west as a whole developed ideals of the future of the common man, and
of the grandeur and expansion of the nation."[11] However, with the
settlement process about finished, the stimuli for progress from the West
would diminish. Even worse, the forces of modern technology tended to
lessen sectional characteristics. The web of communications, commerce, and industry sapped the strength of those features that once
helped define the sections. The power of separate regional traditions
diminished together with the limitations imposed on human life by
space. Sections seemed to be the victims of progress rather than its supporters. Instead of defining their difficult relationship with a contemporary innovator, Progressive historians benignly ignored the sectionalist

Turner—an attitude more comfortable for both sides than the hostile neglect accorded to the Turner of the frontier thesis.

On one aspect of history, the economic influence on history, Turner and the Progressive historians came closer together. While Progressive historians (except for Becker, the grateful student) remained generally silent on Turner, any occasional praise, such as Beard voiced in *An Economic Interpretation of the Constitution of the United States* (1913), referred to Turner's emphasis on economic matters. The latter also provided much of the drama in Turner's *Rise of the New West, 1819–1829* as sections struggled with other sections over internal improvements, tariffs, and the economics of slavery. Indeed, the book even lost its sense of unity whenever the issues raised were not easily connected with the economic interests of the sections. Nevertheless, the unbridgeable gulf on the issue of progress, involving Turner's praise of the past and his uncertainty about the future, remained.

As for Turner, he hoped to resolve all problems and still all doubts with what he half-jokingly called the "Big Book": a section-oriented history of America during the decisive period from 1830 to 1850. Such a task would require collecting vast amounts of data, an endless chore for a perfectionist like him; much writing, a sheer agony for him; and a better-defined stand on geographical determinism, an immersion into theory uncomfortable for him. He did not finish it. By 1917, Turner was well on his way to becoming an isolated reformer and underestimated innovator of American historiography. The Scientific historians objected to his daring hypotheses, which lacked the support of the available data, and the Progressive historians had come to understand that space as a history-shaping force had no link to progress. That missing link also made Turner's version of American history not useful to the modernization of the American sense of history, a fact reflected in Turner's waning popularity. On the other hand, Turner's quest for a New History was marked by too strong an emphasis on America's uniqueness to become a model beyond America's border. That stood in stark contrast to those historians who were just setting out to use geographical sections in a more complex manner for constructing a New History. The young Lucien Febvre was doing it in his *Philippe II et la Franche-Comté* (1911). There the uniqueness of the region was a function not of space but of the unique intertwining of a great many forces in a given space. The work would influence American historians only many decades later, when the ideas of the mature *Annales* school on history's connection with geography would flood into America.

Ideas, another force central to traditional historiography, posed a

special dilemma for Robinson and Becker, who accented the transforming power of rationality rather than that of industrialization. On the one
hand, these two historians were in tune with the contemporary redefini-
tion of ideas. Once conceived as spiritual forces that gave order to human life and its accounts, ideas had lost their status as dominant and
autonomous forces. At the turn of the century, vitalistic and pragmatic
philosophers in Europe and America had developed the basic Darwinist
view of ideas as instruments constructed by human beings in the course
of their adjustment to the environment into sophisticated philosophies.
In them, the ideas and values that at one time had served as the moral
and intellectual fixed stars by which human beings navigated now
changed in accordance with the human needs they responded to. Truth
had become wholly a function of context. Apart from specific life situa-
tions, which gave them temporary validity, ideas were useless abstractions. With pungent hostility, Arthur Bentley would call ideas without
an instrumental function in life "soul-stuff." Progressive historians
agreed with that when they rejected Hegel's philosophy of history with
its Absolute Spirit or Idea, Ranke's interpretation of ideas as mediators
between God and human beings, and Bancroft's timeless ideas of liberty
and equality. Such views kept people from the actions needed to keep
the world, now an evolving process, on a progressive course. In this
sense, Progressive historians have generally and correctly been seen as
history's contingent in the pragmatic revolt or the revolt against formalism that accomplished the detachment of American thought from the
long strain in Western tradition which saw in ideas powerful and stable
elements reaching beyond the empirical world.

On the other hand, the link of Progressive historians to that revolt
was more problematic than often assumed. They rejected some versions
of pragmatism and accepted others. Thus, like Charles S. Peirce, they
exempted science from the constant changes induced by the flux of life,
not because they saw in it the path to a not-yet-known truth, but rather
because it secured the idea of progress in a properly modern manner.
William James, who denied the possibility of such an exemption in a
wide-open and forever-changing world, was rejected by the Progressive
historians on that point. They preferred John Dewey's approach, in
which science was a "given" universally valid instrument with an inherently democratic ethos.

Such a selective pragmatism allowed Progressive historians to construct a pragmatically interpreted world with a teleological ordering
principle, progress. A firm objective order could be combined with the
pragmatic need for human action. This required that one idea or
concept—progress—be defined not as an ad hoc adjustment tool with

its validity restricted to one era or area, but as transhistorical—or, to use the new, less-than-elegant term, transcontextual; a telos built into all of history. Its exceptional position was vouchsafed by science, now seen as a shaping force active in human life as well as the proper form for studying that history. However, progress was not timeless and transcendent in the traditional sense. Although it transcended all temporal contexts, it always remained in the midst of human history—a sort of essence in motion.

Nevertheless, the argument amounted to an exemption of the idea of progress from the rejection of timeless and autonomous ideas. It in turn relied on the exemption of the facts needed to shelter progress from all antipositivist critique. The two exemptions depended on each other. Yet regardless of its precarious status, the argument for the certainty of progress facilitated Progressive history's success in becoming America's most influential New History. Until the late 1920s, it also distanced American historiographical developments from the European historiographical mainstream, where ideas were seen mostly in terms of historicism—that is, as the expressions of different periods and cultures, with none possessing authority beyond these contexts. They also were untouched by the French innovators, who, on the basis of a more radical empiricism, moved the discussion of ideas, including that of progress, into the area of collective psychology. More important, the conviction that the idea of progress was an empirically demonstrable reflection of actual life, not a conceptual construct, protected Progressive history from the vicissitudes of the European struggle with relativism in historiography. The temptation remained small to take the step of declaring ideas, including that of progress, to be fictions, used to construct some order in a meaningless world—a step already taken in German pragmatism by Hans Vaihinger's philosophy of the "As If." Instead, the agreement of Progressive history and the American sense of history on a commonsense realism, if not positivism, seemed firm.[12]

The ambiguity besetting the nature of the idea of progress presented special difficulties as well as opportunities for Robinson and Becker, whose versions of Progressive history rested firmly on the growth of rationality. Both men remained under the spell of the French Enlightenment and saw in the ever-increasing rationality of human beings the true motor of progress. Hence they needed to concern themselves more thoroughly with the nature of ideas than Beard had to. The fragile compromise between construction and reality in the area of progress was promptly reflected in Robinson's and Becker's interpretation of the nature of ideas, one that remained suspended between a truly traditional and a truly pragmatic mode.

Robinson put much effort into his intellectual history course at Columbia University and planned to develop from it a comprehensive
work on Western intellectual history. In it, as in all of Robinson's works,
the march of rationality toward its eventual triumph was central. All
other ideas, none of which enjoyed progress's perfect congruence with
reality, remained temporary phenomena. In one context, these ideas
could be true—when they supported progress—and in another one,
false—when they hindered it. Hence, intellectual history in Robinson's
and Becker's manner concerned itself, aside from tracing the pioneers of
progress, with the demonstration and explanation of that dualistic dynamics of ideas throughout history. A special problem for them and
other Progressive historians was the need to explain why once appropriate and therefore good ideas that had outlived their usefulness did not
disappear with the context of their origin, as the pragmatic logic required, but survived as now useless and hence bad ideas. They ascribed
the survival of such ill-fitting elements of the past to inertia, naïveté, or
oversight, but also to their being intentionally and mischievously labeled as timelessly valid. Such suspicions made Progressive historians
proper inhabitants of the Progressive Era, "an age prone to accusations"
(Walter Lippman), when ideas one wished to refute were often called
mere rationalizations in the pre-Freudian sense of being masks for material interests. Thus, Beard granted that the Monroe Doctrine may well
have been intended originally to protect Latin America's liberty, but it
soon served mainly as a disguise for America's economic interests. Most
capitalistic ideas, appropriate for the time when industrialization broke
the dominance of the medieval economic order, also were now outdated,
and were kept alive in contemporary America solely for the benefit of
special interests. The scheme was attractively simple and appealed to
many, but denied intellectual history its full complexity. Robinson never
wrote his magnum opus on intellectual history, for a number of reasons.
Not the least obstacle was the necessity, dictated by the new perception
of the nature of ideas, to replace the history of ideas as a clearly delimited
and autonomous development with one that took account of life's total
reality, because each idea could now be shaped by any of the innumerable aspects of that life. There also was the all-too-schematic understanding and evaluating of ideas as good or bad according to a concept
of progress narrowly defined in terms of economic and social efficiency.
A simple dualism was unavoidable.

Once more, it was Becker who refused to keep the radical modern
doubts about certainty from intruding, this time into the easy certainties
about progress. In him, the idea of an objective and quasi-timeless
progress lost strength in the measure to which he gradually came to in-

terpret ideas as projections by people rather than as elements of reality. Traces of a denial of a substantial link between ideas and reality could be discerned already in his doctoral dissertation.[13] Six years later, in his *Beginnings of the American People* (1915), Becker's evolving doubts about ideas as mirrors of reality surfaced in his expressions of doubts about the genuineness of the causes championed by the American colonials. Ideas had not yet become simply masks people put over reality for selfish purposes—stripping them of any inherent validity—but Becker was traveling toward that destination rather quickly and to his own intellectual discomfort. His purely instrumental interpretation of ideas, soon more consistent than that of his colleagues, would deny Becker any access to certainty, make his persistent inner struggle more acute, and block reason from being the substitute for faith it had been for the French *philosophes* he so admired. Worst of all, the suspicion that ideas were mere rationalizations would eventually destroy in him the central Progressive belief that in the case of progress idea and reality coincided. His always precarious belief in progress facilitated that destruction. Becker, a lover and brilliant analyst of ideas, highlighted a paradox: The rise of American intellectual history occurred at a time when, for many historians, ideas had lost much of their autonomous and elevated status, and when Progressive historians had reduced them to secondary psychological phenomena, affirmed as instruments with which to master "grubby" reality or to buttress rationalizations for economic interests. In that contradiction lies the reason for the failure of Robinson's and Becker's variety of Progressive history to gain prominence. Its pushing force, the increase of rationality so celebrated by Robinson, was decisively weakened by the reduction of the world of ideas to a tool kit for activism or, increasingly for Becker, at best the source of salutary nonsense. Not surprisingly, then, the robustness of economic forces held a much greater appeal.

9

Beard's Economic Interpretation

of History

In turn-of-the-century America, with its well-advanced industrialization, its social and economic dislocations, its discussions of the proper distribution of wealth, its echoes of Marx, and its liking for sturdily earthbound explanations, historians readily joined their European counterparts in acknowledging the economic aspect of life as significant. However, while American Scientific historians accepted economic history as a legitimate field of history, they sensed the danger of speculation and asked scholars to heed the "great difference between economic history and that which calls itself the economic interpretation of history." Particularly objectionable was the contention by some scholars "that even the ideal world is the economic world: that all our notions, beliefs, sciences, manners, morals, law and philosophy find there their first explanation."[1]

Turner agreed with that cautionary approach, although, as a youth, he had occasionally seen American history as a struggle between aristocracies of property and democratic forces. Then in 1891 he had exhorted his colleagues that "far oftener than has yet been shown have these underlying economic facts affecting the breadwinners of the nation been the secret of the nation's rise or fall, by the side of which much that has passed as history is the merest frippery."[2] Although he occasionally ventured beyond caution and stated that "we may trace the contest between capitalist and democratic pioneer from the earliest colonial days," he never joined the proponents of an economic interpretation of history.[3] For Turner, economic history was a matter of collecting facts while the economic interpretation of history utilized these data. The latter became a harmful "economic dogmatism" if it saw all features of an age shaped solely by economic forces. Still, Beard credited Turner with being the first American historian to adhere to the economic interpretation, specifically "the influence of the material circumstances of the frontier on American politics."[4] Notwithstanding such praise, and although Turner's geographical interpretation of American history was indeed attentive to the economic component of life, Turner's grand force remained space, as Beard and other Progressive historians came to acknowledge regretfully. Since Robinson's main interest was directed toward exploring and demonstrating the progress of human rationality and Becker initially agreed with that, the economic interpretation of history became Beard's domain.

The young Beard, whose Quaker upbringing gave him a keen sense of social justice, learned much about the importance of the economic aspect of life, first at DePauw University and then at Oxford's Ruskin Hall. The social conflicts in industrial England convinced him of the dominance of economic phenomena and, until well into the 1930s, that conviction would pervade much of his scholarly work and stimulate his social activism. But, since the latter needed the choosing and acting individual, Beard's economic determinism always had some limits, even at its height.

Beard propounded an economic interpretation of the course of history in his remarkable first book, *The Industrial Revolution* (1901). In it the young and passionate Beard pronounced industrialization to be the universal driving force in modern history, which demanded of all societies that they adapt themselves to the radical restructuring of production and consumption. Modern Western history moved along purposefully, driven by industrialization—seen as an efficient, productive, and rational endeavor—that, in turn, prescribed a cooperative and fully participatory democracy. Beard's English experience, too, persuaded him that all changes pointed to the cooperative society of the future; one that would stand "as a monument to the intelligence, integrity, and capacity of the Democracy of England."[5] Industrialization would subsequently push all societies in that direction. Only human inertia, all too often artificially strengthened by the beneficiaries of the status quo, delayed the needed adjustments, and with them progress. Not much longer, because now historians understood the situation and would become enlightened advocates of reform, thereby preventing the heavy costs of otherwise inevitable social conflicts.

Beard's emphasis on life's economic aspect was thus firmly set when, in 1904, he joined Columbia University's faculty. *An Introduction to the English Historians* (1906) and his collaborative work with Robinson, *The Development of Modern Europe,* showed it, and so did his courses on government and politics. Beard set to work to clear legal and political theory of all obstacles to society's proper progress. From German legal scholars he learned about positive law as growing with society rather than being deduced from timeless principles, and from such American legal pragmatists as Roscoe Pound, Oliver Wendell Holmes, and Frank

Goodnow he learned about the law as a process and the product of social construction. Once freed from artificially fixed values and ideals,
the law would more promptly and fully reflect the ever-changing social
and economic needs of human life. Beard merged his economic interpretation of history with these insights when he insisted that the process
of social change was fueled by economic forces.

He also was familiar with a considerable body of works, among them
Henry Jones Ford's book *The Rise and Growth of American Politics*
(1898), J. Allen Smith's book *The Spirit of American Government*
(1907), Algie Martin Simons's *Social Forces in American History*
(1911), and Gustavus Meyers's exposés of American power arrangements, in which the Constitution appeared as the bulwark against democratic forces, yielding only that measure of democracy that the people
had been able to wring from the wealthy and conservative classes in return for popular consent. At first, in *The Supreme Court and the Constitution* (1911), Beard gave a historical justification for the principle of
judicial review of legislation, but faulted the laissez-faire philosophy in
which the review had been exercised. But already there the Constitution
was seen as having facilitated such wrongful use because its framers had
not been disposed to join in "the assaults on vested rights which legisla-
tive majorities were making throughout the Union."[6] Their class bias—
solidly conservative, favoring commercial and financial interests—had
made them draft a Constitution that favored a judicial review based on
the philosophy of minimal government. This judicial review reinforced
the dike which business interests had built against the recurrent waves of
social reforms the proper course of American history had called for.

An Economic Interpretation of the Constitution of the United States
surprised many but should not have done so, since it followed the basic
lines Beard had developed in earlier writings. The world had been defined as a process and economic forces as dominant. In that spirit he
assigned to the Constitution the fate of other institutions and ideas that
traditionally had been thought to reflect timeless verities: It was totally
integrated into the flux of the historical process. What many perceived
as a radical diminution of the Constitution's stature was necessary, because that basic law was to be deprived of all claims to an ultimate and
timeless authority from which the specific elements of the legal order
could be deduced. For Beard "the devotion to deductions from 'principles' exemplified in particular cases, which is such a distinguishing
sign of American legal thinking, has the same effect upon correct analysis which the adherence to abstract terms had upon the advancement of
learning."[7] A truly useful Constitution had to give up the exalted status
it had so far occupied.

That the Constitution changed with time was not Beard's central message; amendments testified to that, and Turner had already maintained that "the constitution was, with all the constructive powers of the fathers, still a growth."[8] However, Beard did not view laws as "grown," which implied that the Constitution was indeed in harmony with its society at any given point in American history, but as deliberately shaped ("made") by social and economic interest groups.[9] Thus, those who had pushed for replacing the Articles of Confederation with a tighter union had done so because their economic interests had been adversely affected by the Articles. In all of that, Beard did not deny that the Constitution was the work of politically sagacious and exceptionally able men. Nevertheless, they participated in and were motivated by a common struggle between economic interests.

Just as critics accused him of doing, Beard wished to destroy the people's reverence for the Constitution as a document of enduring wisdom and to depict the supreme law as the result of a rather commonplace struggle between economic interests. With that accomplished, the road would be open to transform the Constitution from an anachronistic basic law, serving only special interests, into an instrument for achieving an ideal democracy "where the rule of the majority is frankly recognized (a condition of affairs gravely feared by the framers of our Constitution), government tends toward a type, unified in internal structure, emancipated from formal limitations, and charged with direct responsibility to the source of power [the people]."[10] With the removal of a major reason for the time lag between that which was and that which should be, even had to be, the full emancipation of the masses could proceed.

In order to demonstrate that the actions by the Constitutional Convention were causally connected with the economic status of its participants, specifically that they were the outcome of a battle between economic interests, Beard undertook one of the earliest prosopographical studies in American historiography. Although it was, by his own admission, also a rather fragmentary one, the study demonstrated to him a grand struggle between progressive (good) and retardant (evil) forces. At the Convention, groups of personalty interests, people with financial, manufacturing, and commercial stakes, fought and prevailed over the realty interests, the farmers and debtors. Hence, instead of being the expression of the popular will, "the Constitution was essentially an economic document based upon the concept that the fundamental private rights of property are anterior to government and morally beyond the reach of popular majorities."[11] The Constitution did not just happen to fail to establish majority rule, it was designed to suppress the popular will.

Amidst the enthusiasm and controversy caused by Beard's work, Beard did not find it necessary to clarify the exact and difficult relationship between economic motives and human actions (he saw them as causes and effects respectively). He proceeded simply to justify his economic interpretation of history in general, first in an article and then through a series of lectures at Amherst College.[12] The former intended to show the applicability of the economic interpretive scheme "of a collision of economic interests: [specifically] fluid capital versus agrarianism" to the decades after 1789.[13] The latter was to give the economic interpretation a wider theoretical base as well as a greater aura of respectability by invoking some of the past masters of political thought as supporters. Beard was gratified that these masters confirmed "a vital relation between the forms of state and the distribution of property."[14] Much of the inattention to economic interests in Western political thought he blamed on the influence of the archvillain Rousseau's theory of democracy—a system "so unreal, so ill-adapted to the world of industry and trade, commerce and agriculture, that its implications are astounding."[15] Far removed from economic reality, it espoused a "formalistic" view of the equality of rights that relied on the rule of the numerical majority. The Declaration of Independence, filled with Rousseau's spirit, led Americans into futile attempts to perfect political democracy without economic democracy. Then the war took Beard away from theory, although one may doubt that theory would have held his attention much longer in any case. If, as one reviewer put it, "our generation wants to know the 'connections' of its public men," then Beard thought to have satisfactorily answered the question.[16]

While *An Economic Interpretation of the Constitution of the United States* excited the imagination of some and the wrath of many, historians should have asked Beard to clarify the theoretical assumptions and procedures that shaped his view of American history. From them derived more difficulties for the Beardian thesis than from all the shocked protestations of contemporaries as a whole. The key problem arose from Beard's preference for explaining history in terms of a dualism of two economic interest groups over analyzing the multiple competing interests in life's reality. The dualistic perspective appealed to Beard's personal inclination to find views that gave clear guidance to activism, but also made possible the reconciliation of the contradictory implications of his two key explanatory concepts: industrialization and economic interests.

When Beard argued that in 1789 and in the early 1900s the central problem of the United States was the adaptation of social, economic, and political institutions to economic realities, he argued from his grand scheme of history. In it, industrialization affirmed progress with a telos—the ideal industrial democracy. It gave human history an inexorable thrust toward the expected better future, specifically the ideal industrial democracy. All social ills could be accounted for by means of the concept of a developmental lag between the new economic structure and the existing political and social institutions. In this, his early explanatory scheme, industrialization, the force that caused the lag, would also close it. Industrialization necessitated a cooperative and participatory democracy, and would eventually do away with the competitive laissez-faire capitalism remaining from earlier periods.

Yet, in 1913, Beard gave the concept of economic interests the key role in historical explanation. However, economic interests, as psychological forces with economic motivations, had no clear connection with history's progressive course. They strove for temporary advantages in wealth and power and brought Beard closer than he ever acknowledged to the worldview of classical and neoclassical economists he so despised. This world, with its cyclical patterns of selfish strivings and their satisfaction, knew no fulfillment or "greater" age of humankind, only the temporary triumphs of some interests over others. While industrialization as the key force could support Progressive history's expectations of a radically new human situation in modernity, Beard's second force, economic interests, implied the endless continuance of the old order with its conflict between groups based on common economic interests. When he tried to give even the conflict of interests a progressive direction and maintained that "the whole theory of the economic interpretation of history rests upon the concept that social progress in general is the result of contending interests in society—some favorable, others opposed, to change," he found himself in the unwelcome vicinity of Mandeville's dictum that public benefit came through private gain, guided by an invisible hand.[17] Social conflict represented the "cunning of history" that enhanced progress as it unwittingly supported history's march toward an ever more perfect democracy.

Beard never addressed this crucial contradiction but could not escape it. The vagueness in his explanatory scheme affected his whole economic interpretation of history, specifically his attempts at economic determinism. Later he would disclaim that he had ever adhered to an economic determinism. After 1913, he was more concerned to distance his work on the Constitution from Karl Marx and to associate it with James Madison. Beard delighted in bringing James Madison's "Federalist Number 10" into the discussion. He even stated with considerable exaggeration that his *Economic Interpretation of the Constitution of the United States* was "based upon the political science of James Madison" when he really wished primarily to use his imagined agreement with Madison's views as a defense against suspicions that he depended too much on Marx and other European thinkers.[18] As a means to align Beard's two explanatory principles, the recourse to Madison was not helpful. Madison, although acknowledging the tensions caused by the uneven distribution of property, never spoke of history as a continuous conflict of interest groups. He and Beard would have agreed on the need for government to lessen these tensions, but hardly on the degree and ultimate end of such an involvement. Beard obscured the distance between his and Madison's views by his silence on the fact that he and Madison disagreed fundamentally on whether the factions caused by property and their conflicts could ever be made to disappear. Madison saw these differences in property as rooted in the inherently different capabilities of human beings, while Beard perceived them as historical, hence temporary and remediable.[19] Nowhere did Madison speak of a progress that would either end or even markedly diminish the so far ubiquitous conflicts of economic interests. He was not, like Beard, a proponent of an economic interpretation with a happy ending.

Beard was quite correct, however, when he emphasized his distance from Marx's economic interpretation of history. Beard, who even as a student had gotten to know Marx's views, held in his mature years a position close to that of his colleague at Columbia University, Edwin R. A. Seligman, who "adapted" Marx to America. Sympathetic to Karl Marx's and Achille Loria's ideas, Seligman purged from them the fatalism-inducing determinism of ironclad laws of history and shaped them into a moderate environmentalism in which "men are the products of history, but history is made by men."[20] In his "theory of social environment," both the validity of the economic interpretation and the possibility of taking conscious action to reform society were maintained; a solution that remained in the confines of the American sense of history (*sine* exceptionalism) and appealed to Progressive historians. Robinson greeted Seligman's version of Marxism enthusiastically. "Few, if any, historians would agree that everything can be explained economically, as many of the socialists and some economists of good standing would have us believe. But in the sobered and chastened form in which most economists now accept the doctrine, it serves to explain far more of the phenomena of the past than any other single explanation ever offered."[21] Beard shared that understanding, because he, too, objected to Marx's insistence on rigid classes, the inexorable patterns of class struggle, and history as a foreordained and inescapable dialectical progress toward a utopian classless society. Beard insisted that history constituted no Hegelian system but a development shaped by a direction, firmly set by economic forces, and specific forms, shaped by rational actions. Whether such a combination was logically possible could be questioned; that Beard kept his distance from Marx for more profound reasons than political caution could not. His British experience, the traditional American stress on volition and rationality, and the intended—if not actual—logic of his thought played decisive roles in formulating Beard's stand. As it did in the case of other American scholars, the American sense of history offered to Beard a more congenial progress theory than Marx did. Critics, however, could have pointed out that earlier and closer links to Marxist theory had been present. In 1906, Beard's economic interpretation still wore a cloth woven by Marx and the classical economists when he maintained that "the general direction of the political movements and legislation in Great Britain during the last one hundred years has been determined by the interests and ideals of the three great economic classes: landlords, capitalists, and workingmen."[22] Such a firm link between the positions of individuals in the economic process, with its denial of any truly efficacious thoughts and rational actions by individuals not determined by their economic status, did endure in Beard's work well into the 1920s, despite mitigating declarations. Beard could deny truthfully that *An Economic Interpretation of the Constitution of the United States* was a Marxist work, but not that it was one of historical economic determinism.

However, Beard and Marx shared an important problem. When they both argued for a preset course of history and the role of conflicts of economic interests in it, they were able to reconcile the teleological and the nonteleological principles only by identifying in each age a group whose interests were in harmony with history's course. Only then could their explanatory systems escape from the endlessly repetitive historical mechanisms of group conflict they themselves had stipulated and speak of a future with a harmonious society. Both men, having transformed history into a dualistic struggle between good and evil, needed for the resolution of that dualism the agent of pure goodness. That Marx's inspiration had come from Hegel, and Beard's would derive from American Populism and Progressivism, did not matter in this case.

It mattered, however, that both Beard and Marx needed to break the so far ceaseless cycle of economic conflict in the modern period. Faced with the need to end centuries of class struggle through a group that ushered in the scientifically sound social order, Marx had found his pure agent in the industrial proletariat. In the spirit of the Progressive Era, Beard would hail the "people" because their interests would lead them to fight for the participatory democracy with full majority rule—in a sense the end stage. Much like Marx's industrial proletariat, Beard's people (those whose interests had lost out so far) would be, at the same time, the liberating force and the liberated group. Both the proletariat and the people would differ from past dominant interests only if their economic interests were so perfectly attuned to progress that the gratification of their interests would lead directly to progress's goal. In this, Marx's proletariat (always hard to define) had the easier task, because its emancipation was seen as bringing with it the institutional order that, by the general ownership of all means of production, would end the cycle of economically induced conflicts.

Beard had a more difficult task in defining the "people" and in which way they would assure not a static new institutional order but the constant, rational, and frictionless adjustment of institutions to ever new circumstances of life; in short, the democratic society that resolved conflicts through rational argument and economic planning. Yet within the logic of his economic interpretation, the people could not be defined as such a pure agent. Beard had labeled as fiction the notion of a "whole" people, even had poured sarcasm on Bancroft's notion that "the Constitution proceeds from the whole people; the people are the original source of all political authority exercised under it; it is founded on broad general principles of liberty and government entertained, for some reason, by the whole people and having no reference to the interest or advantage of any particular group or class."[23] In his own writings vague references abounded to the people as the large homogeneous part of society dominated throughout by selfish business elites. But who were these people? According to Beard's *Economic Interpretation of the Constitution of the United States,* the Constitutional Convention brought a clear victory of the personalty interests, represented by owners of public securities, money, and stakes in manufacturing and shipping. Beard, who loved landholding and had a deep-seated dislike for "paper" wealth, readily placed himself on the side of the losers, the realty interests. By implication, the realty interests represented the people, although, when speaking about the personalty interests, he emphasized that "the representation of one interest was as legitimate as the other."[24]

Actually, in Beard's work on the Constitution, the term *people* had a dual reference—those who lost out at the convention (the realty interest) and those who were disenfranchised, "the slaves, the intended servants, the mass of men who could not qualify for voting under the property tests imposed by the state constitutions and laws, and women, disfranchised and subjected to the discriminations of the common law."[25] Yet the logic of Beard's interpretation spoke against subsuming the two groups under one concept, the people, because the losers on the convention floor, the realty interests, for whom Beard clearly held sympathies, were after all themselves only a selfish interest group. By implication they, too, would have thrown up their own constitutional bulwark against other interest groups and the disenfranchised multitude. And even that multitude was itself an amalgam of interest groups, lacking "purity" of motive, and could not be, as Beard and other Progressive historians often implied, the people who were simultaneously the main beneficiaries and the agents of historical progress. It, too, could not have formed a union based on a supreme law devoid of the shaping influence of self-interest. Beard would have had to agree that full majority rule meant only that the greatest possible number of economic interest groups could assert themselves. Such a conclusion was at an intolerable distance from the cooperative, rational, and relatively harmonious society seen as the mandate of an industrial society. In his own way, Beard had made the expectation of a "new order of the ages," essential to the traditional American sense of history, a part of his vision of the future society. Although that expectation was potentially universal in scope, it conformed remarkably well to the element of American exceptionalism. Eventually, it would become clear that modernity's true historical mediating agent would be the group of new reform-minded intellectuals, seen as being imbued with the modern spirit. Considered selfless, enlightened, and professional, they would lead the masses to the society in which all conflicts would be resolved not by interests prevailing over other interests but through rational argument and economic planning.

Unfortunately for Beard, the issue never found its clarification; it simply faded away, partially because, after 1916, Beard gave up writing directly on the economic interpretation, but mainly because Beard never sorted things out. He had forged his economic interpretation and was eager to get on with applying it as an instrument of reform, never having been one who found pleasure in the exploration of theoretical subtleties or just plain exactness. Most historians who subsequently counted themselves to be Progressive historians adopted Beard's dualistic version of the economic interpretation of history, problems and all.

Conflict, understood in the Beardian manner as economic in origin and dualistic in nature, would be pivotal for Progressive history's view of the American past.[26] The progress model relying on industrialization's advance remained the optimistic framework for history's course, safely embedding all conflicts. Only some of Beard's later followers softened his stark dualism that excluded a proper analysis of the complex network of conflicts in societies and the realization of the usually inconclusive settlements of social conflicts. For the time being, the unsatisfactory resolution of conflicts was ascribed to conspiracies by interest groups against the people. Thus, when Progressive historians interpreted the events of the 1770s and 1780s, they began with the assumption that the American Revolution could have instituted a democracy with full-fledged, even perfect majority rule. Only a conspiracy against the people could explain the failure to do so in 1789. In a vague form, the idea of a frustrated Revolution had already been proposed by the young Turner. But Turner later found the explanation for the failure in the peculiar Eastern settlement conditions rather than in willful acts. True democracy emerged in the course of the westward expansion.

Becker formulated the standard position of the Progressive historians on the American Revolution. He, like other Progressive historians, assumed that the American Revolution could have led not only to independence but also to a complete social reconstruction. America would suffer from the split result of the successful external revolution against English dominance in favor of home rule and the failed social revolution against the ruling economic interest groups over who should rule at home. Becker and others had observed correctly how even large-scale social and political rearrangements have been marked by shifting group interests, but had made no analysis of the varying degree to which each interest group strove for radical change, before and after its desire for change was partially satisfied, and how the waxing and waning of its enthusiasm for change influenced the dynamics of the Revolution. Progressive historians made no comparative studies of revolutions— mandatory for a modern New History—which would have shown that the American Revolution followed the typical dynamic pattern of revolutionary changes: that after a revolution with its radically accelerated pace of change, the desire for stabilization has always made itself felt, and that the ideas that fire the revolutionary fervor have never kept their purity in their realization.[27] Progressive history permitted no such insight, since stability had a purely negative connotation in a world striving relentlessly for a better, if not perfect, future; hence the view of the Constitution with its checks and balances as an ad hoc conspiracy by certain classes to deprive the people of their democratic rights by preventing majority rule. Even worse, when measured against the ideals of an egalitarian future, America never had been a real democracy. Such condemnations denied the founding period an assessment either in historicist terms by its own standards or in comparative terms by general human standards. They did so even in terms of the traditional American sense of history as well as those of Progressive history itself, which stipulated just such a gradual process for an ever more perfect realization of ideas and rights. Also unnecessary became the continuation of the Founding Fathers' debate on whether all of those who exercised power needed limitations, even those in a republic—the people. The discussions about checks and balances, reaching back to Plato, Polybius, and Montesquieu, could be considered irrelevant if one could cite the emancipated people as a force of purity or rely on the inherently beneficial quality of the historical process. Both were seen as assuring a healthy republic then and in the future.

10

A Sense of Triumph

By 1914, Progressive history had emerged as a New History with identifiable tenets and a tolerable internal consistency. It had been formulated in a still-isolated America where the ascendancy of industry, commerce, and technology fostered a boundless optimism about the mastery of human destiny. Accordingly, Progressive historians did not share the European *fin de siècle* mood, but expressed a *commencement de siècle* excitement. They would have agreed with the young Turner's answer to some contemporary poets, who saw themselves as "idle singers of an empty day," that the age's "myriad of inventions, its schools, its newborn knowledge of nature, all cry 'No.' " The age was magnificent; "it is the poets that are lacking." Now, the age had acquired perhaps not its poets, but its historians. Later, they would be known as Progressive historians, because their faith in the modern version of progress held together, made sense of, and gave an ultimate justification to their historiographical views. That faith reasserted hope and confidence at a time when science had "swept aside the ancients' firmaments—and set us floating on the ocean of infinity."[1] It reassured those who were keenly aware of being at a turning point. Even in 1910, with the doubts of the 1890s having long vanished, Turner still spoke earnestly of "witnessing the birth of a new nation" and declared that the sum of the social and economic changes "during the past two decades is comparable to what occurred when independence was declared and the Constitution was formed, or to the changes wrought by the era which began half a century ago, the era of Civil War and Reconstruction."[2] Progressive history would owe much of its success to the assurances it gave about the future, which removed all negative connotations from the term *turning point*.

Such optimism and confidence about the quest for a New History stood in stark contrast to the expectations in the two other countries with active modernization attempts in historiography: Germany and France. There the problem of integrating the worker into society, with the attendant fears and hopes invested in Marxism, and the question of the *raison d'état* for the new German empire and the Third French Republic generated sufficient uneasiness to dampen the expectation for progress. Doubts about a rational, scientifically shaped future, even a strong tendency to affirm life as irrational, could flourish in that intellectual climate. Still, the difference surprises, since in each case the forces pushing the cause of a New History were the same: the pervasive power of science, industrialization, and urbanization. In America, Progressive historians could rely on what European scholars lacked, a deeply embedded faith in progress. Their conviction that progress had now been empirically ascertained also left their concept of progress unaffected by the Scientific historians' suspicion of the old and distrusted philosophies of history; particularly by the injunction that "our philosophy of history should be our conviction as to the direction in which our scientific study is tending, our belief as to the ultimate nature of history and the final destinies of the race, our answer to the riddle of human existence. It should be to us a source of inspiration and of courage, but we should not confuse it with our science."[3]

Such certainty carried with it the obligation to define the shape of the future for which the historian as activist had to work. For it, the Progressive historians had the advantage that they thought to know which specific attitudes, habits, and institutions the major driving force in modern history—be it industrialization or the increase in rationality—prescribed: democratic cooperation, scientific management, and the acceptance of modern technology. For Beard, the future society would show the full conformity between instrumental scientific thought, technological mastery of the material circumstances, and democratic and cooperative values. Specifically he spoke of full employment, at least minimal care for the underprivileged, overall economic planning, the absence of exploitation, and unlimited possibilities for participation in public, including economic, affairs. For Robinson it meant the triumph of rationality, which favored scientific and pragmatic-instrumentalist approaches with their correlate, a rationally guided, democratic, and cooperative society. Once more, the prestabilized harmony between life seen as a never-ending process of adjustment and its progressive goal made possible the logical tour de force of speaking simultaneously of the historical process as "open" (not determined) and of the future as essentially known. All of that also seemed to have a tolerable fit with the American sense of history. The rejection of the traditional, timeless verities in the process, as static in nature and a priori in justification, escaped unnoticed in the Progressive Era's enthusiasm for a managed progress and did not matter to those who were critical of the status quo.

Becker, whose doubts about the beneficial nature of the cosmos, including progress, were growing with every year, kept mostly silent on the matter of the future. General affirmations of "the rising demand for social regeneration" had to suffice.[4] His faith in progress was still strong enough to subdue the doubts he had about reforming society; doubts he had formulated as an undergraduate when he warned "don't try to reform man, it can't be done" and held that the true job was for people to reform themselves.[5] Indeed, when he faulted Robinson for establishing progress as the centerpiece of historiography without giving it a clear definition, it was really prompted more by Becker's unsureness about progress than by Robinson's vagueness about it. Robinson's work was quite clear on the standards for measuring progress.[6] While what Becker wrote at that time carried the implications of a progressive future, he rarely spoke of it directly. However, at that point the three men agreed on the greatest virtue of the Good Society: the ability of its institutions to adjust to ever-new conditions without frictions and, hence, without a time lag. With it, all fundamental tensions that had beset human life in the past would be resolved, including that between capital and labor (Beard) and ignorance and rational knowledge (Robinson and Becker).

With the shape of the future known, the Progressive historians' analysis of social change could only be a limited one. The inherently beneficent nature and structure of both the social process and the future society made superfluous the inquiry into the vast complexity of modern society. The latter was not seen as the result of new social forces reshaping age-old problems of human life. Thus, for example, no questions were asked about the machine age's impact on the relationship between individual freedom and the call for the extensive management of human affairs in the new social order. The future Good Society, the product of a beneficent historical development, pervaded by the spirit of scientific efficiency and marked by full majority rule, would presumably take care of the proper balance without difficulties. The social theory of Progressive history could thus focus exclusively on how to facilitate the quick and efficient emergence of the proper society by clearing away obstacles in its path. The struggle to remedy social problems, reflected in the discussions throughout the centuries, became a matter of combat against opponents to the transformation of American society from its traditional to its modern form. Progressive historians had succeeded in compressing a bewildering array of conflicts (such as those between farmers and banks, workers and capitalists, and the poor and the rich) into the dualism of right and wrong they felt so comfortable with. In historical accounts, all societies and social theories, past and present, could be judged according to their attitudes toward the Good Society of the future. Right and wrong or good and evil were separated neatly and rigidly, with no dialectic connection that could turn even a good into a grievous wrong. In this Manichaean scheme, three types of opponents were singled out: first, those who agreed on the need for change but wished to rely on evolution, unguided by human mastery, for a better future; second, those who expected the better future to result from a radical, one-time institutional change; finally, the mass of anonymous resisters to change who were motivated by selfish interests, traditionalism, or sheer inertia.

The first group substituted the forces of natural evolution for those marshaled by human intelligence. In the laissez-faire philosophy of life, history, and government, most prominently that of William Graham Sumner, intelligent action became a matter of passive adjustment to the naturally beneficent course of history. These were difficult opponents for Progressive historians because they, too, aimed at the liberation of American life from the outdated forms of the past—too many of them transfers from Europe—that so far had deprived the United States of being Western civilization's pioneer in defeating the old order. But, since the course of evolution was set unalterably to the benefit of nature and human history, the good American society of the future would emerge more surely and quickly if scholars taught noninterference in social processes and gave free rein to the natural laws governing human life. Deliberate reforms, such as those sought by the Progressive historians, could well be in error, and thus create new obstacles to progress.

Progressive historians attacked these claims vigorously. First, they denied that the laissez-faire approach derived its authority and truth from the natural order, and insisted that it represented a historical phenomenon. Originating in a certain context, the laissez-faire approach was subject to becoming outdated. As Beard put it, it was "tenable enough before the universal extension of the factory process and the organization of business in national and international forms."[7] Now, in twentieth-century America, the laissez-faire philosophy served only certain class interests; its arguments were mere rationalizations. Its reliance on competition as the driving force of social development was a degrading and inefficient survival from early capitalism. Second, they used the argument of efficiency. As a young scholar, Beard already had argued that the structure of industry prescribed an organization of the economy and society that shifted from laissez-faire to planning so that "the energy and wealth wasted in an irrational system may be saved to humanity."[8] The human progress produced by reason, science, and a proper view of history would accomplish the adjustment of American society to the industrial age speedier and at a much lower human cost than the progress brought about by the natural process. That argument from efficiency could even serve as a general resolution of the bothersome contradiction in Progressive history itself between the simultaneous assertions of progress as a given evolutionary process and the need for the active participation of the people in shaping and facilitating that progress.

Unfortunately, the Progressive historians also curtailed the range of their social history when they discussed the complex transition from a predominantly agrarian to an industrial and urban society in America merely in the context of the laissez-faire controversy. This enabled them to couch the debate in terms of a Manichaean battle between two models for American society: agrarianism with a natural kinship for laissez-faire thinking versus industrialism and urbanism with a built-in need for intelligent mastery.

Jefferson and Hamilton came to be the symbolic figures for the laissez-faire approach to the social order (the past) and the deliberate building of a national order (the future). The choice was, as the title of a best-selling book put it, between *Drift and Mastery* (Walter Lippmann, 1914). Drift was the curse of Jeffersonianism. Beard, who otherwise saw in Jefferson a kindred soul against capitalism, castigated the Jeffersonian antipathy to a strong national government. While Progressive historians regretted Hamilton's "aristocratic" tendencies, they praised his policy as one of energetic and intelligent assertion of the national good. In the end, even his "elitist" tendencies were not so objectionable to historians who knew that, for some decades to come, the few who in minds and habits had already joined the future would need to lead America. Hamilton's vigorous, positive, constructive national policy compensated for his fear of democracy; in any case, Hamilton's emphasis on the state as initiator and actor was preferable to Jefferson's love of a democracy linked to an exaggerated individualism that fit only a small-scale America.

In contemporary history, the decisive criterion for choosing between Theodore Roosevelt's New Nationalism and Woodrow Wilson's New Freedom would be which of the two men held the greater promise for doing away with the lag between America's well-advanced economy and technology and her backward social and political institutions. At first, Theodore Roosevelt engendered much hope, because he was seen as a Hamiltonian, but one who would not commit Hamilton's mistake and make federal power into a bulwark against the rising tide of democracy. In the end, Wilson's New Freedom won out. Initially distrusted for its perceived Jeffersonian traces, it was eventually accepted for its federal activism by most of those with a Progressive vision of history.

The condemnation of Jeffersonianism, thus perceived, also engulfed Turner and his New History, despite his intermittent and hesitant conciliatory amendments. Turner's defense of individualism was well expressed in the argument pioneer settlers used in a petition for statehood:

" 'Some of our fellow citizens may think we are not able to conduct our affairs and consult our interests; but if our society is rude, much wisdom is not necessary to supply our wants, and a fool can sometimes put on his clothes better than a wise man can do it for him.' This forest philosophy is the philosophy of American democracy."[9] Government, once grown beyond a certain point, stifled such individualism. Eventually Turner tried to redefine the relationship between individual and social order by accentuating the voluntary cooperation among pioneers and by acknowledging that two ideals had shaped America: "One was that of individual freedom to compete unrestrictedly for the resources of a continent—the squatter ideal. To the pioneer government was an evil. The other was the ideal of a democracy—'government of the people, by the people and for the people.' The operation of these ideals took place contemporaneously with the passing into private possession of the free public domain and the natural resources of the United States."[10] The amendments did not go far enough to make Turner an acceptable Hamiltonian or a Progressive historian, but they hinted at the true complexity of the issue at hand.

While Progressive historians saw the attachment of Turner to the agrarian mode of life as an error, they viewed that of others as a conspiracy against the proper future. Big business advocated laissez-faire politics, because business people were unproductive, selfish, idle, greedy, and bent on producing not useful goods or services but those that yielded the most profit. Against it were arrayed all the productive elements, from workers to engineers, oriented toward productivity and the public welfare. Once more, the two groups came to incarnate the irrational past and the rational future.

The second type of opponents also envisioned a much better future. However, they hoped to reach it not by gradually reforming America's traditional, liberal institutions, but by making radical institutional changes. Among them, those who had an intellectual kinship to Marx figured most prominently. None of the American innovative historians commented on a Marxist socialism with much sympathy. Turner stressed socialism's European origins and treated socialism as a threat to America's greatness, as being " 'socialized into an average' and placed 'under the tutelage of the mass of us.' "[11] Beard, Robinson, and Becker accepted Seligman's modification of Marxism. Beard's image of socialism carried the imprint of the Fabian socialists, with their preferences for gradual and democratic reforms brought about by individual actions. Their version of socialism lacked Marx's Hegelian dialectics and relentless historical mechanisms, particularly the class struggle. Not radical changes in the concept and institutions of private property were needed, but gradual modifications by rational actions in accordance with the modern social and economic reality. As has often been stated, the mobile American society offered few incentives for the adoption of an orthodox Marxism. It was equally important that Marxism carried a historical message of hope for a better future that Americans could gain from their own sense of history, in a manner more akin to the American tradition and experience. That resistance to a European import, which many considered subversive because of its revolutionary overtones, stifled Marxism's acceptance in America. Progressive historians offered a much more congenial path to the Good Society. Orthodox Marxism's insistence on the one revolutionary reconstruction of society would not do in a world seen as continuous progress. In turn, Beard would be labeled a Victorian moralist for his reliance on appeals to the moral sense and his refusal to be more structurally minded.[12] Others would call him too conservative, trying, like the German *Kathedersozialisten,* to shore up the old order rather than to work for its radical change.

American Progressive historians shared H. G. Wells's confidence that "the essential fact in man's history to my sense is the slow unfolding of a sense of community with his kind, of the possibilities of co-operations leading to scarce dreamt-of collective powers, of a synthesis of the species, of the development of a common general idea, a common general purpose out of a present confusion."[13] The creation of such a new community was a matter of changing the attitudes of individuals through education and of social and economic policies by a government with a truly modern spirit. Intelligent social control was the key.[14] Beard was particularly adamant on the stringent regulation of business, even public ownership of some sections of the economy. He also added an emphasis on sound administration—one technically well developed, empirically oriented, and always flexible.[15] No doubts arose on whether the long-standing tendency of institutions to become static and encrusted would not be applicable to the new "flexible" institutions, too. Progressive historians, viewing planning and regulation of the economy as evolutionary phenomena, felt no need to concern themselves with those problems contemporary European scholars worried about, such as bureaucratization and oligarchic tendencies.

The third and most formidable obstacle on the way to the Good Society of the future was traditionalism. The traditionalists of all kinds sensed no reason for reform because they considered things well arranged and relied on the values and ideas supplied by the past for either explaining or mastering the present and the future. Such a reliance on the past was anathema to Progressive historians because they saw in the concept of timeless values, be they philosophical, religious, or natural, limits to the continuous creative innovation necessary for progress. These limits to human ingenuity were not given in human nature but were merely temporary limits resulting from ignorance, self-seeking, and false reverence for tradition. Hence, a torrent of condemnations was loosed against the "tyranny of tradition and routine" in order to destroy the past's dominant influence. Beard called on Americans to let go of institutions created in the eighteenth century for that century. He also rejected Turner's attempt to identify the traits of nineteenth-century pioneers and freeholders with those of the permanent American character. Institutions and ideals obtained their validity and authority solely from the degree to which they were properly adjusted to the requirements of the future, not from being in accordance with precedent or timeless values and verities. The latter were themselves no more than remainders of former adjustment processes, now out of step with the modern period's thrust toward the unfolding of the future. In the absence of transtemporal standards and values, all past social institutions were to be judged solely on their effectiveness for preparing the future in the present. What, in previous centuries, had been useful as a carefully hedged and consoling interpretation of history had, with the increased human mastery of the world assuring the swift and beneficial course of progress, become useless. Worse, old views and institutions, lacking any instrumental value, turned into obstacles. The conservatives, who kept them afloat for reasons of nostalgia or economic self-interest, committed a sin; indeed, "at last, perhaps, the long-disputed sin against the Holy Ghost has been found; it may be the refusal to cooperate with the vital principle of betterment."[16]

The conviction that the "static" truth of tradition could be abandoned quickly and without fear for the dynamic order of progress showed in the remarks by the young Beard as he ushered in the new century at Ruskin Hall.

Mr. Beard was present, and gave us, during the last three minutes of the Old Century, a retrospect of its morality; and during the first three minutes of the New Century, a prospect of the future ethics. He told us that the absolute moral code, which had for so long dominated the civilized world, was, with the Old Century, to pass away for ever, to give place to the higher morality in which—more fully and clearly regarding his brother's rights—each man must be "a law unto himself." . . . Now that our old moral basis had gone, we were told we had to seek a new foundation.[17]

Beard's confidence in the moral righteousness of history's course would survive, albeit in a more mature form, for three decades.

Unlike Beard's approach, Becker's destruction of the claims made for traditional concepts came not in the context of his analysis of the social order but in that of historical truth. "We are most of us quite proud of having reduced the universe to [an] unstable equilibrium, and yet there is one thing that seems to be exempt from the operation of this law of change and adaptation which incessantly transforms everything else—truth itself. . . . Whatever scientists may think of this notion, historians have not yet been disturbed by it. For them, certainly, truth is a fixed quality." He then ridiculed the notion that "the truth, which alone changes not, is what must be got at. The objective reality must be caught, as it were and mounted like a specimen for the instruction of future ages."[18] Characteristically and unlike Beard, Becker offered no reassurances about an alternative certainty.

Progressive historians saw in Protestantism a most formidable support for traditionalism. They ignored the contemporary Social Gospel proponents, who—in the manner of the Progressive historians—prided themselves on having freed Christianity from the shackles of the past—asceticism, dogmatism, and ceremonialism—and on having transformed it into a message befitting the future—brotherly love in a truly democratic society. They, too, wished to overcome a perceived cultural lag vis-à-vis modernity. Yet dualism knew no middle ground, particularly in a case where the antagonism was driven not only by the logic of arguments, but also by deep resentments that had taken root in some of the Progressive historians since their early years and had driven them to their revolt against Protestantism as a mainstay of the status quo.

Characteristically, Turner, who had no obligation to that dualism and who loved rural America, benevolently ignored the role religion played in American life. Beard, with a happy childhood, also treated religious phenomena as being beside the point, although he carried much of his Quaker background into his social activism. Robinson and Becker rejected more vigorously their traditional Protestant upbringing in small towns, places seen as bastions of social inertia, outdated traditions, and failure to yield to modernity.

Robinson, the son of a devoutly Presbyterian business family in a small Illinois town, praised the medieval church for its contribution to the preservation of knowledge and the advancement of administration, but denied the existence of a religious dimension in life and condemned all contemporary religious ideas as detrimental habits from the past.

By far the most fateful reaction to Protestantism turned out to be that of Becker. His rejection of Methodism, deliberate and traumatic, led him into the Progressive ranks. His thoroughly skeptical attitude toward any claim by religion, philosophy, or science to offer definitive answers, and the resultant lack of spiritual comfort, rooted in the increasing conviction that he lived in an uncaring, meaningless universe, burdened him personally and spurred on his intense attempts to reconcile such a universe with a firm historical truth. Up to 1917, Becker persisted in "doing history" in search of such a meaning—a philosophy of history that would be rational, deliver the historical truth, and quiet his intellectual restlessness. For a while, it appeared as if Progressive history had answered his quest. Yet even in those days of his relative youth and of Progressive history's Sturm und Drang, Becker's pronouncements on progress remained a bit tentative. In his address to the American Sociological Society, whose members in 1912 certainly would have welcomed a supportive statement on evolutionary progress, he dispelled all ideas that progress could be gleaned from the course of history without the value judgment that he, unlike other Progressive historians, could not deduce from the facts. To the contrary, the importance of a fact "can no longer be measured by the fact itself; it must, on the contrary, be judged by some standard of value derived from a conception of what it is that constitutes social progress."[19] Becker's rejection of Protestant certainly was to be followed by that of all certainty.

The most formidable opponent of the progress toward the Good Society was an anonymous one, the force of inertia. It also proved a most perplexing one, because it cast suspicion on the masses, the very people whose emancipation was to be the ultimate act of progress's consummation. Progressive historians had become aware of the problem early on, but in their opposition to political history, had praised long-term, slow-moving developments and located their carrier in the masses. As a scholar, Robinson had called on historians to realize that "no abrupt change has ever taken place in all of the customs of a people, and that it cannot, in the nature of things, take place," and had located in this tendency "the *unity* or *continuity of history*" (emphasis in original).[20] However, in their role as activists, Progressive historians could not see in these habits a necessary force of continuity, but only a harmful support for the existing, mostly outdated order. Hostile to all quasi-static structures, Progressive historians interpreted any prevalence of habits and routine among the masses solely as an uncritical love of routine. In the words of a congenial publicist, it "has all the appearance of activity with few of its burdens."[21] Such inertia, consciously fostered by those who benefited from it, made the masses defenders of harmful institutions. The paradox was obvious: With their unwillingness to innovate or simply to change, the masses held back their own emancipation and, for the time being, deserved mistrust. Progressive historians could plead that their distrust of the masses was not rooted in the fear of majority rule, as it would last only until the lag in enlightenment had vanished and the emancipated masses had become fully process-oriented. However, as Robinson had repeatedly demonstrated, changes in the habits of the masses had throughout the centuries moved with glacial speed. The transition to the Good Society might well take much longer than expected. Even worse, Robinson's findings cast doubt on the likelihood of the masses' ever acquiring the promptness in adjusting to new circumstances so essential for the society of the future. Yet Progressive historians also could not concede that inertia was a permanent, partially constructive feature of life, because that would have acknowledged limits to their activism and contradicted some of their basic assumptions about the human condition.

Ignoring the complex role of inertia in society, the Progressive historians were convinced that they could lift from Americans the burden of the useless past—for them, much of tradition—by replacing the authority of precedent with that of intelligence. When they viewed themselves as visionaries and agents of the future amidst widespread ignorance about or even resistance to that future, the issue of elites reentered Progressive history. Robinson praised an elite of knowledge—the great outsiders—whose work destroyed the existing routines of thought and action, and thereby pioneered progress. The new elite was justified because it differed decisively from old elites. In claiming authority, the old elites had reached into the past for their legitimacy; the new elite called on the future. The old elites tried to perpetuate themselves forever in the interest of their power and wealth; the new elite considered itself a temporary agent on behalf of the emancipation of the masses. The millennia-old tendency of elites to hold on to power would be negated— a unique feature that made all insights gained from comparative studies of elites irrelevant, because they were based on the denial of the genuinely new in human affairs.

Beard, who himself doubted that a full emancipation of the masses could ever happen in a technologically and economically complex society, defused the dangers posed by the new elite with the comforting thought that, in the participatory democracy of the future, the masses would match the power and control of the new elite of knowledge despite the differential in expertise. Particularly so, because the federal, executive, and judiciary institutions—imbued with the pragmatic and egalitarian spirit—would then be on the side of the people.

From all appearances, the modernization of American society had become a manageable task. Progressive history's message was full of hope. People would listen gladly to an interpretation of history that contradicted so thoroughly one of Henry Adams's fears about a New History. If historians were forced "to announce that the present evils of the world . . . were to be continued, exaggerated, over another thousand years, no one would listen to us with satisfaction. Society would shut its eyes and ears."[22] Safely removed from that prospect, Progressive historians held and pronounced a supreme promise for the perfection of human life—a promise they trusted was backed up by history's reality. How radically all of that revised the traditional American sense of history could not be easily discerned as long as progress, as the teleological process of history, made up for the rejected timeless values; progress, buttressed by facts, safeguarded the scientific status of the new view; and reform, guided by intelligence and awareness of the needs of the new American society, would lead to the emancipation from all social and individual evils and from those limits once perceived as constants but now shown to be ephemeral. In the absence of sufficient stress exerted by life, the apparent congruence of the traditional American sense of history and Progressive history found no real test. But Progressive history was not only clear, simple, and cheerful; it also was fragile. Its faith in the beneficial direction of history's flow made possible the trust in the technical solution to all social problems, including the delayed emancipation of minorities and women. In essence, these problems were mere maladjustments that could and would be remedied once they were seen as such. Complex phenomena were simplified to the point of trivializing them. Religion, for example, was denied a permanent functional status in human life, and seen purely as a temporarily useful superstition. All of life's darker colors, tragic dimensions, and sufferings, ironically even its conflicts, lost their true range and appeared as temporary problems accessible to technical remedies. None of life's stubborn dialectic remained, which allowed even intelligent—thus, good—actions to have detrimental consequences. As the price for their certainty, Progressive historians also had reduced most of the past to virtual insignificance. Life's pending challenges would soon test this interpretation of the human condition. Then would show the Progressive historians' dependence on their context—the relatively isolated and sheltered America of the Progressive Era, with its multitude of problems, but also with a sense of the possible total mastery of human life by technical means.

Also unresolved remained the important question of how the envisaged reformed America would fit into the universality of progress, still assumed to be a feature of the modern world. Even in the traditional American sense of history it had been implied that America's exceptionalism would be shared universally, once the *novus ordo seclorum* had been extended to the world. For Progressive history, its universal validity was given by the recognition of the universalizing forces of modernity, such as industrialization and the growth of rationality. In his *In-*

dustrial Revolution (1901) Beard prophesied that steam and electricity would be great unifiers of the world by fostering an increasingly common consciousness among people, and that industrialism and commerce would be great equilizers of nations. Robinson spoke of the denser net of communication and world commerce as suggesting "boundless possibilities of human brotherhood" based on a shared rationality.[23]

Up to 1914, doubts about American progress fitting smoothly into a universal progress left no traces in Robinson's work and only sketchy ones in Beard's. The latter were triggered by one of the early manifestations that not all consequences of industrialization were as beneficial as expected. Influenced by Hobson's work on imperialism, Beard observed a link between modernization, commercial expansion, and imperialism. Now, America, the technologically advanced nation, also followed the logic of the technological and capitalist era by reaching out into the world in the interest of commerce and gearing her foreign policy to it, tempted by her technological sophistication to be a great power and to abandon her isolation. In this, to Beard, disturbing linkage of progress's benevolent force with what he considered malevolent means and correspondingly undesirable effects, he confronted an early manifestation of the problem that would haunt him after 1917: the proper relation of reforms at home to the obligation to universal progress, as prescribed both by the universal character of modernity and the implied missionary duty in the American sense of history.

In these years of great expectations, only Becker's hopes were tinged with fundamental doubts. In 1910, he had spoken out on historiographical issues in the very theoretical foundations of Progressive history. Soon, sensitivity to the complexity of human life made Becker's doubts spread to historical interpretation itself. He was losing gradually whatever confidence he ever had been able to muster in Progressive history's alluring mix of science, progress, and action. Ironically, his Robinson-induced studies of eighteenth-century French history led him not only to the Enlightenment's certainties, but also to Denis Diderot's uncertainties. That *philosophe*'s intellectual crisis he understood only too well. When Diderot reflected on the successful destruction of much of the ancien régime's cultural heritage—one in which he had participated —he pointed for Becker to the similar destruction brought about in contemporary America.

But then what was the bearing of such a [rationalistic] philosophy upon the problem of morality and conduct? No question that it destroyed the intellectual basis of morality as taught by the Church; but it was one of the ironies of fate that the speculative thinking of Diderot, of which the principal purpose was to furnish a firm foundation for natural morality, ended by destroying the foundation of all morality as he understood it. This was the dilemma, that if the conclusions of Diderot the speculative philosopher were valid, the aspirations of Diderot the moral man, all the vital purposes and sustaining hopes of his life, were but as the substance of a dream.[24]

These were strange doubts for a participant in the Progressive revolution in American historiography. Becker no longer was sure that an established tradition could be effectively, quickly, and totally replaced with a new tradition designed by the use of the very same reason whose propensity to doubt would not stop after the transition was accomplished. In the case of Progressive history he would have to question whether it could deliver what, at one time, historians in concert with tradition had delivered, and that needed to be delivered in order to safeguard the social usefulness of history: a sense of stability, certainty, and continuity. Now, only the assumption that a body of ascertained facts spelled out progress, together with the stipulation that natural evolution also vouched for human progress toward a grander future, kept in check a total relativism. For another decade and a half, Becker would be alone with his insights and his inner struggle with relativism.

In the meantime, a much smaller certainty would have to do for Becker, as he pronounced history's value to be primarily moral and not scientific. Inasmuch as it liberated the mind, fortified the will, and deepened compassion, it enabled us "to control, not society, but ourselves,— a much more important thing; it prepares us to live more humanely in the present and to meet rather than to foretell the future," an assertion of history as an instrument of activism at a considerable distance from Beard's and Robinson's reformist zeal, and about as gung ho as Becker ever became.[25]

Other Progressive historians remained convinced that the old views of history with their certainties could be replaced by one grander and more proper to the modern age. Theirs was a Wellsian vision. "We are creatures of the twilight. . . . All this world is heavy with the promise of greater things, and a day will come . . . when beings, beings who are now latent in our thoughts and hidden in our loins, will stand upon this earth as one stands upon a footstool, and laugh, and reach out their hands amidst the stars."[26] The logic of actual life would soon raise its own questions that would tax sorely a view of history that had purchased its certainty, interpretation, and message of hope by calling a truce in its war against positivism long enough to gain from it certainty about progress; rejecting much of the human past as irrelevant, if not detrimental; denying any permanent structure in the human condition;

reducing the complexity of human history to a grand dualism; transforming human life's perennial problems into temporary adjustment difficulties that could be remedied by technical measures; and leaving the tension between national and universal progress unresolved. Questions would be raised inevitably on how satisfactory Progressive history was as a New American History or as an American New History.

Into the Progressive historians' celebrations of the future the guns of August 1914 interjected discordant sounds.

3

A DECADE OF FRUITION

AND STAGNATION

1920–1929

In every social progress, the great and the only difficult work
is the destruction of the past. We need not be anxious about
what we shall place in the stead of the ruins. The force of
things and of life will undertake the rebuilding.

Maurice Maeterlinck
The Measure of the Hours

11

A Defiant Reaffirmation

By 1919, Progressive historians had experienced a double shock. In the fateful summer of 1914, the architects of Progressive history were proceeding full of optimism to define further its major tenets and win converts for their vision of history. Beard tried to elaborate on his economic decoding of history; Becker, with his years in Kansas coming to a close and beset by doubts, wrote occasional reflective pieces on society and education; Robinson basked in the afterglow of *The New History*'s success, looking forward to writing his magnum opus on the progress of human thought. Then the guns of August interrupted all of that. Three years later, the three historians were drawn into a conflict that, at first, had been seen as a distant "midsummer madness" befitting the Old World, but soon was defined as a moral contest. In it the Allied powers became the forces fighting for democratic progress (with Russia the quietly passed-over exception), while the Central powers appeared as the forces of the past, representing tyranny and autocracy. Beard, Robinson, and Becker served in various groups that delivered propaganda material for the war effort. They, together with many other historians, became combatants in the great battle for the minds of Americans and "the verdict of mankind," or, put less heroically, participants "in the world's greatest adventure in advertising."[1] In those years, even Becker, cheered by the "upward" direction of his career as he moved first to the University of Minnesota and then to Cornell University, experienced one of his rare periods of enthusiasm. Then the postwar settlements brought a cruel disillusionment to those who had expected a reformed America, if not world, to result from the war. Even though Robinson, ten years later, regretted that historians "blew trumpets and grasped halberds," the true issue for Progressive historians never was their participation in the war effort, but the apparent failure of their expectations.[2] They, who interpreted the war economy's stunning success in production, planning, and coordination, and in offering opportunities for work to all as an incipient realization of the future order, observed with disbelief how America returned to the old laissez-faire order. Progressive historians also had expected that the general horror over the destructiveness of technologically enhanced warfare would prevent the restoration of the old international order. But the European allies—those imagined allies in the struggle for a new order—did restore the old order. The envisioned future had not only failed to arrive, it had not even come closer. Some hope was kindled by the plans for an organization of nations to preserve world peace and cooperation. It was only partially fulfilled by the League of Nations.

Already during the war signs had appeared that should have shed doubt on some of the expectations of Progressive historians. The events that led to Beard's resignation from Columbia University in 1917 proved that the war to make the world safe for democracy could be quite inimical to civil rights.[3] Civil liberties were seen as threatened when administrators and board members, whose ideas and habits reflected the past, were given the power of judgment over professors. There was irony in his protest, since Beard did not really view the professoriat on the whole as banner carriers for the cause of the future, but rather resented the academic world as one filled with a few curious and many apathetic students, as well as with professors who produced works with measured words, contemplated rather than acted, affirmed the status quo, and remained detached from society. Thus, Beard's action on behalf of professional liberty became his liberation from academe. Robinson's resignation, two months later, was a milder protest. After all, while objecting to any censorship, he had maintained "that the revived restraints due to the war are transient, and need not be a serious cause of apprehension to anyone."[4] He would, therefore, grumble when told to revise a passage in one of his textbooks because it did not paint Germany's behavior in sufficiently dark colors, but he would do it anyway. The whole civil liberties controversy had a more sinister implication. Aside from demonstrating to the Progressive historians' satisfaction the still formidable strength of the forces of inertia, the civil liberties debate should have raised doubts about the great hopes most of them invested in a much more powerful national government for the realization of the proper future. Could any authority, even a progressive one, ever be completely free of the tendency to coercion, and thus not be a threat to the substance of progress itself? A negative answer would have contradicted main tenets of Progressive history, ruling the question itself out of bounds.

Only one Progressive historian tested these bounds. Becker took what had happened as a horrendous contradiction to Progressive history's stipulation of a steady progress toward a thoroughly civilized world. The shock proved most destructive in Becker's case not because his enthusiasm had been so high, but because it had been so fragile a barrier to corrosive doubts; one only strong enough to offer a brief reprieve from his growing skepticism and relativism. Becker was angry at himself that as an experienced historian he could have been naive enough to suppose that Wilson could ever accomplish those ideal objects that were so well formulated in Wilson's state papers. He "should have known that in this war, as in all wars, men would profess to be fighting for justice and liberty, but in the end would demand the spoils of victory if they won. It was futile from the beginning to suppose that a new international order could be founded on the old national order."[5] It was too easy to seek the source of the disappointment in Wilson, when in reality it resided at the core of Progressive history; its fundamental assertion was wrong. Far from having a progressive telos, life was futile.

The war and what has come out of it has carried me very rapidly along certain lines of thought which have always been more congenial to my temperament than yours. I have always been susceptible to the impression of the futility of life, and always easily persuaded to regard history as no more than the meaningless resolution of blind forces which struggling men—good men and bad—do not understand and cannot control, although they amuse themselves with the pleasing illusion that they do.[6]

In the cold cosmos of anonymous forces without "good" purpose, both Wilson and the opponents of the League of Nations talked nonsense. The hope for a full human mastery of life was futile. In the relative isolation of Ithaca, Becker looked at the aftermath of what had seemed a noble endeavor and remarked with sarcasm: "This is the result of some thousand of years of what men like to speak of as 'political, economic, intellectual, and moral Progress.'"[7] The collapse of his Progressive faith would be the fateful context in which Becker's destruction of Progressive history's theoretical framework would proceed.

On the opposite end of the spectrum of reactions to what had happened, the broad American public was much less troubled than the Progressive historians. After an initial disappointment with the war's results, Americans went on with their lives. For them "normalcy" meant to enjoy the fruits of victory and a renewed isolation. It held none of the sinister meanings that Progressive historians connected with it: the neglect, if not betrayal, of the needed reforms of American society and, to a lesser extent, of the expected new world order. Normalcy also had no objectionable connotation for Scientific historians, who resumed their explorations of the past, based on documentary research and done in a positivist manner. Herein lay the strength of Scientific history that, with its fact-finding process detached from the influence of the historian's context, it could take all changes in the world, even such stupendous ones as the Great War, simply as data that only in the distant future would affect the historian's interpretations. In that, American Scientific historians resembled their German and French colleagues. The former could resume their work and take shelter in historicism, although a momentous discontinuity had appeared in German history. They failed signally in establishing a continuity with the German past that would have given support to the new German republic. Victory made it even easier for the French historians to go on with their version of Scientific history that implicitly supported the heritage of the French Revolution. The two innovators, Lucien Febvre and Marc Bloch, were given academic appointments at the University of Strasbourg, at a safe distance from Paris. Even the Marxists, who were most adamant about the solution of the social question (the integration of the worker into society), saw their orthodoxy confirmed and not imperiled by the Great War.

In this atmosphere, hostile to reflection, the Progressive historians returned to their own "normalcy" when they reaffirmed the historical theory they had worked out before 1917. With the exception of Becker, they declined to see in the contradictions that the war and contemporary life posed to their historiography a mandate to reevaluate their assumptions and conclusions. Instead, they maintained that the discrepancy between their expectations and reality stemmed not from fundamental flaws in their views, but only from an overly optimistic estimate of when the proper future would arrive. Progressive history had acquired the characteristics of a mature historical interpretation. It had a sufficiently developed interpretation to find answers to all problems in its own confines. Affirming their version of the American sense of history, they were not tempted by the available alternatives.

By the early 1920s, the allure of Turner's geographical interpretation was diminishing as the frontier thesis faded in both popularity and scholarly impact. Occasionally, even Turner conceded that in the present the "urban side" and "the capital and labor side" had surpassed the frontier in importance for America.[8] Also, he had not published a major work since 1907, only a collection of mainly old articles in 1920. Those who noticed would wonder with Dunning about "how potent has been the influence, and how disproportionately scanty, alas! the historiographic output, of our own Turner."[9] The chase after the data for his Big Book on American history between 1830 and 1850 from the sectional perspective was proving endless, as the data base never was good enough for the perfectionist Turner; the lure of the outdoors, particularly fishing, grew ever more powerful; and the first signs of heart trouble made sustained efforts over longer periods difficult. It also became obvious that the sectionalist Turner did not excite the reading public to the degree that the frontier Turner had, and did not convert young historians in the old numbers. In 1924, Turner retired, although the hope for the Big Book stayed alive until his last years, which he spent at the Huntington Library in San Marino, California. Turner's diminishing prominence made it easier for Progressive historians to ignore his views, which had not been able to support convincingly a progress view that included the industrial and urban aspects of modernity. Only Becker still maintained a warm personal relationship with Turner. He used the frontier thesis liberally in *The United States: An Experiment in Democracy* (1920), and then wrote about Turner one of the best brief accounts of any American historian's personality and work. Beard provided a negative exception to the benign neglect when he dissented from the general praise for Turner's essay collection, *The Frontier in American History,* with a sharp criticism of Turner's excessive claims for the frontier's role in shaping American history and of Turner's poor documentation.[10] In general, geographical interpretations held no fascination for Progressive historians. Even Febvre's pioneering work, *La terre et l'évolution humaine,* translated into English in 1925, with its more sophisticated view of the relationship between culture and geography, even with a touch of evolutionary theory, had no impact.

Another alternative—one seemingly more akin to Progressive history—was presented by Arthur M. Schlesinger, Sr., who perceived "that interest in social and cultural history has been growing very rapidly among the younger generation of American historians in recent years."[11] But his social history shifted the accent from the amelioration of social conditions through basic reforms to the comprehension of American society's complex totality. The grand conflict between business and people, still present in Schlesinger's book *The Colonial Merchants and the American Revolution, 1763–1776* (1918), gave way in his *New Viewpoints in American History* (1922) to a plea for studying history's so far ignored aspects and groups. In general the "great many" must prevail over the "great men." Historians must explore all aspects of life, including Turner's geographic space, the role of women, immigration and related ethnic issues, economic influences, social and political radicalism and conservatism, and the "riddle of the parties." The culmination of Schlesinger's work came with the History of American Life series, which he coedited with Dixon Ryan Fox. It was to be a social history that intended "to grasp and depict both the inner and outer life of society and to integrate the two, and for this there must be found a unifying theme inferred from the painstaking examination of the data."[12] Although the theme proved elusive, the series brought "a revision of American history with the purpose of depicting those every-day concerns of the American people which have molded their social and intellectual development."[13] When Schlesinger offered Harry Elmer Barnes the authorship of volume 12 (tentatively entitled "America in War and Peace, 1914–1926"), early signs of differences with the Progressive historians surfaced. Barnes appeared to be a fine choice because he had as strong an interest in sociology, especially criminology, as he had in history. A report on the prison system in New Jersey had been accepted as his dissertation, and his books *World Politics and the Expansion of Western Civilization* (1920), *Social History of the Western World* (1921), and *History: Its Rise and Development* (1922) showed him to be a historian in a social science mold. However, Barnes espoused an aggressively accented Progressive history. Upon Barnes's inquiry concerning the thrust of the series, Schlesinger assured him that it would not be an apologia for any of the groups Barnes disliked, but also admonished him that the editors did "not want *propaganda* in favor of those principles and policies which mean most to you and me (aren't you sick of Upton Sinclair?). This means that what we want is an objective presentation of the facts, without exclamation points, let the chips fall where they may" (emphasis in original).[14] While Barnes accepted the offer, he never wrote the volume in a series that, for him, had its scholarly locus too far afield from Progressive history.[15]

Although the series did emphasize social change, it was criticized for its lack of a pronounced progressive telos and its neglect to focus on political power and conflict. Beard suspected the series of old-fashioned positivism and aimless eclecticism, while Becker, its figurehead consulting editor, pronounced the series mired in facts. A New History that described and assessed American history as a whole, studying all aspects of American life, without giving it or discovering in it a telos, remained for Progressive historians too close to Scientific history.[16]

In their approach, the initiators of the History of American Life series resembled their French contemporaries Berr, Febvre, and Marc Bloch, who in their country competed with teleologically minded historians inspired by the ideals and ideas of the French Revolution. They, too, deemphasized politics, and, as Febvre put it later, suspended judgment on "whether the whole of the political, social, economic and intellectual history of human groups should be ordered around one history of thoughts, feelings and desires, seized in all its changes over time."[17] Yet the strong comparative emphasis, already visible in Marc Bloch's works of the 1920s, would hardly have appealed to Progressive historians.[18] Once more, the French developments in the 1920s, admittedly not yet fully developed or recognized in France herself, had no influence on American historians; that despite a full wartime-inspired suspension of German influence. Barnes, who had some familiarity with the contemporary French historiographical currents, made some fleeting attempts to bring his knowledge to the attention of others. Unfortunately, his single-minded activism made him list and praise theoretical innovations rather than assess them thoroughly or even use them to modify the theoretical base of Progressive history. Until well into the 1960s, empirical and encompassing historiographies (including social histories) without a direct message of progress played a significant, but not a decisive, role in the American context. Only then, in a period of widespread skepticism about progress, would the nonteleological social history in the vein of the History of American Life series and the, by then, mature *Annales* school capture the interest of American historians.

Again, Becker highlighted the future of Progressive history. In the years that saw the collapse of his faith in progress, he published some works in which readers with a sense of nuance could observe how Becker's destruction of the positivist concept of pure empirical facts was gradually widening to that of the truth claims of historical interpretations, including the Progressive one. He began the fusion of consciousness and "outer world" that, if left unchecked, would destroy the foundation of contemporary American historiography and its ability to modernize the American sense of history in a manner satisfactory to modern doubts. In *The Eve of the Revolution* (1918) he intended "to convey to the reader, not a record of what men did, but a sense of how they thought and felt about what they did." The arguments of the Patriots resonated no longer with echoes of timeless rights and ideas, but reflected only what was useful to say, given the situation and the psychological dispositions of the revolutionaries. When they drew on English and Roman history for parallels, Becker saw in these parallels no indications for the past's capacity to speak about the perennial structure of human life, but only ad hoc arguments invented for the occasion. While this approach seemed to shift interpretation from reading the facts to spinning a web of relationships at a safe distance from "a mere verification of references," things were not yet sorted out in Becker's mind.[19] The endorsement of the reality of natural rights in the conclusion, though highly qualified, still left things unsettled. The subsequent book, *The United States: An Experiment in Democracy* (1920), written for a broad public, was surprisingly affirmative for a man already deeply troubled about all certainty. It used Turner's concepts liberally, Progressive history's ideas sparingly, and his usually brilliant style insufficiently.

With *The Declaration of Independence* (1922), Becker's doubts had acquired enough strength and sophistication to put his deliberation on the nature of ideas and concepts well outside of Progressive history's affirmative pragmatism. Ideas and concepts, now increasingly detached from the world of experience, were resettled in the realm of imagination. In the eighteenth century, human rights had been called natural rights because nature had become the surrogate for God, but the rights had still been considered timeless and absolute. The conception of the instrumentality of all truth transformed such natural rights into historical rights. However, Becker was not yet ready to proceed to the logical corollary that historical interpretations reflected no more than the economic interests and psychological needs of the collective life. With major problems in his historiographical views as yet unresolved, Becker spent the early 1920s perfecting his knowledge of European history— his new teaching field at Cornell University—and sorting out the theoretical implications of his radical skepticism for historiography. With the exception of some book reviews and shorter pieces, he remained quiet. Plagued by recurrent and energy-sapping stomach ulcers (a suffering stoically borne) and convinced that the world would never improve much anyway, he found that the silence suited him well.

Neither Robinson nor Beard nor the new advocate of Progressive history, Harry Elmer Barnes, found the alternative avenues toward a differed New History convincing, and none of them shared Becker's doubts. Instead, they undertook a supreme effort to persuade Americans to see history in the proper way. They wrote and lectured about how contemporary America's failure to establish the *novus ordo seclorum* had its cause in the lack of a truly modern understanding of the course of history. With a palpable sense of urgency, they demanded the alignment of American policies with the overall trend of history toward the Good Society or, in Graham Wallas's term, the Great Society.[20] Robinson, Beard, and Barnes betrayed a conviction, colored by anxiety, that the final effort to clear away the obstacles to the future's arrival had entered its decisive stage. Robinson agreed with H. G. Wells when he assessed the situation as "a race between education and catastrophe."[21] Such apocalyptic visions provided no incentives for ruminations about historiography's theoretical underpinnings. They excluded doubts. When, in the 1920s, they collided with the broad public indifference to reforms, activism turned into a near frantic activity to enlighten the people about the "real" situation and enlist them as co-workers. In a period of self-conscious "normalcy," Robinson, Beard, and Barnes went into the public square to change the old routines, pit intelligence against unthinking repetition, and preach a "new doctrine of salvation loosely comprehended by the term 'social intelligence.'"[22] They were convinced that Progressive history provided the sure guide for both America's adjustment to the modern world, properly aligned with the principles of science, technology, democracy, and social justice, and the proper pursuit of happiness. For accomplishing the task, Progressive history could rely on its stalwarts Robinson and Beard, on their former student Harry Elmer Barnes, on the literary historian Vernon L. Parrington, and on a small group of Progressive scholars in other disciplines, among them the historically minded psychologist G. Stanley Hall. During the 1920s, they brought forth some of the most prominent works of Progressive history. However, these works also represented, in the main, a brilliant exposition of the ideas formulated prior to 1917, rather than their future creative development.

Robinson, entering his sixties and seeing the end of his scholarly career approaching, felt a special sense of urgency. Exasperated by what he saw as threats to the progress of rationality from the reappearance of "primitivism" and worried about the fragile edifice of modern civilization, he suspended his plan for a scholarly magnum opus on the whole sweep of Western civilization's cultural history, based on his popular course at Columbia University.[23] Friends had already begun to regret that "Robinson's *Scriptum principale* seems as unlikely as Roger Bacon's to be ever completed."[24] Instead, Robinson used the material he had collected on the topic as the central part of his *Mind in the Making* (1921). The book, whose title was patterned after H. G. Wells's *Mankind in the Making,* became a best-seller, although it offered a curious mixture of essential, but by then well-known Progressive themes with excessively lengthy condemnations of some thoroughly ephemeral phenomena (such as the work of the Lusk Committee of the New York State Assembly, which Robinson considered dangerously reactionary). Still, many readers found the depiction of intellectual history as a clear struggle between good (the future) and evil (the "survivals" of the past) most attractive, even at the cost of a vast simplification of the complex intellectual development. Novel ideas were absent from this book as well as from the next one, *The Humanizing of Knowledge* (1923), which marked the end point of Robinson's creative career.[25] *The Ordeal of Civilization* (1926), a textbook, was essentially a reformulation of his *Medieval and Modern Times* (1918). A number of articles, published in the mid-1920s, repeated what he had said before, but their exhortations were now occasionally touched by melancholy. As the years went by and the gap between the existing world and the Progressive vision of the future did not narrow, there built in Robinson a hard-to-bear tension between his desperate feeling of running out of time and his flagging creativity. The death of his wife, in early 1927, was another blow to a man who said of himself that he became "more and more retiring every year. I do not have much strength and what I have is drained into piddling channels others dig."[26] The latter remark referred to the presidency of the American Historical Association (1929), which he regretted having accepted. A turning back to an interest of his youth, biology, led to retreats to the microscopic analysis of aquatic life in Woods Hole.[27] He was not quite ready yet to fade away completely, and opposed a memorial volume honoring him. At one time, he still dreamed of writing the book on the course of Western civilization—fifteen years overdue to the Macmillan Company—by expanding his recent article on civilization for the *Encyclopaedia Britannica*.[28] However, Robinson, depressed about the course of things, betrayed the exhaustion of his creativity in his uninspired presidential address at the meeting of the American Historical Association in 1929.[29]

The 1920s were glorious years for Charles Beard, who, eleven years younger than Robinson, produced together with his wife, Mary, the best-selling *Rise of American Civilization*. Splendidly written, the work's first two volumes reached the then fabulous sales figure of 130,000 copies in its early editions, increased the already solid financial independence of the Beards, and made Charles Beard a much sought-after contributor, who could command from ten to twenty cents per word for his writing. But more important, *The Rise of American Civilization* represented the culmination of the Progressive attempt to rewrite American history in the modern manner—a sort of *summa historiae progressiva*—that shaped the outlook of a generation of intellectual leaders. For decades, it would be the "new Bancroft." Whoever missed that central work was nearly sure to encounter Beard in articles, pamphlets, book reviews, and textbooks, or to hear him speak. Those who read much of his material were either reassured about the course of history or somewhat taken aback by the repetitiveness and predictability of his views, since Beard, too, did little to clarify or further develop the Progressive view of history. Even *The Rise of American Civilization*, with its novel concept of the second American revolution and its earnest, although often sketchy, attempts to shape also cultural history in the mold of Beard's economic interpretation, derived its celebrity status less from innovation or an increase in interpretive sophistication than from being a brilliant carrier of a message.

Harry Elmer Barnes, still searching for a firm foothold in academe, poured forth articles and books at an amazing speed. Besides the already mentioned works on Western civilization's expansion, a social history, and a brief history of historiography (all between 1920 and 1922), he published the programmatic *New History and Social Studies* (1925), an enlarged section of which appeared as *Psychology and History* (1925); *The Genesis of the World War* (1926), which would garner lasting renown and foes for him; publications on sociology and penol-

ogy; and the polemical *Twilight of Christianity* (1929). He also collected many of his articles in *History and Social Intelligence* (1926). The
desire to help accomplish a quick turn of American society toward the
right future, a journalistic bent, and the total absence of any doubt drove
him to write so much so fast. Some friends cautioned him that it was too
much and too fast, although they put their admonition kindly—"if you
are not careful, young man, you will exhaust the paper supply in this
country."[30] Speed made his writings, as H. L. Mencken put it, also "in-
fernally long," although editors' pencils could curb Barnes's discursive-
ness to some extent.[31] Critics would question the profundity of these
works, but Barnes's rigidly dualistic worldview and his combativeness—
his "method of dancing a jig on [his] opponents' corns," as somebody
described it—endeared him to many.[32] That aspect of his writing, more
than its substance, moved him steadily further away from the edges of
the mainstream of American historians. In 1920, Jameson still welcomed Barnes to his annual *Convivium historicum* of history professors. Six years later he refused to publish Barnes's letter concerning a
review in the *American Historical Review,* reminding Barnes that sarcasm was not evidence.[33] Nevertheless, throughout the 1920s, Barnes
remained close to traditional history in one important aspect: his strong
affirmation of a positivistic methodological stance. He openly asserted it
in his revisionist writings about the First World War, with their masses of
documentary research and emphasis on individuals. More decisively, he
would refuse to abandon that stance even in the 1930s.

Merle Curti, who at the time also attempted to establish himself in
academe, would eventually prove to be a much more creative scholar,
but his important intellectual history in the Progressive vein appeared
only much later as *The Growth of American Thought* (1943). He also
was the temperamental opposite of Barnes, once admitting that he was
reticent as an activist: "I wish I knew better how to preach the gospel,
and follow it."[34]

In 1927, Vernon L. Parrington, a professor at the University of Washington, began to render splendid help. He had come to Seattle after a
career in which he had acquired a resentment not only of Harvard's
social world, but also of the general conformity to existing social and
political conventions prevalent in higher education. Parrington's experiences of rejection in academe, the influences of English and Marxist socialism, Populism, and the ideas of his new faculty colleague, J.
Allen Smith, helped shape his *Main Currents of American Literature.*
That enormously popular work seemed to fulfill, at least partially, the
hopes for a Progressive history of ideas that Robinson had only raised.
Judgments about its scholarly value would vary, but there was no doubt

about its quality as a passionate account of the struggle between good and bad ideas in the world of literature and the intellect. The neat dualism was made possible by subordinating all aesthetic considerations to the economic and political dimensions of life, seen in the perspective of Progressive history. Parrington had even planned to title the book "An Economic Interpretation of Literature." Once more, innovators struggled on behalf of the people against dominant, oppressive, and exploitative interests, this time in the realm of ideas and literary creativity. Parrington's work was a Progressive manifesto in the form of a literary history that appealed to Americans to take heart, because "intelligent America is in revolt. The artist is in revolt, the intellectual is in revolt, the conscience of America is in revolt."[35] In the end, despite such enthusiasm, Parrington would be less sure about progress than other Progressive historians.

In the 1920s, Progressive historians vigorously did what Robinson had declared to be the task of the historians, "to arouse an intelligent discontent, to foster a fruitful radicalism."[36] For that endeavor it proved unimportant that Parrington was at the remote University of Washington and that Robinson and Beard remained outsiders to academe (except for their brief tenure in the New School of Social Research), and hence never established anything like a school in the sense of sending forth a whole generation of academicians with clear directions in methodology and interpretation. Their work at Columbia University had shown how powerful such an academic position could be, judging by the influence their years spent there had yielded. These scholars had to exert their impact through books and textbooks. They succeeded splendidly when *The Mind in the Making, The Rise of American Civilization,* and *Main Currents in American Thought* penetrated deeply into the consciousness of those whose intellectual formation occurred in the 1920s and 1930s. A subsequent gradual shift of accent in historical scholarship and an increasing number of revisionist works were clear indicators of their impact.

Who was affected by the Progressive historians' appeals? The broad masses, the ultimate target of the campaign, proved rather resistant to the Progressive message. Most Americans did not read the Progressive historians' books and articles. The *Nation* and the *New Republic* were not mass publications. At the latter journal, its editor, Herbert Croly, now had great difficulties in keeping a stable of good writers together, and he himself experienced a weakening confidence in the rational reconstruction of society. After 1918, the world no longer looked so simple as it had when a relatively isolated America seemed at liberty to chart her history's course. Progressive historians ascribed their failure to reach the masses too readily to deeply ingrained habits, maintained by inertial forces and reinforced by the enemies of majority rule, although they experienced no more than the universal tendency of the masses not to make major changes except under duress. The normalcy of the 1920s hardly qualified as such a circumstance. Isolated attempts to speak directly to the blue-collar population proved short-lived. In the early 1920s, Robinson and the Beards cooperated with the Workers Education Bureau of New York City in an effort at adult education, particularly through the Workers Bookshelf. Robinson supplied his *Humanizing of Knowledge,* hoping to replace the prejudices fed by ignorance with sound scientific insights. But his plan of a whole series of books designed to advance that reform did not come to fruition, because of a lack of willing authors. The failure of the endeavor especially disappointed the Beards, who, still influenced by their English experience, had held even higher expectations. Hoping for an American Labor Party, they had seen the Workers Education Bureau as an effective instrument for such a party's creation and its eventual victory.[37]

In the midst of an overwhelming sense of normalcy, the response to Progressive history's appeal came mainly from liberal members of the educated American middle class. They had a greater predisposition for doubt and reform after their hopes for a new social and political order had been dashed in the aftermath of the Great War. To them Progressive historians gave a new sense of certainty, direction, and hope, or, at least, a better definition of their discontent. For influencing these readers the Progressive historians had found the proper media outside of academe. The dissemination of ideas through books (including bestsellers and textbooks), journals, and magazines proved effective in changing the perspective of a whole generation of citizens intent on reforms, among them a host of educators and young historians.

12

The Quasi Alliance with the

Social Sciences

In the battle against normalcy, Progressive historians could not rely on an alliance with the social sciences. Talk of such an alliance persisted, while ad hoc relationships still substituted for a common and clearly defined theoretical base. That was just as well, since a close scrutiny would have revealed the dwindling chances for an agreement on theoretical issues between Progressive historians and social scientists. On their part, Progressive historians continued to speak of the essential role of the social sciences as well as of the obligation of historians to take note of it. The spokesman for the alliance now was not so much Robinson as Barnes. The latter, a historian, who at first worked in the field of criminology, came to be seen as a prominent sociologist on the basis of numerous books on sociology, social thought, and penology.[1] His message was the same as Robinson's, although its strong accent on science, to the point of scientism, foretold his refusal to join other Progressive historians in the relativist experiment of the early 1930s. "It is becoming ever more apparent that the complex difficulties of the present scientific and industrial age can in no way be completely dealt with by excellent intentions, single-track schemes of social and economic reconstruction, metaphysical idealism or religious zeal," but through the application of the research findings of social scientists. Historians had to accept the social scientists as allies because these sciences were mandated by history. They alone could secure the means for the "adequate and intelligent control, direction and reorganization" of society.[2] Robinson did little more than add a stronger historical rationale to his previous admonitions. Only if historians and social scientists strove to match the level of scientific quality of the natural sciences could progress be enhanced and even a temporary backward slide in human rationality be prevented. In Roger Bacon, Giordano Bruno, and the modern scientists, Robinson found assurance that, this time, the great failure of the Greeks would not be repeated. After having secularized human thought, they had left a philosophical heritage that made possible a useless spinning of "laborious webs of learning" that had resulted in scholars with "their wits being shut up in the cells of a few authors (chiefly Aristotle, their dictator), as their persons were shut up in the cells of monasteries and colleges."[3] Now, in the modern period, a pragmatically reshaped rationality must and would pervade all thought permanently. In the vein of the Comtean history, Barnes argued that modern science had created a world that necessitated the social sciences (including Progressive history) as the corresponding instrument for the mastery of human life.

In all of these exhortations for historians to be more scientific it was never made explicit what it really meant for history to be or become scientific in the image of the natural sciences. Robinson admitted that he was "not advocating any particular method of treating human affairs, but rather *such a general frame of mind, such a critical open-minded attitude,* as has hitherto been but sparsely developed among those who aspire to be men's guides, whether religious, political, economic, or academic" (emphasis in original).[4] Although familiar with the contemporary French and German debates on the matter, Barnes never bothered to formulate concrete suggestions either. The implication was that the progressive-evolutionary perspective had set history on the right course, one in line with the scientific mandates of progress. Life would give the answers the scholars were too busy to seek. However, the haziness on what the term *scientific* meant in Progressive history left the basis for an alliance ill defined. The preoccupation with activism prevented any profound explorations of the topic. That, in turn, hid developments in social science theory, which made all talk of an alliance more and more illusory.

In principle, nothing so far had stood in the way of an eventual fuller union between history and the social sciences. Yet after the war, the conditions for such an alliance changed when social scientists, by and large, retained a reformist attitude but abandoned the evolutionary framework for their work. John Dewey's observations on recent tendencies in the social sciences should have warned Progressive historians, who continued to argue in what social scientists now would deride as the grand speculative manner. Social scientists became more and more convinced that if they devoted their "compelling attention to details, to particulars, it safeguards one from seclusion in universals; one is obliged, as William James was always saying, to get down from the noble aloofness into the muddy stream of concrete things."[5] When, during the 1920s, they strove to become empirical in the positivist sense, they found the evolutionary framework of thought, particularly its teleological historical perspective, incompatible with detailed empirical studies. They turned to problems of a small scale to find or illuminate the mechanisms, even laws, that regulated social relations. That meant a slowing down or even suspension of social reforms until they could be based on the authority of social science. The new social scientists were cautious members of by now well-defined disciplines, professionals with a definite analytical approach to inquiry, possible beneficiaries of financial support from grant-awarding agencies (such as the new Social Science Research Council), and researchers content with achievements on a small scale. Of progress or a historical perspective little was left except an implicit recognition of the American sense of history in the scope of explorations. Its metaphysical foundation in the divine and natural rights was rejected, while the centrality of the individual as the actor and beneficiary of history was retained. Individual social processes might not be tightly linked to an objectively given progress, but the progressive tenor of thought was still present. That historical residue justified the tenuous hope for an alliance with the Progressive historians.

Nevertheless, Progressive historians continued to speak of such an alliance. Thus, in his 1929 presidential address to the American Historical Association, Robinson blithely declared the alliance to be a given. The harsh facts of the increasing estrangement were partially veiled, because on the issue of social activism the division did not exist. Many social scientists still were not only concerned with how things were but also with how they ought to be. And, until the late 1920s, the two groups of scholars still shared a methodology with a sufficiently positivistic core that kept away the radical doubts—already powerful in Europe—about the reliability of the historians' interpretations based on facts. When German epistemological theories and the writings of Freud, Vilfredo Pareto, Karl Mannheim, and others gradually seeped into the intellectual worlds of Beard and Becker, they would erode the last foundation for an alliance, this time from the side of the historians.

The overt parting of ways between Progressive historians and social scientists on the issue of the proper scientific language was important as a symptom of greater problems. Most social scientists now wrote primarily for specialists. Those who wished to reform society could then be more effective by basing the social technology on new scientific findings. However, the Progressive historians, for whom activism held a more immediate priority, wrote so as to appeal directly to the broad public.

Thus, just like the definition of the term *scientific*, the issue of a scientific language could wait. Progressive historians had not heeded Robinson's earlier advice to free history from the tyranny of having to conform to the dictates of popular tastes. Now, in the 1920s, they were even less inclined to do so as they were urgently trying to convince their readers of the immediate necessity for reforms. On the contrary,

Robinson perceived the need for "a new form of literary ambition if scientific knowledge is to reach a fair proportion of the population and the scientific mood is to be widely cultivated. This ambition should be to bring home to the greatest possible number of readers as much knowledge as possible, in the most pleasing, effective, and least misleading manner."[6] Impatient with historical works he considered overly erudite, Barnes chose a style of writing not so much pleasing, but forceful—some would even call it badgering.

Beard, never an author of dry theoretical treatises, understood the problem superbly. He used vivid word pictures, colorful phrasings, emotion-packed appeals, and devastating irony to make the Progressive case. The abstract was banned from his writings when he spoke of the "rolling tide of migration," of "the man with a rifle—grim, silent, fearless," or of "the hunters, nerves kept taut with watchfulness." He never released his hold on the readers' minds as he bent their thinking about the past in the desired direction.

Robinson's writings, more precise than exciting, could not make up for the great loss Progressive history suffered when Becker published little more than a few minor pieces during the 1920s. Becker's style—marked by clarity, irony, and elegance—fascinated readers. His student diaries testified to his early concern with good writing, and his studies of eighteenth-century France enhanced his determination to write elegantly. Nevertheless, Becker kept in check the temptation to imitate the French writers of that age. He understood what the democratic age demanded of the historian. Referring to Bancroft, he wondered "why a Harvard man with sufficient independence to become a Jacksonian democrat, should not have realized that a 'style' suitable for telling the story of the Trojan War or the Fall of Lucifer is not the best for relating the history of the United States."[7]

The disagreement with social scientists on language and style was joined by others on substance. Robinson and Barnes praised especially anthropology for establishing the uninterrupted story of human life and thereby destroying the concept of "prehistory" as well as the biblical story's dominance of early human history. Evolutionary anthropology, with its orderly stage-by-stage development toward a more rational culture, even supplied one of the core concepts of the Progressive historians' social thought. Edward Tylor's term *survivals* was frequently used to describe dysfunctional remnants of past cultural stages. Ironically, while Barnes proclaimed that anthropology constituted "the indispensible prolegomena" for historical studies, much of anthropology followed already thoroughly nonevolutionary precepts, like those of Franz Boas.[8] Anthropologists, too, turned to empirical studies without long-term vistas. They accepted the concept of societies as functional structures that changed not in conformity with a universal progress but with the need for the optimal adjustments to different environments. In this perspective the cherished achievements of Western civilization, such as science, increasing rationality, and even the idea of progress, had no more value than the folkways of other cultures.

Robinson and other Progressive historians had never been quite so enthusiastic about sociology, but they were nevertheless affected when sociology distanced itself from Progressive history. The historical perspective in sociology was waning together with the popularity of Comte's and Spencer's grand schemes. Indeed, Barnes noted, "historical sociology . . . seems to have become a non-existent phase of sociological study." He agreed with social scientists that their turn toward the empirical study of problems with a short time range, taken in the interest of the "scientific purity" of sociology, could also make sociology a more effective instrument in the amelioration of society. However, the long-range view must not be abandoned, because "without a sound knowledge of the genesis of the various forms of human culture and the leading social institutions there can be no complete understanding of contemporary life and problems, and no valid plan for improvement in the future."[9]

Although, in the 1920s, sociologists were unreliable allies of Progressive history, they at least shared the view of society as a body of individuals whose relationships needed to be brought into conformity with the needs of the modern context. Little heed was paid to Durkheim's insistence on the structural reality of society or the German sociologists' intermediate positions (Georg Simmel and Max Weber). That left intact an agreement with Progressive historians on the centrality of social control through the mechanisms discovered by social psychology and applied by enlightened government action. Sociologists simply pleaded for time to get enough insight into the microprocesses of society from which to derive useful generalizations. Others were more ambitious and reached for macroconcepts. Yet William I. Thomas's social laws, based on a fixed human nature, were of little use to Progressive historians. They could not reconcile themselves to sociological theories that promised insight into and mastery of ethical and cultural phenomena at the price of defining progress in a quasi-natural manner. More akin to them was William Ogburn's concept of the "cultural lag" between material and nonmaterial culture and its remedy through enlightenment.

Given the widespread conviction that economic forces were the most decisive ones in history, economics should have been Progressive history's most solid ally. Beard, who in 1916 had given up writing on the economic interpretation of history, still published his Amherst lectures of that year as *The Economic Basis of Politics* (1922). Nevertheless, *The Rise of American Civilization* (1927) proclaimed the economic interpretation of history just as lucidly, grandly, and fervently when it depicted the shifts of political power as always following the lines drawn by the forces of economic life. The activist implication of that view was spelled out when Barnes applauded Beard's insistence that all changes pointed toward the social and economic emancipation of the people, overcoming the resistance of those who held that "the path of the Almighty lay in the direction of the creditor interests."[10] His European and Asian experiences evoked in Beard much puzzlement, but no reformulation of the economic interpretation of history. Yet even doubts of a strength sufficient to shake Beard's confidence could not have led to a thorough reassessment, because he had cut himself off from the concepts and theories of mainstream economic theory. He had always opposed classical economics and its offspring, among which he counted both Marxist and all utility-based marginalist economics. Although classical economics with its inescapable mechanisms and limits still had had a long-range dimension, it had projected a grim future filled with endless oscillations between temporary improvements and deteriorations in the lot of the masses. Marxism offered an acceptably positive future, but one that Beard considered utopian and reachable only by a rigidly deterministic path. As for the contemporary neoclassicists, their reliance on the perceptions of utility for explaining the workings of the economic realm stressed short-range market mechanisms, for which psychological rather than historical explanations sufficed. Nevertheless, most American neoclassicists found that the endless sequence of equilibriums of gratifications could be combined with the element of progress in the American sense of history. One needed only to see the sequence as leading to ever better living standards through competition. But instead of vistas of a future with collective control of the economy on behalf of rational production, they stressed the limits to human control drawn by the laws of the market.

Beard and like-minded historians had always felt more kinship with the small group of historically minded economists, including Richard R. Ely, E. R. A. Seligman, Simon Patten, and Thorstein Veblen. Progressive historians shared with them some major tenets: the need to see economic phenomena in the context of life; the insistence that the *homo economicus* was a useless fiction; and the demand that production would have to be geared to social needs rather than to profit. In that light capitalism looked far from efficient, given to conspicuous consumption and a production of goods with little if any social usefulness. Such a perspective yielded the Progressive historians' basic argument against mainstream economics, namely that self-interest was no natural human trait, but merely a historical phenomenon peculiar to the capitalist phase of Western civilization, and therefore need not be the regulative force in a future economic order. Thus the prevailing economic theories themselves appeared as unfortunate remnants of the past's heritage. Yet in the 1920s, historically minded economists struggled to transcend the limits of description and had difficulties in competing with the neo-classicists. Such institutionalists as John R. Commons, Walton M. Hamilton, and Robert F. Hoxie produced new theorems which, how-ever, left no traces in Beard's stock of ideas and concepts; neither did Beard's and Veblen's tenure at the New School for Social Research, par-tially because Veblen's tenure proved even shorter than Beard's. Without a sufficiently developed theoretical base, Beard's economic interpreta-tion could not be developed further. It remained an unsatisfactory frag-ment, which facilitated Beard's eventual turning away from the claim of absolute primacy for the economic aspect of life.

The increased use of psychological forces in economics was only one more manifestation of the great strides psychology was making in be-coming the basic discipline for all of the social sciences and history. Ap-proval of that trend by Progressive historians could only be conditional on a satisfactory resolution of the old problem of a fixed human nature. Hence, it was easy to see that such Progressive historians as Robinson and Barnes would find behaviorism's rise to dominance attractive. Its view of human beings as endowed only with a few basic unalterable mechanisms of stimuli and responses, and thus as totally open to condi-tioning by the environment, promised the widest possible scope to the remaking of social attitudes and institutions. At first glance, therefore, the praise Robinson lavished on Thorndike's associationist psychology was not surprising. Yet its exclusive explanation of human behavior through habitual and learned stimulus-response patterns would appear to fit poorly to the conviction of Progressive historians that modernity needed human beings of a highly developed rationality who were called upon to make rational choices. Robinson simply ignored behaviorism's basic presuppositions about human life and treated the conditioning process as an effective technique for the destruction of outdated thought and behavior patterns.

Barnes's justification of behaviorist theories was more complex. Along the lines of an evolutionary adaptation theory, he praised be-haviorist psychology's rigorous attention to social conditioning as "all-important to the historian who desires to interpret a personality in relation to his early life and social surroundings." He found it especially useful, since "human behavior cannot be understood when sharply separated from that of other animals, particularly of our fellow simians."[11] But Barnes's further arguments showed a tendency to accent the deterministic element in behavior theories that grew out of his strong faith in science and his increasing impatience with the slow pace of reforms. He would say that "human motives are the product of stimuli and impulses derived from the chemical properties and processes in the human body, the biological past and the personal experiences of the individual; and conduct is, in a psychological sense, strictly determined, there being no place in modern psychology for the old metaphysical doctrine of freewill."[12] Historians would have to add to the traditional theoretical equipment the study of physiological chemistry and endocrinology because "it is probable that adrenalin played as large a part as pan-Slavism in Sazonov's decision upon war in July, 1914," and the study of the behavior patterns caused by arteriosclerosis and senile dementia because "statesmen, diplomats, and supreme court judges have usually been men of advanced age."[13]

The acceptance of so significant a degree of immutability in human beings was hard to reconcile with the basic views of Progressive history. Nevertheless Barnes found reassurance in the openness of the cultural environment to human mastery. He was applauding the views of Lucien Febvre, who considered the environment as relatively stable and the human adaptation as of a broad range. The people of an area "chose" from among a number of possible adaptations the one that would become their set of traditions (their culture). The environment did not rigidly prescribe the forms of life, although it influenced the shaping of the repertory of popular thoughts and habits. All of that was eventually incorporated into the concept of *mentalité*. Such an approach to culture could have reconciled psychological forces of a purely individual scope and the search for a source for and proper degree of social control—at the price of abandoning the grand scheme of progress. But Barnes, like other Progressive historians, was not ready to accept the view of history as a mere sequence of cultures. Indeed, Barnes, unlike Beard and Becker, would never abandon the conviction that progress was a feature of reality to be explored scientifically. That and his inability to study problems and theories in depth made him miss the insights offered by French alternatives in social history, of which he alone among Progressive historians was aware.

The works of Freud and Pareto met with an equally ambivalent response. Freud's inescapably irrational world, and Pareto's view of history as the endless cyclical rise and fall of elites, caused by fixed psychological traits, cast a pall over the views of history as progress. Only an eclectic approach made Freud's and Pareto's works useful for Progressive historians. They could find support for their assertion that the disturbing inertia of the masses had been facilitated all along by those who loved the status quo and filled the minds of the masses with illusory reasons and ideals for keeping it intact. Freud and Pareto, Robinson thought, helped explain and even prove these assertions in their discussions of rationalizations, although the suspicion arises that Robinson neither studied thoroughly nor assessed systematically the implications of either Freud's or Pareto's works—a suspicion that is reinforced by his declaration that the "best presentation of the bias and implications of psychoanalysis I have met is embodied in a recent novel by Elsa Barker."[14]

Barnes's brashly naive eclecticism made him accept many elements of the psychoanalytic approach, unhedged by considerations of whether they were consistent with Progressive history.[15] He conceded, for example, that the power of reason, on whose steady increase Progressive history based its very explanation of history, was not at all decisive, since "the motives for many human activities are not revealed to the conscious mind, being derived from the subconscious, and much of our explanation of motives and purposes is but elaborate secondary rationalization, which is more congenial than the actuality to the content, sets and attitudes of the conscious mind."[16] He would call Freud's biography of Leonardo da Vinci dubious and exaggerated, but still maintain "that history is the record of the 'collective sublimation of the neuroses and psychoses' of the great personalities of history."[17] With the irrationality of the individual irremediable, the ideal world of Progressive history, based on the expectation of full rationality and intelligent action, became a superficial and deceptive construct; a fate Progressive historians had intended only for the traditional view of history. From now on, any lack in rationality could no longer be seen as a matter of inertia, remediable in time by rational appeals and social reforms. It had its roots in deep-seated psychological structures. The concept of rationalization was extended until all past actions, views, and convictions became gratification substitutes. Samuel Adams's radicalism was really a compensation for his failures in life; George Washington's efforts served to gratify his "Jehovah complex"; President Coolidge's espousal of "a philosophy of frugality, piety, candor, sincerity, and uprightness" compensated for his abject service to the plutocracy.[18] Hamilton's and Jefferson's divergent stands on important issues were not so much the result of rational reflections on the structure of American life as of their personal psychological development. Barnes, of course, never subjected Progressive history as a scientific endeavor to that interpretation.

Ironically, Becker would eventually receive the highest critical acclaim for the most fruitful use of psychology by a Progressive historian, although he never showed any interest in academic psychology. He had developed his gift for observation into a tool for understanding people to a degree that few of his contemporaries could match. As a historian he perused eagerly "the more personal writings . . . in which individuals consciously or unconsciously reveal the hidden springs of conduct."[19] Unfortunately for Becker, when he transformed ideas into psychological phenomena, he also enhanced his skepticism, which a philosophical understanding of ideas could have checked.

The initial call for an alliance between the social sciences and history had made sense at a time when historians understood that "the program of the 'New History' with regard to the scope of its interests is by definition all-inclusive."[20] Progressive historians and social scientists could join in the collection, evaluation, and interpretation of data. Hope for an alliance was possible as long as both partners subscribed to an evolutionary worldview and shared a determination to be pioneers of progressive reform. In reality, even in those early years, the relationship never amounted to an alliance. The ad hoc use of social science findings remained typical, because Progressive historians already knew the structure and dynamics of history. They used the findings of the social sciences for the substantiation and "fleshing out" of their view of history, and hence were not really available for a joint venture in discovery. Then, when the social sciences discarded the evolutionary model of explanation, the Progressive historians hardly acknowledged the change, perhaps not even noticing it, because the partial use of some new views and concepts suggested by the social sciences was still possible, even if their full implications were clearly incompatible with Progressive history. There was in the United States no room for an alliance in terms of contemporary developments in France. Febvre and Marc Bloch could cooperate more fully with the social sciences because both groups accepted a historicist egalitarianism of cultures and abandoned all aspirations to a direct public usefulness.[21] Their journal, *Annales d'histoire économique et sociale,* founded in 1929, differed sharply in the form and substance of its deliberations from the writings of American social scientists and Progressive historians. Not surprisingly, the incipient *Annales* school exerted no influence on American historiography, not even on Barnes, who knew about its development. Instead, the rhetoric of an alliance with the social sciences stayed intact, while the reality of such an alliance became more and more distant. Had the two groups of scholars been more fully cognizant of each other, the Progressive historians would have criticized the social scientists' flight from the evolutionary-progressive approach, while the social scientists would have asked whether the Progressive historians had not done what Robinson accused Plato of doing—having fled the real world of the leaky pot and having established an orthodoxy estranged from real life.

13

The Battle for Progress

America, victorious in war, was spared a postwar depression of her spirit. No group of pessimists came forth, such as the one led by Oswald Spengler in Germany, who, "unable to endure the necessary strain of the age, . . . announced the doom of western civilization."[1] Americans also were not impressed by Henry Adams's prophecy of a move toward the final "equilibrium of death and extinction" in accordance with the Second Law of Thermodynamics. Neither had the horrors of technological warfare created any serious doubts about the thoroughly beneficent nature of science. The war had been a shock, but in the end it mattered most that Americans had not lost the war. In a decade of general prosperity and confidence, the American public and Progressive historians affirmed their varieties of the American sense of history with progress at the core. Beard spoke for many when he ascribed to technology the role of a benevolent Leviathan. "Like time, it devours the old. Ever fed by the irrepressible curiosity of the scientist and inventor, . . . technology marches in seven-league boots from one ruthless, revolutionary conquest to another."[2] Nevertheless, as the 1920s went on, doubts about the promise of ever greater prosperity, stability, and peace would increase among the public and the intellectuals.

In those years, Progressive historians sailed along smoothly on their theoretical ship despite the ambiguities, if not contradictions, in their arguments for progress. It mattered most to move as rapidly as possible toward the harbor of destiny. They agreed with Dewey that the society of the future was already known as one in which "human beings can get together cooperatively and bring their physical resources and their intellectual resources to bear upon the problem of managing their society, instead of letting society drift along more or less at the mercy of accident."[3] Even occasional doubts were rhetorical, as when Beard asked "whether man, long the victim of natural forces and many delusions, can emancipate himself from the involution of life and environment that produced him and assume the Jovian role of interpreter and director."[4] The positive attitude relied on the identity of the ideas and institutions advocated by Progressive history with the dynamic principle of life itself. In this situation, Progressive historians required what Barnes, in his blunt ways, described as dropping "esoteric research" and shifting to "popular exhibition." All efforts needed to be directed at abolishing the lag between what was and what should be in American culture. For this decisive battle Progressive historians shaped no truly new plans or weapons.

The masses were still seen as the huge inertial body blocking the path of progress. Explanations were formulated that were really more accusations. Barnes ascribed the inertia to the herd instinct, which made it possible for the people's minds to stay filled with "archaic debris of past attitudes and interpretations."[5] Robinson offered a subtler version of that explanation when he explored the psychological reasons for the disturbing phenomenon.

We are tremendously suggestible. Our mechanism is much better adapted to credulity than to questioning. All of us *believe* nearly all the time. Few doubt, and only now and then. The past exercises an almost irresistible fascination over us. . . . Mankind is lethargic, easily pledged to routine, timid, suspicious of innovation. That is his nature. He is only artificially, partially, and very recently "progressive." [Emphasis in original][6]

Their enthusiasm for the desirable future and their minimal appreciation of past human life kept Progressive historians from the constructive assessment of inertial forces in human history that future New Historians would produce. They would see inertia as a powerful structural element that accounted for much of that continuity and stability of human life to which Progressive historians gave a mainly negative value. Robinson and others, who knew how slowly in the past the habits of the people had changed, viewed that knowledge as a spur not to further inquiries, but to liberating human beings from that inertia. Full emancipation from inertia was necessary to free "the vast potential reserves of energy and intelligence which [now] are paralyzed through the influence of custom, tradition, habit, superstition and other specific traits and practices."[7]

In the early 1920s, Vilfredo Pareto, who had triggered a positive, even faddish response among American intellectuals, brought a challenge to Progressive history's stand on elites. His view of the masses as inert and easily misled found no contradiction. The reaction was different to his stipulation that elites emerged by virtue of some fortuitous combination of psychological characteristics and faded due to the failure of later generations to keep intact that favorable combination. In Progressive history, past elites failed not because cyclical patterns decreed it, but because they eventually stood in the way of progress once their special interests lacked any common benefit. In Becker's harsh view, old elites represented not just outdated groups but conspiracies of wealth, who widened participation in government only when they needed the support of the masses. Even if, so far, history had been Pareto's coming and going of elites—the dreary "graveyard of elites"— it would not be that in the future, because the new elite would be always open, properly motivated, attuned to modernity, and immune to corruption by power. For their approach they cited statements by Jefferson and John Adams on the "natural aristocracy of virtue and talents," and that "that government is best which provides the most effectively for selection of these natural aristocrats into the offices of government."[8] The Progressive historians would have agreed more fully if Jefferson had said "aristocracy of the enlightened intellect," because it would have assured that in the egalitarian social order of the future all of the people could be part of the elite.

Traces of doubt about the new elite were present. Beard could not quite convince himself that the new elite's superior mastery of the natural and social sciences could ever be shared with a sufficiently large segment of the people. Robinson was troubled by his own insight into the glacial speed of changes in popular habits and the conclusion that, for centuries, the masses had enabled the old elite to govern through their conspiracy of silence. Resigned to some imperfections in the future full democracy, he took heart from the fact that creative individuals such as St. Francis, Dante, Voltaire, and Darwin had changed the "character and ambitions of innumerable inferior members of the species" who, throughout history, have been the passive and dependent consumers of ideas.[9] Even worse, the inert masses had haunted those who wished to push human life beyond the primitive stage. Without the new elite, among them the scientists, inventors, and engineers, there would be no hope for a new world. Instead, the future would see class struggles in which "capitalists and laborers would find themselves lapsing back into the stage of savage incompetence."[10]

In the campaign for the future, the opponents changed. Traditional religion faded as a major antagonist, although even at the end of the decade Barnes mounted a sharp attack on it in his *Twilight of Christianity* (1929), and Robinson still considered it one of the major distorting forces. Increasingly, Progressive historians turned toward a new quasi-religious target, a perceived secular national religion. It required "that solemn and unreasoning reverence towards the cultures and institutions of the past which is the chief cause of that distressing contemporary lack of competence and insight everywhere in evidence in man's seeming inability to cope with the issues which confront him." At its core stood an "American epic" that cast its spell on American historiography and all actions guided by it.[11] Americans were too caught up in the worship of the founding period, in which depiction of the Founding Fathers as "mental giants" and elevation of the Constitution to a timeless status featured prominently. Using one of William Trotter's pronouncements in *Instincts of the Herd* (1916), Robinson labeled that attitude simply a "childish impression we have never carefully scrutinized."[12] Progressive historians would not have objected to using the term *myth* in this connection (indeed, on occasion they did), but rather than replacing it with another myth they intended to replace all myths with a rationally explicable and therefore true view.

The rectification came down to the question: "*Is not the moral overrating of the past our besetting danger?*" (emphasis in original).[13] Caught in a web of restraints, how could Americans change what needed to be changed? "Such heavy words of approval as 'venerable,' 'sanctified,' and 'revered' all suggest great age rather than fresh discoveries."[14] Hoping that ancient Rome could instruct modern America was just as futile as consulting "the mechanism of the ancient Roman ox-cart in order to diagnose the engine trouble which has caused a Packard speedster to become stalled by the roadside."[15] Instead, history must act "as the sovereign solvent of prejudice and the necessary preliminary to readjustments and reforms."[16] Americans must understand that the inertia-induced veneration of the past had always been used as a bulwark against change erected by special interests, especially business.

While in attitudes and habits the national religion was replacing Protestantism, in institutional life business had long replaced religion as the major obstacle to progress. It had "produced new evils and reenforced old ones which no thoughtful person can possibly overlook." The "sickness of an acquisitive society" could only be cured by breaking the dominance of business's philosophy, which claimed to be based on the "immutable traits of human nature."[17] The great slaughters and sufferings of the First World War, the "Frankenstein side" of the modern world, could happen only because selfish economic interests had made irrational use of science, industry, and technology. Robinson even suspected that the traditional secular orthodoxy was guarded not only by the inertia of habits and the pervasive influence of economic interests, but also by the new Inquisition, the Secret Service. Writing during the Red Scare, he saw in the socialists and communists the Waldensians and Albigensians of the modern period, although he usually considered communists to be dogmatists themselves.

To this definition of a basic conflict Parrington supplied another version rather than any new insights. He demonstrated how one could ascertain a fundamental conflict between democratic and antidemocratic forces in American ideas and literature by penetrating the surface phenomena of philosophical and aesthetic concepts and forms. For Parrington, the latter were mere subordinate phenomena to the basic forces. American intellectual and literary history was a drama in which theologians, philosophers, and literati had acted out roles assigned to them by one of the two basic forces. Ideas and works acquired importance solely as the visible manifestations of the raging conflict over full democracy, one that also included economic democracy. However, Parrington did not agree with other Progressive historians on the central role for a strong federal government in the resolution of that struggle, since he celebrated a vague mixture of physiocratic agrarianism and Jeffersonianism as the proper American worldview. Thus, for him, the democratic forces in American history were the Jeffersonian, Jacksonian, and successive third-party movements. The people would have to wrest full democracy from their opponents in a society which had distorted the concept of progress. "The idea of a beneficent progress, which was the flower of the doctrine of human perfectibility, came to be interpreted as material expansion with constantly augmenting profits; and the idea of democracy came to be interpreted as the right to use the government of the whole for the benefit of the few."[18]

Despite the centrality of conflict in these views of American history, the Progressive historians never sided with those who wished to respond to the awareness of a decisive turning point in history with radical and quick institutional rearrangements. Their view of history called for an overcoming of the gap between the present and the future by means of reforms in accordance with the American evolutionary spirit. When Progressive historians spoke of the future development of liberal democracy into a social democracy, which would have the "improvement in the lot of the people as the goal of industry, business, and government," they affirmed the gradualism of reform.[19] Abrupt and radical changes in American society, particularly any noteworthy infringements on private property, were rejected. Critics would assert that, as members of the middle class, Progressive historians were bound to favor such a moderate and gradual approach. Some awareness of that showed when Becker mockingly accused Dodd of being a well-to-do property holder (Dodd had a dairy farm), and he could have said the same about Robinson and Beard.[20] The critics have been correct, but for a complete explanation they would need to add the prevailing gradualist temper of American society and the logic of the Progressive evolutionary view— both of them indebted to the basic American understanding of history.

The nature of Progressive history's diagnosis made education the battlefield in the imminent age of *"imperative social reconstruction"* (emphasis in original).[21] On it the new human being would be formed and progress freed to go unimpeded on its course. As a first step, progressive reformers called for wresting control of schools from those authorities that, being subservient to special interests, oriented education toward the past instead of the future. Progressive history could supply the core insight for the new pedagogical program: All human problems were historically explainable, and hence solvable. Educational considerations could, therefore, be detached from the centuries-old and vexing debate about human nature. The philosophical problems, involving elements of fixity, became psychological and hence remedial ones. With human nature no longer marked by timeless features, perceived purely negatively as limits, and the world becoming genuinely new, education could no longer aim at instilling tradition. In design and method, the new curriculum had to draw on the insights of Progressive history and the social sciences.

As for the teaching of history, its traditional version—now seen as obsessed with facts, uninteresting, dry, and, above all, past-oriented—had to yield to one that stressed incessant and innovative change and made students reject rather than revere most of the past. That would also expunge the prevailing competitive and aggressive mind-set. Instead, education must result in the cooperative citizen of the reformed American republic, not the competitive isolated individual. Most Progressive historians would rely on installing a new democratic discipline rather than on an appeal to an inherent goodness to rectify human nature deformed by previous societies, most recently by the capitalist ideals and institutions.[22]

The most ambitious educational endeavor involving Progressive historians, the New School for Social Research, started during the period of disillusionment with the result of the war and concern over the intolerance of the Red Scare. The triggers were the resignations of Beard and Robinson from Columbia University. Both men had long viewed American academe as dedicated to the preservation of the status quo and controlled by governing boards that were, not unlike that at Columbia University, composed of men "reactionary and visionless in politics, and narrow and mediaeval in religion." Such a situation damaged not only the war effort, but also the educational enterprise at a moment when "we stand on the threshold of an era which will call for all the emancipated thinking that America can command."[23]

The New School was not to be just another innovative pedagogical venture, but one that was to redirect American history. From it, an island of the Progressive future existing in the present, the reformers for the conversion of America would go forth. But from the moment the New

School opened its doors in a burst of enthusiasm in January 1919, life brought into the open some of the ambiguities in Progressive history. The issue of whether to emphasize either the elite or the masses pitted those who wished to create an elite school—an American *École des sciences politiques* that trained the leaders of business, government, education, and labor (Croly's "democratic saints")—against others who aimed at an institution that, through an extensive adult education program, would have a broad impact on many people. Against both groups stood those who wished for a pure research institution. Beard, leery of the static quality of all organizational schemes, wished only to rent some rooms, employ teachers, announce lectures, and proceed. Against that were arrayed the pressures of life: Students needed credits and diplomas for the still "old" world; the laws of the country prescribed a charter and a board; and the school needed a steady supply of money. In 1922, with the endeavor in peril, a major reform of the New School signaled that some ideals had to be sacrificed in order for the institution to survive. The New School acquired a more workable organization and trimmed its goal to being a Progressive island that would only slowly expand to become the American mainland. Eventually, Veblen was fired, Beard, Croly, and Robinson left, and Barnes became an irregular member, while John Dewey had returned earlier to Columbia University. Once more, the time-lag thesis served as an explanation, if not consolation, for the failure of the future to arrive. A critical scrutiny of the unresolved, often bitter disagreements on the purposes of the New School and the victory of stability and routine over the spontaneity of change would have cast serious doubts on the viability of some basic assumptions of Progressive history.

More serious and comprehensive were the challenges from abroad to the type of faith in progress that was underpinning Progressive history's social philosophy. Italian fascism and Russian communism contested those liberal tenets that buttressed Progressive history's claim to be the authentic modern interpretation of history. Italian fascism with its diffuse, if not crude, theory evoked a sympathetic response from a variety of Americans, who invested either anticapitalist, anti-Bolshevist, or neo-aristocratic hopes in it, or simply were impressed by the regime's actions on behalf of a stable order. The ever-present disenchantment with the inertia of the masses, and the fascination with the imposition of a modern order on a society perceived to be outdated, enhanced fascism's attractiveness for reformed-minded historians. Early fascism interested Beard because of its experiment with the corporate organization of the state. It seemed to enable the state to play to the full the role of economic planner, reformer, and social mediator. As for democracy,

Beard was satisfied with the hope that fascism "may work out in a new democratic direction."[24] However, Beard and others with a Progressive vision of history soon became disenchanted with fascism. The worship of brute power, militarism, and imperialism was perceived to be an element of the old order.

The Russian Revolution with its suddenness, brutal force, radical incisions in Russian life, and universal ambitions at once fascinated and repelled Progressive historians more intensely. A most serious future-oriented competitor in the interpretation of history had arrived. Beard predicted "that the historian of the next century will count the Russian revolution among the most significant acts in the great drama of the present age."[25] In a rare venture into comparative history—one neither in line with the precepts of Progressive history nor free of hyperbole and ineptness—Beard found the destruction of Carthage in 146 B.C. to have been the last event of equal importance. No less ponderous was John Dewey's view of the revolution as a "liberation of a people to consciousness of themselves as a determining power in the shaping of their ultimate fate."[26] Because of the revolution's immense importance, Beard called, in the midst of the widespread shock, for an assessment of bolshevism "built, not upon the frothy essays of frenzied propagandists, but upon the soberest accounts given by Bolshevik and anti-Bolshevik writers."[27]

Beard soon became uneasy about the potential for oppression in a state that was the "master of all economic and intellectual life" and about the continuation of the revolutionary brutal force originally used to replace the ancien régime. He nevertheless joined the reassuring Progressive consensus that communism only temporarily deviated from the truly modern approach to life: pragmatism. The revolution and its horror was an interlude, objectionable but necessary. In the end, as Dewey formulated the Progressive historical view magnificently, the "smells of outworn absolutistic metaphysics and bygone theories of straight-line, one way 'evolution'" would evaporate and a modern pragmatic society emerge; indeed, orthodox Marxists would not like it. He was certain that the proletarian revolution was only a dialectical response to the "dictatorship of bourgeois capitalism" that would end in a pragmatically democratic synthesis.[28] The Soviet Union of the 1920s did not deliver sufficient shocks to dislodge such comforting views.

The postwar period posed another problem for Progressive historians. The global interlocking of national destinies was becoming ever more discernible, which highlighted the issue of universal progress. Until the late 1920s, Progressive historians usually counted nationalism among the negative forces. Even the disillusioned Becker still diagnosed a world order based on the unlimited sovereignty of nations as a major cause for the ills of the international situation; it no longer accorded with economic internationalism, the driving force of progress. Robinson and Barnes pointed to the contradiction between the senseless passions and interests stirred by national aspirations and the rational insights into the necessities of an increasingly interdependent world. Robinson called nationalism an "*ancient tribal insolence* [that] *has been developed on a stupendous scale*" (emphasis in original).[29] Barnes saw it connected with the "psychology of the hunting-pack." Consequently, Robinson, Beard, and Barnes supported the League of Nations although they did not like its constitution. It had become a league of governments rather than of people and concerned itself nearly solely with politics, to the detriment of important economic and social matters. Still, they were not ready to be part of the shameful "Great Refusal of History."[30] On this issue Beard still argued against the opponents' contention that America's tradition and historical role prescribed isolationism. Whatever the past showed, isolationism had become impossible, because distances and oceans had ceased to be barriers. Though not perfect, the League of Nations could function as a way station on the road to the peaceful cooperative world appropriate to modernity. Becker had his usual doubts. As early as 1918, he had questioned the excessive hopes invested in the League of Nations. The abstractions of international law could never withstand the concrete force of national self-interest, especially since the people would never really love peace or act on the basis of common sense.[31]

In the perspective of general progress, Europe proved a more perplexing problem. While, in the view of Progressive historians, some European countries were ahead in legislation for the social democracy of the future, the continent was still mired in its old order despite the radical social and political changes after 1918. Its international system signaled no progress toward a peaceful order. Indeed, European experiences tinged Beard's early findings on postwar Europe with an unusual air of resignation. Yet he clung to industrialization as the great hope for the modernization of the world, even when he confronted the grave problems of one of the new states created in the Wilsonian spirit: Yugoslavia. Industrialization alone, he thought, could tie the feuding nationalities of that state together and thus loosen the grip of the past. Beard held to his central argument from the primacy of economic motives, but history would not.[32]

The contrast between expectations for worldwide progress and the empirical evidence struck Beard most forcefully when he faced life's reality in Japan and China. As a consultant for Goto, the mayor of Tokyo,

Beard felt unexpectedly touched by features of Japanese traditional culture; "the glories of the past," he called them. Yet he was puzzled that the economic modernity of Japan could coexist in such seeming tranquillity with a tradition-bound society. His explanatory scheme for history, including the usual time-lag scheme, failed him here, since social and economic adaptations to modernity were too few. Even after the Tokyo earthquake of 1923 had created a near tabula rasa, the Japanese did not follow Beard's advice to create a modern Western-style city, but restored the old city in a slightly updated form. Disappointed, Beard praised the absence of such a dominant past in the United States. But his encounters with the complexities besetting universal progress impressed Beard deeply. He would eventually confess that after his travels "I became a changed person. I have never been the same again!"[33]

Yet the logic of Progressive history could not concede to traditions more than a retarding role and ascribe the vast cultural differences to anything other than temporary deviations from the universal industrial-technological civilization. Nevertheless, under the impact of the disappointing political conditions in the 1920s, faith in quick universal progress faded fast. At this point, Progressive historians took advantage of the ambiguity in the American understanding of history on the issue of America's role in the universality of progress. She could be the example for the realized new order of the future (the shining "city set upon a hill") or the active missionary. Given the turmoil and stubborn adherence to old forms in the postwar world, the building of a progressive America, in a deliberate though not complete isolation from a world that went on in its old ways, came gradually to be seen as a reasonable choice; not one of despair, but still one of hope for an ultimate universal emancipation.

Already in Robinson's *Mind in the Making,* whose author so far had viewed history in the wide perspective of Western civilization, the appeal for Americans to institute the future in their own country overwhelmed all. The material for his planned magnum opus, a grand intellectual history of Western civilization as a testimony to the universality of progress, now was employed in an elaborate justification for American reforms.

In Becker's case, the enthusiasm for universal progress had died together with that for progress in general. He confessed to his lack of spirit to be a reformer at home and abroad when he admitted to Barnes, "As you know, I have much less faith in the possibility of setting the world right than you have."[34] He could no longer concur in the contention "that the world is divided into good men and bad, intelligent and ignorant, and that all will be well when the bad men are circumvented and the ignorant are enlightened."[35]

In 1922, Beard strayed far from his insistence on a universal progress when, disillusioned by the turbulence as well as the persistence of many Old World features in Europe, he spoke warmly about the concentration of all reform efforts on America. He tried to avoid the connotations of isolationism by using the term *Little Americanism.* More than a decade later, *continentalism* would refer to the same ideal. Adhering to "progress at home first," America would "bend all national energies and all national genius upon the creation of a civilization which, in power and glory and noble living, would rise above all the achievements of the past."[36] That did not necessarily mean an abandonment of universal progress, only an acknowledgment that the time to elapse before humanity had received all its benefits would be much longer than expected.

Thus, during the 1920s, Beard could still argue in two seemingly contradictory ways. On the one hand, Americans must let European statesmen settle the "old quarrels" of Europe and apply themselves to the construction in America of the civilization of the future. On the other hand, Beard repeatedly argued for the impossibility of an isolated America, partially because the current American foreign policy would involve the United States in any new European war and partially because America had even a moral obligation to stay linked to the world. Although the United States had repudiated the League of Nations, it was "a member in spite of its myth of isolation."[37]

This ambiguity points to a conceptual problem with Beard's "Little Americanism." Beard's concept encountered its logical nemesis in his own economic interpretation of history, which insisted not only on the transnational character of progress due to the nature of industrialization, but also on the unbreakable link between economic and political power—the root of imperialism.

The linkage between economic and political power in foreign policy never ceased to trouble Beard. As a young man, he had still discerned a progressive component in imperialism; it modernized and integrated the world. In this vein, he had defended the British Empire for its civilizing role. But at the same time, he had been even more impressed by Hobson's arguments on the evils of imperialism. Thus, in the 1920s, a thoroughly negative judgment on all economic expansion, if enforced by political and military power, became typical of Beard. Without such a link Beard could even praise the pacific influence of international finance and financiers with the surprising declaration that "the best pledge of peace lies in the decline of feudal aristocracy and the towering rise of international capitalism."[38] Usually Beard would hedge his praise for a purely economic internationalism with the proviso that only in a new world order would it not carry the danger of a subsequent transformation into a political and military imperialism. In the meantime, Beard feared for America. Even though he did not subscribe to the stipulation of an innate and irresistible urge of human beings to expand, conquer, and dominate, he found that the capitalist need for ever new markets for the sake of prosperity introduced a new kind of fate into history. With all land for colonization already taken, America was left with a vaguer form of imperialism, that of commerce in which economic and political power merged into each other. The Monroe Doctrine served as a favorite example, because it was seen as a mere disguise for American commercial imperialism.

Beard worried much about the threat that America, having grown to be "first in investing, industrial, commercial, maritime, and naval powers of the earth," would be lured into making war rather than building the advanced civilization of the future. The danger was enhanced when the population of a great and powerful country combined ambition with the "philosophy of Buncombe County" and thereby could bring the nation to the "gates of destruction."[39] While that problem could be alleviated through education, the major preventive measure would have to be the strict separation of economic expansionism from foreign policy. The empire of trade was inevitable; that of political domination was not. That argument would be the basis for his later campaign against a large navy, fostered by the pursuit of commerce and used in the interest of the nation's merchants and financiers.

The assertion that one could separate by an act of will the sphere of economics from that of politics was startling, since in his interpretation of history Beard had branded just such a separation as a traditionalist heresy. On this point it was disingenuous for Beard to argue that such a separation would indeed occur in the future order, because he wished for it to happen right then and there, in the "old" America. Here, the needs of activism prevailed over consistency of historical interpretation.

In his attempt to educate Americans about the imminent danger posed by their foreign economic policies, Beard reached back into the past for arguments against imperialism. Rather than arguing from the available insights into the life cycles of past empires and the role of the exhaustion of resources through empire building, he simply mentioned the fate of Alexander and Caesar, thereby hinting at a comparative argument without really making one. In the end, Beard himself was not sure that Americans would prefer to build the Great Society rather than to proceed along imperial lines. Then, in an unusual nonprogressive mood, he mused that even America's avoidance of imperialism might not save her from eventual decay or destruction. He found some consolation in that tragic fate. "The great power that pursued it [the avoidance of imperialism] might, indeed, sink down into dust like the empires of Tamerlane or Augustus, but at the least the world's experiences would be enriched."[40] Soon such discussions were overtaken by events. The Great Depression provided a powerful incentive for turning inward while letting the world drift toward a state of war. The issue of the universality of progress, left unresolved in the 1920s, would next re-emerge in the debate over America's intervention in already ongoing wars.

14

The Twilight of Certainty

Robinson's presidential address to the American Historical Association in December 1929, by projecting two different moods, showed that all was not well in Progressive history. As the representative of a mature and now influential school of thought, Robinson called on historians to emulate him and his turn-of-the-century colleagues and "trace the aggressions, oppressions, surrenders, and compromises, together with the persistent defense of habits and beliefs originating in venerated ignorance and gross misapprehensions of man and his world, which had debouched in the situation as we found it at the opening of this century." But the address also had a somber tone, not all of it due to the onset of America's great economic crisis. Impressed by the contradictions between his high expectations and the actual course of life, and haunted by bouts of depression, he confessed to being "filled with a sort of dismay, which I did not feel so keenly twenty years ago."[1] Nevertheless, that dark mood was not yet reflected in a lessening assertion of progress. Critics were rebuked for insisting that the limits to human knowledge and the mastery of life made impossible any social order free of the problems that had marked the past. Beard condemned those who did not see history as the *Weltgericht*. Barnes focused his wrath on scholars who asserted that "'there is neither any known law of human progress nor any likelihood that one will ever be discovered.'"[2]

Indeed, the doubts that would eventually erode the very foundation of Progressive history were not caused by the impediments life piled across the path of progress. The doubts that in the end would cause a dramatic change in the Progressive interpretation of history grew in an area well out of the limelight: epistemology, or, more modestly, historical truth finding. After 1926, they would diminish the trust in the ability of facts to shape interpretations authoritatively, and with it lift Progressive history's anchor of certainty.

At this writing that decisive development is being praised as the step that integrated American historiography fully into modernity. Yet unless one subscribes to a new Whig history in favor of relativism, it is more fruitful to observe that all theories of history have been simplifications of human life's complexity and, therefore, have been subject to revisions, if not rejection by life. Internal inconsistencies are highlighted in new contexts that no longer support so smoothly the prevailing tenets. Disenchantments with the peace settlements, the shock of America's Progressive Era ending in the period of "normalcy" (interpreted as the triumph of inertia), and, at the end of the decade, the onset of the Great Depression, reshaped the American context. New links of America with Europe and the fading of the Progressive Era's confidence in the human ability to establish a progressive order would be important contributors to the shift.

Immediately after 1919, European influences were less important than could have been expected. German historians struggled for the normalcy Americans had found so easily. They tried to redefine national history in the light of the new republican Germany. In the face of the sudden end to centuries of monarchical rule, continuity proved elusive, particularly to historians who connected the republic with the lost war. Even more than in other countries, these historians devoted much effort to the documentation of and the debate about the war guilt. All of that had only one connection with American historiography: with the work of Barnes and other revisionists on the question of war guilt.[3] It stimulated interest in the problem of historical truth only in reference to the causes of the First World War, and there strictly in a traditional, document-oriented way. German historians could not alleviate a profound postwar Kulturpessimismus. The crisis of historicism was deepened by the stark realization that historicists could give neither assistance in matters of national self-definition nor assurance on the course of history. The epistemological explorations that had begun in the 1880s and had involved Dilthey, Rickert, Windelband, and Weber had not yet produced interpretive results. Indeed, the hope had been abandoned that one truth could be discovered, one method be found, and one meaning of historical phenomena be revealed. The potential of Weber's temporary islands of meaning, rationally constructed and called the ideal types, was not appreciated at that point. In the late 1920s, Beard, prompted by his son-in-law, Alfred Vagts, began reading some of these works, created in the context of the decline of German historicism. Even earlier, however, he and Becker had become enamored by Benedetto Croce's views, which owed so much to the German intellectual tradition.

French influence would have been just as disruptive in its own way. The works by the French innovators—Berr, Febvre, and Marc Bloch—were empirical, often comparative, still significantly positivistic in method, and directed at finding the structures of historical phenomena in an encompassing social history. Even better links than those that existed to American historians could not have overcome the obstacle presented by the nonprogressive tenor of what, from 1929 on, would be known as the *Annales* school of historiography. Barnes, alone in being familiar with the French works, presented some of Berr's and Febvre's ideas on epistemology and geographical influences on history, yet did not make any use of them.

For one brief moment, Robinson hinted in his *Mind in the Making* at some doubts about the solidity of historical knowledge when he spoke of historical reality as located only in the mind and seemed to question language's ability to reflect thought accurately. However, Robinson did not link that issue to the then emerging understanding of concepts as symbolic constructs with a complex relationship to reality. Instead, he found a simple dualism between the language of facts and the language of rhetoric. The first was scientific and reflected reality, and the second, that of conservatism and tradition, offered a medium for "pious ejaculation," where "language is not primarily a vehicle of ideas and information, but an emotional outlet, corresponding to various cooings, growlings, snarls, crowings, and brayings."[4] Robinson, far from doubting the potentially full correspondence of reality and language, once more affirmed it. His suggestion turned out to be no harbinger of epistemological innovation, but only a tactical position of an activist who wished to facilitate the reform of popular attitudes through the use of the proper language. It was related to his view that any discrepancy between historical interpretation and past reality was only one of a temporary "not-yet" correspondence, not at all a permanent condition of historiography. The alignment of mental images with the objective (that is, progressive) reality of the past remained the central goal. "*We should proceed to the thorough reconstruction of our mind, with a view to understanding actual human conduct and organization.* We must examine the facts freshly, critically, and dispassionately, and then allow our philosophy to formulate itself as a result of this examination, instead of permitting our observations to be distorted by archaic philosophy, political economy, and ethics" (emphasis in original) and, not the least, by the wrong language.[5]

In the 1920s, the systematic formulation of radical doubt advanced most swiftly in the private scholarly world of Carl Becker, who was not engaged in the fervent activism on behalf of speeding up progress that so dulled all concerns with the theoretical maintenance and reconstruction of Progressive history; who, teaching at Cornell University, was physically far enough removed from the activist centers of Columbia University and New York City; who, by then, already lacked any genuine commitment to viewing history as progress; and who had time and inclination to bring to a logical conclusion a development that, for him, had begun much earlier and now was favored by a more skeptical climate of opinion (to use Becker's own phrase), the flagging theoretical vitality of Progressive history, and the influx of European ideas on historiography. The war had stilled Becker's epistemological doubts for a few years, but also stimulated them again by destroying the certainty about progress that had offered Becker an absolute reference point. Now would occur a perfect confluence of Becker's personal travel to radical skepticism, the development of a new uncertainty in the American intellectual world, and the lines of the logic of his thought.

In 1910, he had weakened the objectivity of facts by seeing them as composites of evidence and interpretation. Only one year later, in the relative obscurity of a book review, he had indicated much more fundamental doubts when he looked with favor on Houston Stuart Chamberlain's scorn for objectivity, "at least if objectivity means a pale neutrality. He [Chamberlain] has not formed his judgments 'from the Aristophanic cloud-cuckoo-land of the supernatural objectivity.' "[6]

At this stage of his development, it was puzzling, although not important, that Becker was uninterested in all contemporary French historiographical developments, because they would not have supported his radically antipositivistic attitude. It was more important that Becker, who had studied eighteenth-century French thought with Robinson, had become enamored by it, and had referred to it over and over in the course of his work in early American history, was not able to derive some measure of stability for his historiography from the example of the *philosophes*. He no longer shared their confidence about the course of history as the progressive and universal realization of absolute values inherent in the nature of the world. The latter had become pure constructs, important when useful for life, but without either any strength of their own or a correspondence to reality. Soon the facts, too, would become constructs with no privileged connection to reality and little power to shape interpretations. Already in 1921, Becker could say of Wells's *Outline of History* that "a contribution to knowledge the book does not of course pretend to be; but a contribution to meaning which we may, and indeed ought, to attach to the knowledge we have, it does very particularly pretend to be."[7] While truth remained here still in suspension between fact and imagination, Becker's inner struggle was proceeding toward the conclusion that in a meaningless cosmos it made no sense to speak of facts as if they stood in a privileged relation to a stable reality and of historical truth as one.

European influences did not create Becker's doubts, but augmented them. He had pretty much ignored the earlier appeal by Fred Morrow

Fling for American historians to become familiar with the German and French attempts to establish a historical science not imitative of, but autonomous from, the natural sciences. He now encountered Benedetto Croce's *History: Its Theory and Practice,* and perceived a kinship to Croce's central tenet that the world was no more than onrushing life without a firm structure or a direction or goal.[8] Historians could grasp cognitively aspects of past life, but could not build from these abstractions a cumulative system of historical knowledge. Becker agreed with Croce when the latter condemned all history conceived as a record of events, "since this record, apart from the mind which puts meaning into it, is mere lifeless ink and paper. History is none of these; it is just the total reality which the mind at any moment, and at every moment, thinks, and by thinking creates."[9] Only such a historical knowledge, based on will as well as cognition, was useful in life. Croce spoke with exuberance about how liberty, defined as the human ability to create, manifested itself in every creative act—a kind of inevitable progress that realized itself not over the course of time, but in the given present. Becker lacked a similar enthusiasm. He preferred cool analysis to intuitive grasping, saw in life not only the ongoing creation but also the recurrent destruction of what passed as truth, and experienced the groping for certainty as something painful. For him, life and scholarship amounted less to an enthusiastic participation in creation than a resignation to fate; one not without inner turbulence caused by a residual longing for a steady meaning.

When Becker later reflected on the contributors to his growing relativism, he also listed

Sumner's "Folkways," which impressed me with the relativity of customs and ideas. Freud's "Introduction to Psychoanalysis," which made explicit the notion that the wish is the father of thought. Vaihinger's "Als Ob," which came to me in the English translation, "As If," and confirmed me in the notion that social thinking is shaped by certain unexamined preconceptions current at the time. Whitehead's "Science and the Modern World," and "Adventures of Ideas" had the same sort of influence. . . . John Dewey's books I find hard to understand, but his ideas, coming to me through other writers, have confirmed a native tendency to pragmatic theory.[10]

Given those influences and Becker's disposition to doubt, it was the more remarkable that he kept much sympathy for those who still hoped to find "the true and useful" at the end of the journey. His review of Croce's work was coupled to that of Robinson's *Mind in the Making.* It was more than kindness for his former teacher that made Becker assess sympathetically Robinson's book, which spoke of cumulative progress and affirmed one objective and knowable reality. In the early 1920s, Becker was willing to abandon all certainty, but not yet all hope.

In 1926, the private struggle of Becker, so far only discernible in intermittent signals, became semipublic through the paper that he read at the meeting of the American Historical Association. Becker had arrived at firm conclusions not on how to get to the truth about history, but about the impossibility of obtaining an objective truth. He had reached that insight after destroying all notions that facts were solid, substantive, possessing definite shape, ready to use, able to give a sense of stability, or make historians feel safe, and, when sufficient in numbers, would yield true accounts of the past. Facts impressed Becker as "pale reflections, and impalpable images [of vanished realities] which cannot be touched or handled." Even the sources offered no access to facts. "In a sense the fact is there [in the records], but in what sense? The records are after all only paper, over the surface of which ink has been distributed in certain patterns." Both the context of the occurrence and the context in which the historian wrote made something into a fact; the actual occurrence mattered less. The patterns in which facts were grouped so as to yield meaningful configurations were "themselves only 'histories' of the event, made by someone who had in *his* mind an image or idea" (emphasis in original).[11]

Becker had solved the persistent problem of historians, the closing of the gap between the *res gestae* (what actually happened in the past) and the *historia rerum gestarum* (the report on those happenings), not by carefully weighing the degrees of certainty that could be obtained for facts and interpretive statements, but by declaring the gap to be unbridgeable. Historians standing on one rim of the gap were condemned to gaze across it and make the best—really the most useful to them—of the hazy images visible on the other rim—the reality of the past. Without saying so Becker had collapsed the crucial compromise at the core of Progressive history that had made possible the discernment of objective progress from selected facts, and then had progress offer the principle for selection of what was a fact. In the absence of reliable facts about the past, one could not assert an objective progress or any other objective meaning. When facts lacked all autonomy from interpretations and, hence, interpretations could not be backed up by facts, truth became the truth in the given context; it simply pleasured our experience. It, like the fact, was a symbol, and "of a symbol it is hardly worthwhile to say that it is cold or hard. It is dangerous to say even that it is true or false. The safest thing to say about a symbol is that it is more or less appropriate." That made the past "a kind of a screen upon which we project our vision of the future; and it is indeed a moving picture, borrowing much of its form and color from our fears and aspirations." Becker, a prominent member of the American profession, softened the impact of his message a bit by granting Scientific history some usefulness. "Doubtless the proper function of erudite historical research is to be forever correcting the common image of the past by bringing it to the test of reliable information."[12] But Becker failed to specify in which manner such data could correct historical interpretations, which now were projections occasioned by powerful promptings from the historian's external and internal contexts.

After 1926, Becker remained silent on his findings. He never published the paper because he considered it not well enough argued and fit only for testing the waters.[13] Five years later, he would say it all more clearly and elegantly in his presidential address to the American Historical Association. In the meantime, keen observers could detect traces of his now well-formed relativistic outlook in some occasional pieces where, for example, he delighted in agreeing with an author "that history is not a 'science,' that the facts do not 'speak for themselves,' and that 'history for history's sake' is a played-out game."[14] His reluctance to speak out was certainly not the reluctance of Descartes, who was "very careful to say that philosophic doubt was not to be carried over to daily conduct. This should for the time being conform to accepted standards, unenlightened as they might be."[15]

Becker's had been a lonesome struggle, with its rigors and far-from-consoling insights borne with his usual stoic resolution. Encouragement came from seeing the intellectual world, year by year, becoming more sympathetic to his conclusions. The twilight of certainty had spread beyond history to those disciplines on which historians had relied as a wellspring of authority, the natural sciences. The actual theories of the New Physics exerted less influence on historians than such fascinating new phrases and terms as *relativity of time and space, discontinuity, uncertainty principle, quantum jumps,* and *indeterminacy.* The latter were popularized in numerous books and articles on the New Physics of Bohr, Einstein, and Heisenberg. The old perceptions of the world with a neat space-time continuum, in which cause-and-effect chains established continuity and a rationally explicable order, were fading. Scholars were beginning to view concepts and ideas more and more as constructs, deliberately designed for understanding, mastery, or domination. In the world of signs and symbols there would be no room for or striving after an absolute certainty; reality, past and present, would remain in large part an enigma.

Still, in 1926, the majority of American historians remained at a far distance from Becker's hard-won relativism. At the session, Fling's sharply different views found much more resonance among the audience. None did what Barnes later would do—hail the relativism of Becker as history's equivalent of the theory of relativity in physics, and hence as the proper response of history to modernity. Traditional Scientific historians understood that Becker's arguments destroyed history as an endeavor that, with a stable and truthful account of the past at its base, could accomplish an ever more authoritative reconciliation of the past, present, and expectations for the future. Most historians agreed with Fling that the possibility of historians to be "observers" with a sufficient independence from their contexts must not be abandoned. Historians must continue to assert "that the aim of history is a scientific aim—to determine the facts of man's past." Many of Becker's colleagues would indeed have agreed with the flat statement: "No, fact, no history!"[16]

Beard cheered Becker but did not join him. He simply was delighted that, once more, the orthodoxy had been challenged, and was unconcerned about the paper's implications. In those years, Beard himself spoke in two languages. The language of certainty about objective progress pervaded *The Rise of American Civilization,* with which Beard wished to counter the "visions of despair" with "a more cheerful outlook upon the future of modern civilization."[17] However, gradually the vocabulary of the language of uncertainty and the view of concepts as constructs were intruding into Beard's world as he read Croce's work and became familiar with the discussions on historical truth in the wake of the crisis in German historicism. Occasional hints surfaced that Beard was beginning to sympathize with Becker's view of histories as interpretations impressed by historians upon a world without intrinsic order and meaning.[18]

Although Barnes had cheered Becker's paper, he never became Becker's companion on the journey to relativism. He would never abandon the original frame of reference of Progressive history wherein only those historical interpretations were constructs that did not conform to the standards of science and rationality (in the Progressive spirit). Among them were the myths foisted on a gullible public by special interest groups. As for progress, Barnes still considered it real indeed.

Barnes's reluctance to make the turn to relativism was emulated by most of those who, after 1930, counted themselves among Progressive historians or owed much to that perspective's conceptual world. Indeed, the broad impact of Progressive history on American historiography was made by its prerelativist form, which still affirmed the power of facts and an objective progress. Becker and Beard, however, were willing to apply radical doubt to that conviction. Becker sought no limits to the dissolution of certainty into useful illusions. "Without our best illusions life would be a poor thing. Illusion is after all the best reality; and truly the most convenient form of error."[19] Beard had no inclination toward such a Stoicism, and his ambivalent relativism would demonstrate that. In the routine world of a scholarly meeting the opening shot of a revolution had been fired in the so far quiet segment of American historiography, the epistemology of history. Its soon-to-come public manifestations would undermine the American sense of history in both its traditional and Progressive versions.

4

THE RELATIVIST EXPERIMENT

AND ITS REASSESSMENT

1929–1948

The Woods of Arcady are dead,
And over is their antique joy;
Of old the world on dreaming fed;
Grey Truth is now her painted joy;
Yet still she turns her restless head.

William B. Yeats
"The Song of the Happy Shepherd," from *Crossways*

15

Collapse in a Triumphant Mode

The Great Depression brought into this situation of a weakening certainty about truth an experience that shook the faith in the intrinsic benevolence of the industrial age more violently than the horrors of the First World War had. While it did not destroy the faith in the American sense of history, it helped open the already unstable intellectual American landscape to the influx of radical modern doubts about traditional certainties. Becker's doubts entered the scholarly debate, and so did European influences that undermined the theoretical base of American mainline Scientific history, as well as that of Progressive history. The early compromise of Progressive history with the positivism of facts, which had made easy the building of a progressive interpretation of history, now became a severe liability. It had precluded the creation of a more elaborate epistemology (such as the incorporation of symbolic interpretations) that would have prevented what Becker and Beard saw now: a stark alternative between total certainty or no certainty at all. Unfortunately, the European influences that penetrated into American historiography were understood primarily in terms of that dualism. Their supportive explanatory philosophical frameworks, which would have softened some of the impact, remained mostly unused. There was irony in the fact that just when Progressive history was in need of a sturdy theoretical basis on which its message of hope for the future could rest, it would be drawn into the reassessment of the potentials for and limits of human knowledge its proponents had avoided for two decades.

The task of responding to the new challenges fell to Beard and Becker. Parrington had died in 1929; Robinson had, for all practical purposes, ended his scholarly career after that year; and Barnes had two reasons for not joining in. First, he did not share the fundamental doubts about positivist truth finding that now counseled the abandonment of basic positions of Progressive history. Instead, he reasserted a substantial connection between ascertainable facts and interpretation, despite his praise for those—like Freud—who considered life to be intrinsically irrational. It was telling that, even in the 1930s, he tried to have works by Ernst Bernheim, Johann Gustav Droysen, and Eduard Fueter translated—

none of which showed any signs of either a sociological or instrumental view of the concept of truth. Second, Barnes could not render help in the developing debate on theory, since he had left academe for journalism. Throughout the thirties, he served as a "highbrow editor" with the Scripps-Howard newspapers, who could be relied upon to persuade readers of the necessity for liberal reform policies—hardly a position conducive to theoretical reflections.[1] Barnes could have been a significant steadying influence in the developing theoretical debate. Quite contrary to Beard and Becker, who now became receptive to those European influences that declared it impossible to ascertain a substantial body of knowledge that was not decisively shaped by the personality and existential context of the historian, he derived from his studies of European scholars support for continuing to assert the attainability of knowledge that corresponded to objective reality. They were primarily the innovative French scholars, Henri Berr and Lucien Febvre.

When, in the early 1930s, Becker and Beard took a new look at the theoretical underpinning of Progressive history (for Becker already well under way), their scrutiny would bring a destructive clarity to matters in which Progressive history had benefited greatly from an unexamined opaqueness. Progressive history's pragmatism, so far comfortably hedged by the assertion of an objective progress, would have its safety net destroyed, and with it the reassuring knowledge of the true order of things. Progressive history entered its relativistic phase, in which it abandoned all more-than-temporary reference points for historical truth, even degrees of probability. The magnificent unity of fact and interpretation in the concept of progress disappeared. Without its so far well-hidden source of stability and continuity, Progressive history was set adrift. Hence, while Beard's and Becker's works brought them fame and acclaim, they destroyed the very foundation of Progressive history.

Becker could be satisfied with the intellectual developments. All along, he had been like an antenna, finely attuned to the radical denials of all certainties inherent in modern thought. Those who, in 1926, had missed his paper on facts, still tentative and rough-edged in its conclusions, now would witness the culmination of Becker's long scholarly journey in December 1931, when he delivered his presidential address "Everyman His Own Historian" to the American Historical Association. In that address and in the subsequent, widely hailed *Heavenly City of the Eighteenth-Century Philosophers* (1932), he demonstrated that his doubts and ideas of 1926 had developed into a much richer and more mature reflection on historiography.

In his presidential address, Becker developed his arguments for a historical interpretation without stable point of reference on the example of Mr. Smith's (Everyman's) coal bill and humdrum life, because he wished to highlight history as an endeavor forced on human beings by life. Mr. Smith's attempts to orient himself in the world by means of a memory geared to practical purposes constituted a legitimate form of history; indeed, one closer to the basic function of history, since it lacked the "superficial and irrelevant accretions" of academic history.[2] Mr. Smith's history was that of the short range, prescribed by the everyday practical purposes it served. Yet even in the short range of his daily life, Mr. Everyman was forced to become a more complex historian when he ascertained a need in the present, coped with it by calling on the past with the help of his unaided memory as well as documents, and then made provisions for the future. Thus, history on "its lowest terms" shared its basic structure with that on higher terms, because both histories were based on the "specious present"—the present that included stretches of the past and anticipations for the future. From it derived the historical character of life as well as the necessity of "doing history" for every person.

When Mr. Smith was forced to venture beyond the short-range specious present, where history could be defined simply as "the memory of things said and done in the past," he, like the academic historians, had to venture into the long range.[3] There, they shared one crucial dilemma. As the range of the specious present increased, the gap between what Becker called the actual and ideal histories—the reality of the past and the constructed past—widened and needed to be bridged by interpretations for which life provided neither ready nor efficient correctives. Mr. Everyman's faulty memory that the coal bill had been paid would soon be challenged by a bill collector as the agent of reality. Life's corrections, in short-range historical accounts usually quick and clear, became less easy, if not impossible, to discern in long-range history. Becker failed to detect in or stipulate for that history any ready corrective mechanism. His failure was linked to his conviction that the cosmos was without any ascertainable objective order. In it any quest for long-range clarifications changed from seeking the truth to striving for a "mere compensation for the intolerable dullness and vexation of the fleeting present moment," and, as such, could be satisfied by the richly embroidered "pattern of artificial memories." Thus, when Mr. Everyman and the academic historians put together their accounts that reconciled past, present, and the expectations for the future, these accounts needed neither to be "complete [nor] completely true"; indeed they could only be useful at a given time.[4]

The memory (history) of the short range had to be accurate, since life would not tolerate anything else. But the memory (history) serving the long range lacked the quickly ascertainable pragmatic standard of truth, and allowed Mr. Everyman to concoct "an engaging blend of fact and fancy, a mythical adaptation of that which actually happened."[5] With that, Becker had set historical interpretation of anything beyond the immediate past free to float. Now, he had to clarify what he saw as the connection between past life and its historical account while being forced to forego a necessary link between facts and interpretation. It would be a struggle that Becker never quite resolved. He would at heart be dissatisfied with the role he now had assigned to the historian: to be the passive keeper of myths that neither were based on nor offered rational certainties.

Becker had denied facts a significant role in the construction of historical interpretations, although he was cautious in his rejection statements because of his own uncertainty and the wish to ruffle as few feathers as possible. Facts were still seen as the traditional barrier to fiction. As the guarantor of accuracy their gathering was "always in order, and is indeed the first duty of the historian."[6] Becker even spoke, at times, of facts as "stubborn and irreducible," even yielding whole clusters of facts that were certain.[7] Interestingly, Becker's defense of relativism in his correspondence was much less ardent and sure than that in his public statements. Yet, at this point, Becker's mind was too firmly set against the objectivists to make much of facts. They could have no significant role in interpretation; at best they were a defense against being "duped."

Becker introduced a different element of stability when he tied what now seemed free-floating historical interpretations to temporary climates of opinion. As a matrix for truth, each of these climates had a set of accepted views and explanations, and thereby gave to society a coherence of ideas and to the individual a sense of familiarity and security. The key to that solution was a change in the idealist concept of the zeitgeist. The world no longer was understood as a manifestation (objectification) of an "absolute spirit"—manifestations that changed in time and space in accord with that spirit's development. The absolute spirit was replaced by relatively long-lasting psychological structures in the minds of members of a group.[8] Explanatory schemes derived from them Becker called "myths," a word that, he knew, would not please his colleagues. So he urged them not to let "the harmless, necessary word 'myth' put us out of countenance." A myth was merely a view of history that, in retrospect, would be looked upon as "a once valid but now discarded version of the human story."[9] Even in the modern age, with its desire to be sure of its facts, the historical accounts were no more true than before. The changes in the climates of opinion and their myths did not add up to a grand approximation of truth. An old myth was transformed into a new myth because the latter was seen to be more useful. In that scheme there was no necessary link between a myth and its environment, nor was there room for developments of any rational element that transcended the sequence of myths.

Becker's argumentation, careful and elegant as always, had made Progressive history itself into a temporary myth without privileged status. All talk of history moving toward an ideal future had become nonsensical, at best a myth. The future, no longer the ascertainable result of a causal or logical development, could not provide the standard for all historical interpretations and judgments. The original Progressive history definitely had ceased to be Becker's intellectual home. Historians were no longer the leaders toward a better future, prophets of what was to come. Instead, they yielded to the insight that the myths of the people prevailed because "Mr. Everyman is stronger than we are, and sooner or later we must adapt our knowledge to his necessities." The new chore of historians was to tend to the myths.

When historians affirmed prevailing myths as appropriate for their periods, they could tolerate the presence of elements of older myths in them, not because of any assumed timeless value but in the interest of continuity. People would reject abrupt changes. Yet even this limited affirmation increased the value of tradition, which, for Becker, now became that web of myths a society accepts at a given time. This also reaffirmed Becker's long-held contention that ideas, such as the ones contained in the Declaration of Independence, could not simply be arbitrarily infused into public opinion but, in order to be accepted, had to conform to the substance of the existing tradition; in other words, historians had to appreciate the inevitable elements of the past in every climate of opinion rather than oppose tradition in principle. The activism against it, which had been at the core of Progressive history, had lost its source of authority and its rationale—the idealized future as perceived by reason.

Such emphasis on the connection of the present with the past rather than with the future accounted for Becker's echoing Edmund Burke in the pronouncement on the role of the historian. "We [the historians] are thus of the ancient and honorable company of wise men of the tribe, of bards and story-tellers and minstrels, of soothsayers and priests, to whom in successive ages has been entrusted the keeping of the useful myths."[10] To a large measure, the historian had become the keeper of tradition. In 1931, Becker, of course, did not speak of tradition in terms of transmitting timeless truths and values, only of tending to ideas and values in a given climate of opinion. After 1936, however, this surprising

by-product of Becker's relativism—the limited affirmation of tradition—
would form the basis from which Becker could proceed in his defense of
liberal democracy, including elements of the American sense of history.

As for Beard, despite some earlier isolated indications of a relativistic
turn in his thought, his eventual pronouncements appeared to be sudden explosions. His relativism not only came about more suddenly but
also was more externally induced than Becker's. To a good measure his
conversion was less the result of logic pushing thought to its last conclusion than of a yielding to a changed climate of opinion. It also was facilitated by a more casual attitude toward the subtleties and intricacies of
the truth-finding process on the part of Beard, the epistemological op-
portunist.

In this light, Beard's eclecticism in accepting new theoretical ideas
and concepts appeared understandable. Once more, German rather
than French historiography had a greater impact due to personal contacts, particularly with Alfred Vagts. When yielding to influences, Beard
regularly ignored the systematic and structural frameworks in which the
accepted elements stood, and proved receptive only to those aspects of
the new ideas and concepts that emphasized the openness of the human
world to rational change. From Karl Mannheim's *Ideologie und Utopie*
(1929) he accepted the assertion that ideas were instrumental constructs
produced by and for social processes and expunged the insight that,
with the total conversion of knowledge into a fabric of constructions,
the mastery of life lost not only its limits but also its authority. From Karl
Heussi's *Die Krisis des Historismus* (1932) he took the depiction of the
fruitless search for a stable truth by German historians since the turn of
the century as an example of the sterility of historicism, but neglected to
see the looming repetition of historicism's problems in his own new theoretical approach. From Theodor Lessing's *Geschichte als Sinngebung
des Sinnlosen* (1919) he learned not about the arbitrariness and futility
of all stipulations of meaning, but about the freedom human beings had
in giving meaning to the world. And from Croce's work—German in a
Mediterranean spirit—he screened out the individualistic and aesthetic
celebration of life's creativity and transformed Croce's assurance of the
inherently creative character of the world into the promise that a better
society could be created. This selective acceptance would make sure that
the influences would not evoke corrosive doubts about progress, but
would contribute to a new understanding of progress. Beard's overall
approach to historical theory owed most to Kurt Riezler's view of life as
equally shaped by a causal structure (interests) and by human freedom
(ideas). It explained and to a degree justified Beard's wavering between
seeing historical interpretations as true reflections of reality and as mere

constructions. Beard's definition of and commitment to relativism never became systematic, complete, or even clear. While he spoke much about the total conditioning of all historians by their social, economic, and political circumstances, he sensed rather than understood the limits on his activism and faith in progress such an abandonment of an authoritative truth would entail.

When Beard made public his conversion to a relativistic view of history in his presidential address to the American Historical Association in 1933, "Written History as an Act of Faith," and in the subsequent article "That Noble Dream," it took the form of celebrating the coming of the age of radical contingency. With pleasure he noticed that the historian had finally done away with the pretensions of the philosopher to be the keeper of the secret of history, if not of life, by "placing him in relation to the movement of ideas and interests in which he stands or floats, by giving to his scheme of thought its appropriate relativity."[11]

However, at about the same time, Beard issued declarations with a different message. The book *The Discussion of Human Affairs* (1936), just as important a contribution to the contemporary theoretical debate, showed that, unlike Becker, Beard derived from the impossibility of demonstrating an objective progress no image of the world as meaningless and no sense that activism was futile, not even the impossibility for progress to be more than an interpretative construct. Typically, Beard reconciled all tensions, if not contradictions, between his theoretical and practical stances by a kind of practical reason. "Since I am no scholastic able to spin out propositions indefinitely by a purely logical process, I cannot proceed to the business of thinking without having some knowledge and concrete realities to work on or with."[12] Beard would never really let go of the assumption that in a vast area of human life, objective knowledge and, hence, an objectively correct mastery could be obtained.

In accordance with his activist stance, much of Beard's argument on behalf of relativism took the form of a broad argument to prove that the prevalent objectivist view of historiography was outdated. He ascribed the obsolescence of that history to its passive observer stance toward the world; its insistence on letting the structure of the past speak for itself; its denial of the supreme importance of contingency; its affirmation of a deterministic world of causes and laws; and its inability to come up with an "overarching hypothesis" of practical value. From this Beard concluded that the fading of Scientific history was no mere passing of a theoretical scheme, but rather a defeat of conservatism in its struggle with liberalism. He would never cease to condemn Scientific history as conservatism disguised as science, an imitation of Ranke's craving for peace and preserving the status quo, which had now "been discarded and laid away in the museum of antiquities. It has ceased to satisfy the human spirit in its historical needs."[13]

Much like Becker, Beard was careful to reassure Scientific historians of his appreciation for facts. Nevertheless, "the distinction between particular facts that may be established by the scientific method and the 'objective' truth of history must be maintained, if illusions are to be dispelled."[14] Actually, distinction was not the real aim, but a sharp separation was. Without the ability or promise to spell out laws, tell clearly of progress, or supply at least elements of a binding structure to interpretations, facts had become rather insignificant in historiography. Facts were valuable as long as they claimed no sovereignty rights over interpretation, although for Beard, the activist, that injunction never really applied to the concept of progress. He declared the act of interpretation now to be free, "after a final declaration of independence," from the natural sciences and its world of causality and laws.

This ambivalence of seeing in progress at the same time a mental construct and a part of objective reality marked all of Beard's pronouncements on matters of theory. On the one hand, he celebrated the new freedom to shape American society unhindered by any traditional structure or static order to human life; a freedom he saw safeguarded by the recognition of the world as purely contingent. On the other hand, Beard wished for a view of history that was useful for the mastery of human life; one with a maximum capacity for accuracy and guidance, or, as he put it, one that contained "all the exactness that is possible and all the bewildering problems inherent in the nature of thought and the relation of the thinker to the thing thought about."[15] Unable to resolve the tension between his celebration of contingency and his activism-induced need for stable elements in reality, Beard straddled the issue of the connection between past reality and historical account, never addressing it fully. In this he was helped by having two kinds of readers: those who read his relativistic pronouncements, but did not relate them to his work on behalf of reforming American society, and those who paid attention to his many books and articles on matters of public policy—full of traditional historical buttressing—but did not care about the theoretical issues. The latter group was not aware of the collapse of the old theoretical framework of the Progressive history on which Beard's own social reform proposals still rested.

Even in his most exuberant profession of relativism, "Written History as an Act of Faith," Beard unearthed the old philosophical argument against pure relativity, namely that "the apostle of relativity will surely be executed by his own logic." The escape and, thus, a possible positive message of history were offered by the insight that the historian could survey the many views of history and ask: "To what are these particular times and circumstances relative? And he [the historian] must go on with receding sets of times and circumstances until he confronts an absolute: the totality of history as actuality which embraces all times and circumstances and all relativities."[16] That absolute totality, which Beard left vague as a concept and considered unknowable with certainty as reality, presented the supreme challenge for historians. They could not be satisfied with studying a mere sequence of views on history stretching endlessly into the distant horizon. "The quality of greatness and endurance lies elsewhere—in the effort to grasp the fulness of history." All great works have derived their distinction from "the attempt to encompass the periphery, the all-enclosing circumstances, that marks those discussions of human affairs which divine and influence history."[17] That fullness that goes beyond particular contexts, which Beard once had viewed as progress, now appeared as the "total absolute."[18]

Beard insisted that the gap between what scholarship could secure and what the total absolute represented could not be closed or even appreciably narrowed by interpretations of history. As a consequence, he spoke of an act of choice between what he thought were three mutually exclusive conceptions of the "total absolute": to assert chaos, cycles, or progress (which Beard coyly did not name directly but circumscribed as a development with "an upward gradient toward a more ideal order").[19] Since the available facts provided inconclusive evidence for all of these alternatives, the choice would always be an act of faith or will. Beard chose progress with an alacrity that posed the question of how thoroughly he really had reassessed his former concept of an objective progress in the light of his new theoretical stance.

Yet only one year before the address, he had still detected a clear progress in the story of historiography, and had declared that "again and again in history, the truth rides over the set conventions of society" and praised history as the superior discipline, "which began with the songs of bards and ends in philosophy."[20] By this and similar pronouncements Beard included himself among those he would blame for being blind to the insight that the historian "speaks or writes at a time and at a place—a fleeting moment is a small corner of the great earth. No wonder that he resorts to God, Nature, Science, the System, or some other universal, toward which his aspirations reach."[21] At best, he could plead that he had kept faith both with his change in theory and with his zeal for activism by blurring the objectivity of progress sufficiently to escape the charge of inconsistency.

Such a tenuous link between reality and historical account at the far periphery of historiography never sufficed for the activist Beard, who continued to assure people that the proper course of history ran along lines he had sketched out. Hence, while he celebrated the ending of the "tyranny of physics and biology" and the casting off of "the shackles of theology" and proceeded with enthusiasm to an unrestrained welcome of the new age of relativity, Beard could not wish to erase completely the cognitive foundation for a rationally guided activism. Although he granted that scholarship was effective only in " 'the narrow land of rational certainty, relative, conditional, experimental,' " and that the world was too complex for a science preoccupied with natural laws, regulations, and repetitions, he still considered scientific work (including that in the social sciences) essential for building the proper society.[22] Short- and mid-range history, too, needed more than a knowledge constructed on the basis of an act of faith. How else could one persuade Americans that their country had arrived at a decisive turning point, comparable only to the years of the Constitutional Convention?

At times, progress was now only a hypothesis according to which "humanity in its long and zigzag march from barbarism is conquering its environment and itself, and may make the nobler aspirations of mankind prevail over material circumstances and the passions of acquisitive conflict."[23] Yet nearly simultaneously, he maintained that progress was more than a theory because "it has achievements to its credit on every hand." It gave him "a faith of power, faith that the world, as Emerson said, 'is all gates, all opportunities, strings of tension to be struck.' " For the man with a progressive faith, "the suffering, ignorance, and folly which drive the timid to the Nirvana of doubt and oblivion are . . . calls to action, to research, planning, and to conquest." Progress was "dissolving the feudal institutions of Europe, disturbing the slumbers of the Orient, arousing lethargic Russia, and finding a naked avowal in the United States of America."[24] This was a remarkable confession of certainty by a man who, later the same year, would make his confession of uncertainty about the interpretation of history.

Sometimes Beard's arguments became wildly mixed. Most often, the idea of progress still derived its capacity to evoke hope from being a real and not just a conceptual force. As this real force, progress was "closely affiliated with democracy, natural science, technology, and social amelioration." They and progress possessed a universal validity as the "gospel of futurism." Therefore, Progressive history was the appropriate historical interpretation for a civilization that believed itself to be "on the threshold of time." It alone was marked "by the buoyancy of youth, not the skepticism and morbidity of old age."[25] Against progress and its promise of a truly modern future the old order of the laissez-faire with its outdated dominance of private over public interests had no chance. Devoted to the profit motive, that order had lost its ability to regulate the centrally important relationship between production and consumption. While guided by necessity, progress demanded activism, specifically that the state mediate between capital and labor; it rejected the "doctrine of fatalism," whose adherents would "leave the world to its folly and withdraw within themselves to contemplate."[26] Then, using the language of his new concept of history, Beard relied on the brave act of choice for proceeding from the "real that oppresses us" to the "ideal that seems possible," since that ideal could no longer be expected to result from life's process or the application of science. America would now have to "dare to assume ethical and esthetic responsibility, and to exercise an intuitive judgment" beyond the body of ascertained knowledge.[27] On that basis, a new prophecy for the future could be created, one still convincing and persuasive, and whose logic called on America to plan its life, especially its economic activities.

Occasionally, Beard tried to clarify his troubled theory of history. Much like Becker with his climates of opinion and subsequent historians with their great variety of temporary structures for human consciousness, Beard allowed for mental structures that lasted over periods of years in order to give some stability to the human world in which whirl now seemed to be king. He spoke of frames of reference that in given periods dominated historical interpretations. These frames were controlled by their historical contexts and modified in each historian by the idiosyncracies of that historian's persona. Objectively valid interpretations were impossible when the historian had to admit that "it is I speaking, this fleeting moment, in this place with its intellectual and social peculiarities." Thus, Pareto should not have said "we find certain facts before us," but "I find certain facts before me"; after all, as Beard pointed out, Pareto did not live on Mount Olympus.[28] Time and time again, Beard referred to Croce's pronouncements about the impossibility of knowing or explaining the past as it actually had been, and the delusion of those who believed otherwise.[29] And he would state his "conclusion that all general discussions of human affairs are in truth assertions of opinions, good, bad, and indifferent."[30]

Yet Beard, who was first of all an activist for the envisioned future, searched for as many assurances as he could get for the progressive course of history. Thus, still in 1932, turning once more to objective truth and the scientific approach to human affairs, he could say that "scholarship has its own imperatives. To say that science exists merely to serve the instant need of things, causes, or parties is to betray a fatal ignorance of the inexorable movements in thought."[31] Neither was he willing to declare his already toned-down economic determinism to be just another imaginative and temporarily valid view of history.

In an interesting attempt to limit the scope of the relativism inherent in the interpretations of history as acts of faith, he suggested that historians should list the possible ways in which history could be interpreted and then address the opportunities and problems each of them posed. After that, the historian could still "seek to escape these issues by silence or by a confession of avoidance or he may face them boldly, aware of intellectual and moral perils inherent in any decision—in his act of faith."[32] In the likely case of disagreements, Beard appealed to his colleagues to be tolerant of different interpretations, clarify what their assumptions and procedures were, and even hold sessions at the annual meetings to discuss them. He asked whether such a survey of philosophies and interpretations, once made available to historians, could not form the basis for attempts to "bring the multitudinous and bewildering facts of history into a coherent and meaningful whole."[33] His conciliatory tone was no mere matter of academic politics, but originated in the desire to remove the act of faith from the area of spontaneity and give it at least a semblance of a firm base.

Becker's and Beard's revisions in historical theory began a new period in American historiography in which the full impact of modernity's radical doubts was being felt. American historians lost their relative isolation from the broader historiographical developments in Western civilization. European ideas, detached from their own contexts, began to intrude into the attempts at modernizing history within the American sense of history. They negated all thoughts of an American exceptionalism, timeless and universal rights, and the definition of history as progress. Instead, they seemed to suggest historicism as the modern interpretation of American history, depicting a sequence of nations and cultures, all of them unique in their modes of life and values and going nowhere in particular. The foundations of Scientific history were eroded, too, when all expectations of a future reconciliation of the "scientific" approach with the traditional American understanding of history (as more than a myth) vanished. As for Progressive history, its source of strength—the certainty that the world as a continuous process had the inherent direction of progress—had become a useful myth or the result of an act of faith.

The earthquake in historical theory should have produced a fundamental debate among historians. It did not. A relativism debate would have involved not only a revision of the American understanding of history but even the possibility of its losing the status of a "given." Neither American historians nor the public had much desire for such a debate in

a period when the confidence in the American destiny was already severely tested. Thus, in Becker's case, expressions of praise for the address
"Everyman His Own Historian" and, subsequently, *The Heavenly City*
were too often just kind words for a man one cherished; a-bit-too-
fulsome agreements by former students and younger scholars; or elab-
orations on partial understandings. None of them took the true measure
of Becker's ideas. That Fling and other critics objected to Becker's relativism could not surprise, but that nobody saw the obvious implications
for Progressive history should have. The absence of incisive criticism
could be accounted for by a continued reluctance to engage in theoretical discussions, or by a wish to avoid a public disapproval of the views of
a man recently honored with the presidency of the American Historical
Association who, fortunately, put radically dissenting views into elegant, witty, and therefore less offensive language.

Beard's address, "Written History as an Act of Faith," with its aggressive rather than persuasive tone, did get more hostile responses, but in
his case, too, the needed serious debate did not occur. A discussion of
some crucial issues came in Theodore Clarke Smith's review article,
"The Writing of History in America, from 1884 to 1934," in which the
author criticized the relativism of Beard and Robinson but, surprisingly,
not that of Becker. Limited by the theme to a fairly broad criticism and
also not offering the most cogent arguments, Smith made it easy for
Beard to issue a stinging response, "That Noble Dream." Smith saw in
Progressive history the main challenger to American Scientific history,
which he depicted as the broad mainstream. The latter had its origin in
the works of the pioneering professional historians of the late nineteenth
century, and its accounts of the past were vouchsafed by objectivity.
Beard denied Scientific history the status of a binding orthodoxy. The
founders of professional historiography had never intended an official
creed. Stung by Smith's accusations that Progressive history was "doc-
trinaire" and discarded "impartiality as incompatible with a specific
theory of human activity," he assured his readers that he did not consider the economic interpretation of history a doctrine. As for Smith giving the economic interpretation an origin in "Marxian theories," Beard
cited Plato and James Madison as witnesses in his defense.[34] On the issue of facts and interpretation, Beard did not deny the "far-reaching assaults upon the ideal of historic 'impartiality,'" but made light of it by
the assurance that facts remained indispensable, by labeling histories
that put forth facts with minimal interpretation as trivial, and by once
more calling Scientific history a conservative attempt to use history for
the defense of the social and economic status quo.[35] In this discussion,
dominated by old arguments, each man made one incisive suggestion.

Beard pointed to the absence from the meetings of the association of any thorough analysis of theoretical issues, especially of "the noble dream." And Smith raised the question, which would soon come to engage Progressive historians, how they could argue from their relativistic standpoint that democracy had a better claim to truth than fascism, communism, or nazism.

American historiography would be worse off for the absence of such a debate on the basic issue of the connection between reality and historical interpretation that Becker and Beard had raised. It might have provided a much firmer theoretical foundation for the further development of both Progressive and Scientific histories. A systematic rebuttal of Becker's and Beard's views came only in 1938 with Maurice Mandelbaum's book *The Problem of Historical Knowledge: An Answer to Relativism* (1938). In this book the young philosopher affirmed that historical accounts can, to a sufficient degree, approximate the reality of the past. Mandelbaum rejected the assertion that the historian's context was not only influential but dominant and the erosion of the role of facts to the point where historical accounts could become mere projections of the historian's or the collective's preferences and wishes.

Mandelbaum's rebuttal was given little chance to make its impact on scholars in a world where the imminence of war pushed theoretical considerations even further than usual into the background. But the ideological struggles of the later 1930s had already begun to test Becker's and Beard's new theoretical stance and were forcing them into a piecemeal revision of their brave pronouncements. Traces of it can be detected in Becker's and Beard's responses to Mandelbaum's work. Becker offered a qualified endorsement of relativism. He declared his willingness to renounce his relativism if it meant to disavow the possibility of obtaining a substantial body of objectively historical knowledge or even the striving for it. Beard offered one of his rare clarifications of his relativism, although it was too broad to say much. He saw in relativism the scholarly recognition that "no historian can describe the past as it actually was and that every historian's work—that is, his selection of facts, his emphasis, his omissions, his organization, and his methods of presentation—bears a relation to his personality and to the age and circumstances in which he lives."[36] Life, the relentless corrector of historical interpretations, brought about a debate within the intellectual worlds of Beard and Becker.

16

Becker's Struggle for Usefulness

By 1936, Becker and Beard rode the crest of their fame or, as others would see it, notoriety, with the exact distribution of assent and dissent among American historians impossible to know. Soon after, too, would come the end of the age of joyous discovery for Beard and the relentless driving to a conclusion for Becker. Their new concept of historical truth would undergo a wrenching and inescapable test by ideologies, "those alien systems—communist, fascist, Nazi," which claimed to speak with absolute authority on human life, including its history, and to offer "'liberties,' and institutions to guarantee them, better adapted to the conditions of the modern world."[1] They would ask difficult questions of those historians who professed to have abandoned any certainty, vouched for by a rigorous and disciplined inquiry. That Beard did so only halfheartedly was not obvious to historians. As for the American sense of history, it found no support in the relativist version of Progressive history, and the defense of liberalism became a questionable matter.

Becker would have been content with the calm academic routine of Cornell University, comparatively isolated from the social activism of the period. Inner peace and good health still escaped him. His views on history offered little consolation to him and none to Americans, whose hopes for progress now faced the fate of all ingredients of a climate of opinion—they would vanish together with its context. Becker met with resignation the insight that "time, the enemy of man as the Greeks thought" created a world of ceaseless becoming, in which everything disappeared into the past, growing dimmer with distance; where even grand events "must inevitably, for posterity, fade away into the pale replicas of the original picture, for each succeeding generation losing, as they recede into the more distant past, some significance that once was noted in them, some quality of enchantment that once was theirs."[2] However, as all other interpretations of history must, Becker's new kind had to provide a measure of continuity. Occasionally, remainders of a progressive frame of mind showed. Becker would agree with Santayana on the acquisition of the historical consciousness itself as the civilizing step upward. Human beings had transcended the status of "the barbarian, [who] for want of a trans-personal memory, crawls among superstitions which he cannot understand or revoke and among persons whom he may hate or love, but whom he can never think of raising to a higher plane, to the level of pure happiness."[3] Within his new cognitive frame of reference, Becker would have had difficulty accounting for such terms as *superstitions, higher plane,* and even *pure happiness* as they were tied to the stipulation of an objective progress.

Nevertheless, there was a deeper and, hence, more easily overlooked layer of continuity. Even at his moment of utter despair of anything truly stable, Becker affirmed important elements of universality in the human experience, although he did so by chance and incongruously. The *Heavenly City of the Eighteenth-Century Philosophers* was a hymn to flux in human affairs in which everything material and ideal had to be seen "as no more than 'inconstant modes or fashions,' as the 'concurrence, renewed from moment to moment, of forces parting sooner or later on their way.'"[4] Its thesis stipulated that, at its very essence, the Enlightenment was a secularized Christianity; a transformation brought about not in the course of a gradual approximation of the truth throughout history, but by a change of myths that answered the same basic human concerns in different forms. The Russian Revolution was just one more such transformation in the specific ways in which, all through history, people have attempted to master human life—in this case, to realize liberty and equality. In time, it would undoubtedly be succeeded by other attempts. History as a series of such transformations, as even Becker realized, implied a steady core of history either in a stable human condition or in a "human being in general." Both gave a permanent structure to human life; one that presupposed, among other things, that human beings had a set of hopes, aspirations, and ideals beyond basic needs. Thus, Becker ascribed the success of Christianity to its fitting response to what he now quietly conceded were rather stable human hopes. The explanations of human life might change, but all of them answered stable human quests. Into the place of metaphysical strivings or assertions of natural laws and rights, Becker had put permanent existential features. The cosmos was not quite so meaningless as thought. Had he not left (until late in his life) his thoughts on the matter in an uneasy balance, Becker would have realized that a sequence of worldviews, prompted by the same recurring questions, implied a structure of life that put limits on his view that all ordering elements were pure constructs. The stable human condition with a substantial content provided a referent that put limits on the construction of myths, and thus a standard for verifying the validity—or at least more than temporary usefulness—of historical interpretations. Becker had discovered a guide for the interpretation of long-range history, although Condorcet's call for the priority of the "what ought to be over the what is" would never again find a clearly affirmative response in him. Still, the stability he had found in the facts of human existence would become an important element in Becker's thought.

His defense of liberalism and new attitude toward the American sense of history were spelled out in four major works. As collections of essays or lectures—"annual reflections," Becker called them—they released Becker from the obligation to deliver systematic answers to those historiographical, philosophical, and political questions that the world of the 1930s kept posing, not as theoretical puzzles but as practical problems of life. Liberalism as a form of public life and its associated Progressive version of the American sense of history needed an intelligent defense. The lecture books enabled perceptive readers to observe Becker's struggle to give historical interpretations a certainty sufficient to allow for a modicum of affirmation and activism. He wrote lucidly but, with a triumphant message lacking, in a less than dazzling manner.

Initially, Becker found it difficult to treat the fascist, Nazi, and communist ideologies as opponents rather than as alternative interpretations of life because he viewed liberalism itself as just another ideology. From a secularized Christianity that had been a valuable weapon against the ancien régime, it had developed into a myth justifying bourgeois dominance. What had been a call for the "emancipation of the individual free from class or corporate or governmental restraint" had turned, after the political emancipation, into the justification for a bourgeois democracy.[5]

Becker's troubles proved greatest in answering communism. He was impressed by what he took to be the basic agreement between the Communist and liberal ideologies on history's direction toward a desired end. "In both ideologies the process (progress) toward the desired end ('liberty, equality, fraternity'; 'the classless society') is taken to be an objective activating agency" that shaped and assisted human actions directed toward the ideal end. This agency "in liberal ideology . . . is taken to be a rational intelligence, . . . in communist ideology it is taken to be a nonrational force." From this Becker concluded that "in their fundamental presuppositions, the liberal and the communist ideologies are thus very much alike." Linking his relativistic view directly to the controversy, he could still hold, in 1936, that "the communist no less than the liberal ideology thus belongs to the category of the useful social myths," designed by human beings to align the past, present, and future.[6] Becker's discernment of such morphological similarities and his emphasis on communism's seeming rationality left some people dissatisfied with the doubts about communism he voiced otherwise. Accusations of Communist sympathies surfaced and threatened not only his reputation, but also the lucrative sale of his high school textbooks. Fortunately for Becker, his defense against the accusations proved effective.[7]

Gradually, Becker himself became dissatisfied with the arguments and persuasiveness which his view of historical interpretations as myths provided him in ideological discussions. He could not bring himself to join those who stipulated an ironclad linkage between ideologies and class interests, and denied that the ideas at the basis of ideologies were "consciously or cynically invented" instruments for selfish purposes. Yielding in his insistence on reason as a purely adaptive instrument, he voiced the expectation that "the realm of the matter-of-fact apprehension of experience may be so greatly extended that the effective social ideology will take on the flexible, pragmatic character of a scientific hypothesis." This revival of one old hope in Progressive history—that all rigid interpretations of history would in the end become pragmatic in spirit—was a significant signal that Becker's radically relativistic phase was fading. It was part of what would be a gradual, positive reevaluation of elements in the American understanding of history, including liberal institutions and values as well as objective progress.

The concerns of theory and life linked up first on the issue of progress. Despite Becker's view of progress as one of many myths, he returned to the concept of progress in search of a rudimentary certainty and hope. In his short period of grand hopes, Becker, like other Progressive historians, had judged everything in the past and present in relation to the ideal order of the future; predictably, that had made liberal democracy seem fatally flawed. Then the war had destroyed his already weak belief in the future ideal order, and his relativistic stance had ruled out any possible certainty about it in theory. In the absence of any referential truth, the accepted myths of the past—tradition—appreciated in value as they provided a measure of order and continuity. Now Becker found tradition clearly superior as a source of social cohesion to the alternative: the newly constructed myths, the ideologies, that needed to be instituted by naked force. He confessed that liberal democracy, however sharply he had criticized it for being out of date and flawed, appealed to him and most other Americans considerably more than either fascism or communism. As he put it in 1941, in comparison with Hitler's and Stalin's new order and new liberties "it has become more obvious than it was before that the defects of our democratic way of life . . . are negligible, and that its liberties are of all our possessions the ones we cherish most and least wish to surrender."[8] Such a reaffirmation of a rudimentary certainty provided for the possibility of seeing in historical truth not merely an irrational myth or a pure construct. It recognized in historical interpretation the presence of insights into the actual structure of life, such as those gathered by Americans in the course of their collective existence. These insights contained errors and were open to change. But they spelled out some truth of more than temporary value regarding that permanent structure of the human existence Becker himself had alluded to in his *Heavenly City.*

By 1939, Becker felt comfortable with Bertrand Russell's judgment "that there is good reason for thinking that the American tradition will resist skepticism, whereas other traditions have commonly succumbed to it." As for America, some of her democratic virtues might well disintegrate with time, but for Becker, that was not fatal, "so long as the essential American tradition remains reasonably intact."[9] That in this context he just about equated the American tradition with a set of habits, especially with "the habit of settling our affairs by representative government," was less important than that tradition had at least partially left the realm of useful myths and reacquired a more intrinsic link with the reality of life. Becker celebrated it that the American republic was not sustained by a constructed political myth, but rather relied on enduring habits that yielded guiding values. He concluded his *How New Will the Better World Be? A Discussion of Post-War Reconstruction* (1944) by, at first, repeating once more Burke's view of society as a historically grown "partnership not only between those who are living, but between those who are living, those who are dead, and those who are to be born," and then affirming it by paraphrasing it in a modern manner.[10] Tradition could offer the force of cohesion, and its sanctions could bring about the necessary discipline for a stable democratic society. It spoke with an authority derived from its transcendence of the flux of the immediate. The partnership between the present and future generations could best be maintained if the present generation could not only hand on the legacy, but make contributions to the accumulated knowledge and wisdom as well. The demands of life, specifically Becker's wish to defend liberal democracy, had brought about an affirmation of continuity that was equidistant from the old condemnation of tradition as harmful inertia and its celebration as a purely useful myth. The crisis of authority had found in Becker a precarious solution.

Another significant shift, that in the status of democratic values, was linked to that in the status of tradition. Even when he had affirmed the purely constructed nature of values, Becker, the intellectual historian, had always been uncomfortable with the prevalent consignment of ideas and values to the shadows of the primary "material interests." Instead, he stressed the interdependence, and hence reasonable equality in efficacy, between the two spheres.[11] Thus, he spoke with disdain of theories that reduced the values' source, the mind, to a "survival product"—still extant, though without autonomy, because it was useful in the adjustment to the environment and the achievement of "desired ends."[12] While Becker wavered to the end of his life on the exact nature and authority of values, he did move away from seeing them as purely temporary constructs and toward a well-hedged affirmation of them as rather stable parts of reality.

In 1941, Becker attempted to find values that transcended their contexts, and had listed intelligence, integrity, and good will as three self-evident values.[13] In the same year, he spoke on occasion of the values of liberal democracy as universally valid, despite the error of Americans in limiting the ordering capacity of the state, to the detriment of equality and social justice. Seduced by the safety of a continent surrounded by oceans, spoiled by abundant resources, and lulled by the absence of serious challenges to the republican form of government, Americans had chosen the laissez-faire approach for the realization of liberal democracy. Following the guidance of Jefferson, they were "too much concerned with negative devices designed to obstruct the use of political power for bad ends" instead of directing it toward worthwhile ends.[14] However, that wrong understanding did not invalidate the underlying liberal values and ideas themselves.

When he titled an article "What Is Still Living in the Political Philosophy of Thomas Jefferson" and began it with Jefferson's assertion "I believe . . . that there exists a right independent of force," Becker completed the shift he had begun in 1936. He had discovered a firm foundation on which to stand in the defense of liberal democracy by separating the outmoded aspects of Jefferson's political philosophy—the views on the proper function of government—from the fundamental ones. For Becker that meant to pay attention "to the form of government as distinct from its function and to the essential rights to be secured as distinct from the particular institutional forms for securing them." Jefferson's political philosophy would remain valid in the present and the future to the extent to which the "general presuppositions upon which it rests have a universal validity, the extent to which they express some enduring truth about nature and the life of man." Hence, the period was over when "we were in a mood to ask whether the representative system of government might not be, if not at open, at least too often at secret, war with the rights of mankind." Now the defects of that system appeared to be not fatal but remediable. Hitler had "forced men everywhere to reexamine the validity of half-forgotten ideas and to entertain once more half-discarded convictions as to the substance of things not seen. One of these convictions is that 'liberty, equality, fraternity,' and the 'inalienable rights' of man are phrases, glittering or not, that denote realities—the fundamental realities that men will always fight and die for rather than surrender."[15] That was as ringing a declaration for timeless and universal values at the core of human history as Becker would ever sound on his bell. As if to make sure that after all these assertions his residual uncertainty would not be forgotten, he concluded with a new version of Jefferson's famous "We hold these truths . . ." passage, one a bit longer because of the added modifying and hedging clauses. The latter originated in the conviction, still held fast, that American society needed a radical reform of its institutions, guided by the newly recognized enduring democratic values. After a decades-long reflection on historical matters, Becker had assumed a stance that strikingly resembled an updated traditional understanding of American history. At its core was still the ever better realization of the potentialities for freedom and equality present in the American republic. The American sense of history was again more than a myth that pleasured people temporarily, and historians had reacquired a role beyond that of passive recorders and keepers.

Becker's calls to reform American society had acquired a new authority. Historians, while no longer able to rely on a grand objective progress for guiding the world toward better things, could base their reform activism on more traditional elements of stability in the flux of human events. The problem of reform was now a matter of giving an institutional realization to Jefferson's inalienable rights appropriate for the twentieth century, particularly by extending their applications to the economic sphere. Otherwise "the physical barricades may be up before we realize what it is all about—before we are prepared even to understand the fundamental issues which history has long been preparing for us."[16]

Becker, much like Beard, sensed a historical mandate to reform American society in the direction of a more communal structure. In Becker's new perspective, America's options were no longer the near infinite number of useful but free-floating myths, but encompassed only four choices: socialism, communism, fascism, and "what for lack of a better term we may call Social Democracy," each of them linked to promptings by contemporary life.[17] Becker chose the fourth option for its supposedly greater collective spirit and efficiently planned economy. When such a linkage of the American destiny to a form of social organization seen as European was criticized, Becker pointed out the venerable age of government regulations of economic activity in the United States, visible in tariffs, road building, the Homestead Act of 1862, the mail system, railroad legislation, and many other measures. The choice of so-cial democracy as the American future fit the American sense of history because it affirmed progress and all intellectual, political, and economic liberties. After all, "Social Democracy asks us . . . only to submit to such governmental regulations of private economic enterprise as may be necessary to correct its evils and secure a reasonable degree of equality of possessions and of opportunities for the mass of the people."[18] It was significant that Becker had justified his choice of the future not on the basis of a constructed ideal future, but in line with a sense of the past that reflected reality.

Now that the strength of the values, institutions, and progress inher-ent in the American understanding of history had been at least partially restored, Becker, much like Beard, found it easy to deflate warnings about the consequences of social democracy's concentration of eco-nomic as well as political power in government. The dangers readily ob-servable in Communist countries were not relevant to a collectivized United States. Becker treated the Founding Fathers' anxiety over the de-mise of earlier republican governments through the misuse of excessive power, particularly the Jeffersonian insights, as the expression of an un-necessarily distrustful attitude toward government. It befitted an agri-cultural society of relatively small scale, but not the America of advanced industry and commerce. Since social democracy meant "no more than the governmental regulation or control of the economic life of the community," and since that government would then be controlled by a true majority, no abuse of power could occur. History's mandate, or at least preferred choice, could not be one fraught with danger. The re-jection of collectivism was "a pious wish. It is not a question of what we should like if it were possible to have it, but the question of what we must accept under conditions as they exist."[19] A hint of doubt came only on the right of free speech, where neither the newly powerful na-tional government nor the people were trusted to respect the liberties of those who dissented too strongly. With the knowledge gap between scholars and the community becoming ever wider, the cherished free-dom of research might well be endangered.

In that new perspective and in contrast to Beard, the approach of war and the war itself moved Becker only to weary reflections: on the trivial reasons given for making war that only covered up the self-interests of national states; on the professions of love of peace on the part of the masses whose passions he distrusted; on his agreement with Ernest Lavisse that "war is a habit of civilization"; on William James's finding that wars also solidify a nation and inspire it to cooperation and sacri-fice; on his doubts that any war would bring the end of wars; and on the futility of hopes for a "better world" after the war, discounting the hopes for a United Nations organization and eternal peace, now that those who observed carefully had seen how close the world was to barbarism at any time.[20] Yet while still unable to discern any overriding meaning in history, Becker was willing to follow America in her course after 1939. In that year, he had accepted the possibility of war when he conceded that "'while war can do nothing to safeguard democratic institutions, it may be the only means of preserving the power and independence of democratic countries.'"[21] As for the postwar order, he could only glimpse it from the outcome of the Yalta Conference. In observations made shortly before his death on April 10, 1945, he hinted that his attitudes probably would have been those of a modified continentalism, a view in line with his newly found center in the American tradition. He, like Beard, asked for restraints on America's outward thrust, but his reasoning went along the rationale of *Realpolitik*. Thus, on the then central topic of Eastern Europe, Becker cautioned against any deep American involvement in the affairs of Eastern Europe, because America had an interest there "but not a major interest." The Soviet Union had that major interest, and her sphere should be recognized, particularly since Americans could do nothing about events in that region. America's missionary role was denied completely. The Eastern European problems (especially those of Poland) offered a "complicated conflicted of ideas and interests which simply cannot be solved by saying that every people 'must be permitted to choose the government under which it will live.'"[22] More important for America was the preservation of peace, which needed the cooperation of the great powers, particularly if an international organization was supposed to keep it. To that necessity all other goals had to yield, including the ideals of self-determination of some nations.

Unlike Beard, he did not worry about foreign policy interfering with the great social reform. Even with his now moderately affirmative outlook Becker found it no less difficult to bestir himself on behalf of the human race. "Judged by my private values, very little can be said in its behalf: judged by the private values current at any time, the Human Race must be mostly wrong and thoroughly perverse." Only those who believed in the realization of an absolute truth in the future had "a cheap ticket to salvation." As for himself, he could not "enter their clean but sparsely furnished Heaven."[23] However, the lecture series and the books derived from them demonstrated on ongoing, intense, and partially successful struggle for that meaning and stability he seemed to have written off permanently. Still, every time he found some answer it came with a hedge; every affirmation evoked in him the suspicion of the "as if." He hesitated and, in the end, could not consort easily with any stable truth, just as he had failed to find a satisfactory intellectual home in any school of historiography. Fixity was uncomfortable to him, although the world as nothing but change was not as bearable as he wished it to be. He ardently applauded the trait in "the modern mind to escape 'the illusion of finality,'" but realized the flaws in the relativistic positions, "one of the chief being that they must be prepared, at the appropriate moment, to commit hara-kiri in deference to the ceaseless transformation which they postulate."[24] Perhaps Becker's partial reconciliation with the American tradition was his way of avoiding that hara-kiri. It put him at a discernible distance from his earlier, minimalist assertion—inspired by the Spanish philosopher Miguel de Unamuno—in which he had found that "the significance of man is that he is insignificant and is aware of it," and that, as the universe in the end crushed him, he triumphed over it, since he knew about the universe, "but of all of that the universe knows nothing."[25] The supreme work of art by human beings, their real triumph, had been to create a world in their image. If the universe had no intrinsic meaning, human action could make it more moral than the morally silent universe was by itself. That defiant stipulation of a purely constructed meaning for human life eventually yielded, if not to the stipulation of a grand order or meaning, then at least to one of structural elements of more than an "as if" nature.

17

Beard and Post-1935 Reality

Those who read Becker's works published between 1935 and 1945 could observe his efforts to arrive at a workable reconciliation between his relativism and his desire to defend liberal democracy. The books bore the marks of a scholar who tried to deal with the basic questions that required answers for the collective as well as his own good; all of it done in patient analysis without an exhibition of passion. Beard pursued his struggles more fervently and in the glare of the public square. After a brief venture into theoretical discovery, the ideological struggles forced him, too, to test his new relativist view of the world as one upon which order was impressed by acts of faith and will. The liberal worldview, justified in the new manner, would have to show its mettle against the challenges posed by the fascism of Hitler and Mussolini (itself based on acts of will and faith) and of communism (based on claims to being scientific and progressive).

On the surface, Beard's new view of the world and history enhanced the already strong activism in Progressive history, because no other force but the committed actions by individuals mattered. Will stood against will, faith against faith. Beard seemed to be even liberated from the need to prove his faith in progress through factual argumentation. Yet Beard never abandoned his habit of marshaling the facts for his side. Indeed, as the debate proceeded, his new certainty about progress came to resemble more and more his old faith in an objective progress. His marginal interest in theory and his relentless drive to educate the public to the needed changes in American society would join in preventing Beard from dealing systematically with the ever more visible, wide-open gap between his claims to certainty as a social reformer and his denial of any interpretive certainty as a theoretician. Nevertheless, his desire to redirect American policies forced him to define the situation in the 1930s and 1940s in a manner that brought about fundamental revisions in his historiographical views. The specific issue of the greatest concern to Beard was an old one and one that seemed unlikely to involve historical theory: Ought domestic or foreign policy to have primacy? Yet the question raised anew the historiographical issue of how to reconcile the modern universalizing forces with the universal aspect of the American sense of history.

At the center of Beard's work, after 1936, remained his longtime goal: the American Good Society befitting the proper course of American history. Events in Europe and the Pacific basin, together with worries about a wrong American response to them, guided Beard's attention to the possibility of war; not the threat of war in general but America's involvement in one. The latter became for Beard the darkest shadow over the American future. It would mean the destruction of all hopes that the great domestic task of reform would ever be undertaken. This perception yielded the stark alternatives of "staying at home" or projecting America into the world. Beard would speak, once more, as the voice of history, unmindful of the limitations he had spelled out for the authority of subjective visions of history. In the manner of an Old Testament prophet he warned of certain ruin unless Americans decided to persist in the proven policy: to "stay at home." His fears only temporarily assuaged by the Neutrality Resolutions, he discerned in President Roosevelt's Quarantine speech of October 1937 and his later policies a fatal desire for "world-meddling."

For some time, the mechanisms of early Progressive history seemed to suffice for the interpretation of the new situation. They did in his key article, "We're Blundering into War."[1] At fault was the unchanged, unreformed American foreign policy of outward commercial projection, unneeded but backed by armed force, which drew America into areas of tensions and conflicts; an imperialist capitalism, Beard called it. After his travels in the 1920s and then again in 1935, he prophesied that such a policy would involve America in a war with Japan and also in any new war in Europe—a foreign policy that was illogical even on its own terms, since it was hostile to Japan, a good trading partner, and friendly to China, a country of little consequence commercially. Against that possible course of events Beard put his demand that "*the United States should and can stay out of the next war in Europe and the wars that follow the next war*" (emphasis in original).[2] Beard eagerly assured people that he did not argue his case as an "old isolationist," but as a modern historian who understood the logic of history.[3] The policy of continentalism (earlier he had called it Little Americanism) offered the only possibility of fulfilling America's true destiny. Hence, when in the late 1930s an aroused segment of the public formed various noninterventionist groups, Beard was their close associate. However, although he sympathized with the goals of the America First Committee and the Keep America Out of War Committee, he never joined them. They were really pressure groups, while Beard, never a joiner in the first place, saw things in grand historical terms. In this respect he differed sharply from one of his staunchest supporters, Barnes, now an influential columnist who had much closer connections with the antiwar groups.[4]

When, year by year, the urgency to prevent American intervention grew more acute, Beard pressed his arguments harder. In the process, he modified decisively some of the central tenets of Progressive history concerning the historical role of the masses, the weight given to the past, and the limits to human mastery of life.

In his attempt to sway American foreign policy, Beard put much stake in a grand national debate on the question of intervention. Beard wished to arouse the masses, who then would force the president into a debate and be, without a doubt, on Beard's side. He now took courage from the fact that the people and their representatives had rejected Wilsonianism. A truly participatory democracy, made actual in such a debate, would conform to the thrust of history. The debate would also prevent the resurfacing of the simplistic "devil theories of war," which blamed the calamity of war on specific persons or groups. Because wars occurred in the context of overall policies and developments, their prevention was a collective task. After a thorough national debate historians could never again search for culprits (or devils). The whole nation would be responsible: "War is not the work of a demon. It is our very own work, for which we prepare, wittingly or not, in ways of peace. But we sit blindfolded at the preparation."[5]

His trust in the people's judgment required that Beard declare the people now to be emancipated despite their proven inertia. Such inertial tendencies were no longer seen as merely detrimental. The slow-moving development of the American mind and spirit (a broad collective current, if not entity), formerly bemoaned as the result of too much inertia, now became the great steadying force. This powerful force would reject deviations from America's proper course. The people were its true carriers and agents. Beard quoted with approval from an article published in the *Atlantic Monthly* in 1858, that these people " 'are more in conversation with the heart and pure spiritual fact of humanity, than any other people of equal power and culture.' "[6] In that role, the people had always been opposed to interventionism abroad, as manifested now by their fierce and widespread opposition to interventionist intents in the Quarantine speech.[7] As Beard put it in 1942, "this *demos* in movement, this people in the process of civilization" would carry the cause of American civilization.[8] Despite their diverse national origins, their shared lives had shaped them into a unit with strong political, economic, and moral ties. He would contrast the people's healthy, straightforward sense of history with the errant one of a segment of the American liberal intelligentsia, the new elite from which so much had been expected. Their desertion into the camp of interventionism was especially reprehensible, because they should have known better.

In a second change, the past recouped an important role when Beard attempted to give his warnings substance and authority. Increasingly and contrary to his earlier views, he relied for both of them on demonstrations and verifications from the past. Such arguments from past experience were weightier again, since Beard once more argued clearly on the basis of a logic in history's course. That logic ruled out Progressive history's radical disjunction between the past on one side and the present and future on the other. However, when Beard spoke of lessons from the past, they were derived not from a comparative history of great states, but, because of America's uniqueness, primarily from the American past.

When Beard called history "the lamp of experience for guidance in the present," it now had a strong, once furiously rejected, Ciceronian ring, with the past as the teacher of life.[9] As a corollary to the new emphasis on continuity, the assertions of relativism and the view of historical concepts and interpretations as constructs disappeared from the foreground. Continental Americanism was no mere constructed theory, but part of America's very nature and destiny. It "was realistically framed with reference to the exigencies of the early Republic and was developed during continuous experience with the vicissitudes of European ambitions, controversies, and wars."[10] Whenever America had deviated from that tradition the deviation had proved fruitless, and any advantages gained had been temporary. The most recent deviations, between 1895 and 1920, had cost the country dearly. Accordingly, Beard became moderately supportive of the anti-interventionist tendencies in the revisionism of Barnes and Sidney Fay, as well as the munitions inquiry by Senator Gerald Nye. But for Beard's argument World War I's specific causes were less important than its general cause: the major deviation from the traditional continentalism in the interest of capitalist ventures for markets and of ill-conceived schemes to improve the world. He pointed out to Americans the terrible consequences of the intervention in 1917. The reform enthusiasm of the Progressive Era had been crushed, the wartime national unity as well as economic planning and full employment had proven temporary, and civil liberties had become endangered. Beard was sincerely and passionately convinced that a second world war would abolish the last chances for the historically mandated reforms of American society. This sense of confronting a final turning point in American history accounted for Beard's feverish anti-war activity before 1941 and his bitterness after America's entry into the war. The consequence was an even firmer emphasis on the authority of the past and on continuity. Thus, he urged Americans to rely on the tried and true policies of continentalism "framed by the founders of the American Republic. They were experienced, active, and effective statesmen," who in an equally unsettled period "formed a clear picture of the Republic which they were to maintain and develop, of its practical interests committed to their care, and of the great foreign powers whose policies and arms were involved in their fortunes."[11]

As Beard perceived it, the New Deal, despite its excessive accommodation to the Old Deal, had made a good start in reforming the American civilization. From 1937, however, the policy of continentalism "was whittled away and overshadowed by other policies holding fateful consequences for the American people"—by the doctrine of internationalism.[12] The great American temptation of the late 1930s to deviate from America's destined course came, in Beard's terminology, from the internationalists. They, the governing elite, had already twice "turned the nation away from its continental center of gravity into world adventures, ostensibly in a search for relations with the other countries or regions that would yield prosperity for American industry and a flowering of American prestige."[13] This was especially tragic since, according to Beard, only 10 percent of American production figured in foreign trade, and that amount could be easily absorbed in the domestic market, given the increased power of consumption in a society with greater economic justice. Beard's critical analysis of the elite that diverted America from her proper path was in the by then well-known vein. He traced the modern rejection of "the doctrine of continental independence" to the work of Admiral Alfred Thayer Mahan, who had championed American naval strength for securing American rights abroad. On numerous occasions, he highlighted the expansionist role of the navy in modern American history, including his testimony before a House committee, in February 1938, against the new naval building program.[14] The most detrimental conviction of the internationalists was that "nothing fundamental can be accomplished by *domestic* policies and activities in relieving the American people from the curse of poverty and unemployment, in promoting the characteristic features of American civilization, in lifting the American standard of living to a higher plane, by the fullest possible use of national resources in materials, machines, and labor, which are here in abundance" (emphasis in original).[15] Tirelessly, Beard proclaimed that in reality the surest way to America's peace and prosperity was a strict continentalism. Once more, John A. Hobson's accusation was brought up that imperialism was a futile attempt to escape from domestic problems.[16] On the contrary, no

country that had severe unresolved domestic problems must intervene in
the world on behalf of a better order. The 1890s demonstrated the futility of trying to flee from one's domestic problems; after every external
thrust they had still been there. The heritage of Wilson's internationalist
experiment had been the same.

Beard's analysis condemned all kinds of interventionists, even those
not favorably inclined toward commercial interests. Indeed, he criticized especially the liberal intellectuals for their interventionism. His
criticism was based on a surprising argument. Beard accepted the very
limits to the human mastery of life that Progressive historians had all
along rejected as inappropriate for modernity. The internationalists of
the 1930s, who wanted to employ America's power against fascism,
nazism, and, to a lesser degree, against communism, did not understand
the limits of American power. They saw only that the United States was a
great power and must assume the responsibilities of a great power for
reforming the world. In retrospect, Beard would point to that conviction
as the most detrimental attitude of the post-1936 period. With its ascendancy, the fate of the New Deal was sealed. Until then, the New Deal had
been "guided by the belief that the main business of getting the country
out of the depression belonged to the people and the government of the
United States, and could not be disposed of by trying to get foreign markets in bankrupt Europe and Asia."[17] Once more, it was forgotten that a
nation that lacked a sense of direction in its domestic policies could not
give direction to the world. Beard reiterated the message in *Giddy
Minds and Foreign Quarrels: An Estimate of American Foreign Policy*
(1939).[18] He could agree with Henry R. Luce that the New Deal had
failed to bring about a reinvigorated American civilization, but certainly
not with Luce's conclusion that, in the American century, the perception
of America as the beacon of free enterprise and "the principal guarantor
of the freedom of the seas, the vision of Americas [*sic*] as the dynamic
leader of world trade, has within it the possibilities of such enormous
human progress as to stagger the imagination." He rejected Luce's exhortation that America should "send its engineers, scientists, doctors,
road builders, teachers, educators, and even 'movie men' everywhere
'throughout the world,' providing leadership to all mankind in creating
the right kind of civilization." That, Beard found, was a wild escalation
of the old imperialist designs that had only "promised to do good on a
limited scale to them that sat in darkness."[19]

By 1940, Beard's historical world had regained a clear dualistic nature. On one side were those who saw the ever more urgent need to reaffirm American continentalism, and on the other side those who advocated an American internationalism for either economic or visionary

reasons. Once again, they represented the pair of forces with which Progressive historians had always been most comfortable: historical creativity and retardation. And once more, America's fate depended on the right choice. American society must conform to the objective order in which "with inescapable fatality the mass production made possible by machinery and nourished by our unparalleled natural resources accelerated the leveling democracy implied in the idea of progress." Protected by the umbrella of continentalism, Americans could build the new American society that would differ vastly from Europe's *grand monde,* where "the cultivated classes deliberately recompose the idyll of the past," and that would make "obsolete the *le grand monde* of the lotoseaters." A new age would start as the "iron gates are closing on the dreams of privilege."[20]

In the years immediately preceding the attack on Pearl Harbor, those whom Beard criticized struck back at him. The liberal critics put in question the feasibility and the morality of his continentalism. They denied the authenticity of Beard's reading of America's history. One group of Beard's opponents argued the economic impossibility of an isolated America. Henry Wallace, then secretary of commerce, sympathized with Beard's "open door at home," but treated it as a noble unobtainable ideal, perhaps one not even desirable, because it would be a risky gamble involving enormous costs in money and the dislocation of people. He preferred the experimental approach of President Roosevelt, the object of Beard's distrust. Wallace suspected Beard to be "an aesthetic, a believer in the Good Life according to academic standards."[21] Raymond Buell's *Isolated America* proved most effective in countering Beard's arguments by the recitation of relevant economic facts.[22] Economic nationalism had already destroyed prewar international trade and brought on Hitler, Mussolini, and the Great Depression. Above all, an isolated America would not only give up the production for export, but have its life changed radically. Total regimentation with grave consequences would result. That criticism should have impressed Beard, because by then, he was familiar with works on bureaucratization and its impact on social flexibility and individual freedom. Later, in 1944, he would come to know Friedrich A. Hayek's dire prediction of economic planning as the road to serfdom. But Beard never wavered in his conviction that participatory democracy would remedy all of these problems. He put his trust in the difference between "state intervention by despotisms and state intervention by constitutional governments under popular mandates."[23] Besides, American history was unique and the experiences of others were not applicable. Hence, he also was not impressed by Buell's prediction that, lacking the stimulus for production and the restraint on prices coming from foreign trade, America would suffer a decline in the living standard, lose accustomed freedoms, and see an enormous enhancement of the power of the state, with no guarantee for permanent peace. Turning the table on Beard, Buell viewed continentalism as a refurbished isolationism, an outdated ideal of agrarian America that fit ill to an industrial power—an argument based on progress, which Beard, in previous years, had loved to make in a different vein.

But the criticism that hurt most came from a second group of critics, who denied to continentalism an ethical foundation. Here the theoretical debates about historical relativism took on practical features. In the face of the grave threat from the Fascist and Communist ideologies, these critics now included Beard among those who had lost all proper philosophical foundation to speak of truth and defend it. They conceded that Beard was correct when he pointed to the failure of England and France, still colonial powers, to stand up for liberal democracy when Hitler and Mussolini first flouted international law, and when, in the light of recent experience, he did not grant the Soviet Union a positive judgment. Still, his conclusion that England and France should not expect America to come to their rescue was, to his critics, shortsighted or worse. Lewis Mumford defined the "worse." For him, the phrase *human* (or, at least, *Western) civilization*, which Beard distrusted and considered to be of no practical importance, had real meaning. Pragmatic liberalism (including Progressive history), as opposed to ideal liberalism, had suffered the corruption of its ethical component. "The isolationism of a Charles Beard or a Stuart Chase or a Quincy Howe is indeed almost as much a sign of barbarism as the doctrines of a Rosenberg or a Gottfried Feder."[24] The obsession of pragmatic liberals with nonintervention in the interest of peace blinded them to the fact that they were advocating a "capitulation to the forces that will not merely wipe out liberalism, but will overthrow certain precious principles with which one element of liberalism has been indelibly associated: freedom of thought, belief in an objective reason, belief in human dignity." Here, Progressive history had immunized Beard and other liberals against the threat of a new Dark Age, since it knew only upward progression. Their "liberalism glibly refuses to acknowledge the evidence of its senses. Like the sun-dial, it cannot tell time on a stormy day."[25] All of that was predictable from a school of thought that would not distinguish between the liberalism of the Manchester laissez-faire type and the sound principles of the humanistic tradition, nor between the lasting wisdom of liberalism and its nineteenth-century forms; saw all social evil as stemming from evil interests and institutions; and perceived the future in purely technological terms.[26] What Beard and others had forgotten was the valuative and passionate side of human life. In that regard, Beard's activity on behalf of European refugees counted for little. As his advice was increasingly scorned, Beard stood his ground and suffered an increasing personal isolation—having lost many friends, his once towering standing in the academic world, and outlets for his ideas in the *New Republic* and the *Nation*.

Beard's gradual isolation was shared by Barnes, whose newspaper column "The Liberal Viewpoint," throughout the 1930s, expressed his disappointment with the New Deal and American foreign policy. Many readers were perplexed and chagrined to learn that the American political system was unfit for the now more populous and complex country, party government no longer served democratic aims, the New Deal had achieved only minor reforms, and America was reaching the end of her rope.[27] Publishers began to have second thoughts about Barnes's textbooks, and his attempts to reenter academe proved unsuccessful. Beard regretted that he could not help him, since "not many college authorities ask me for recommendations . . . the war mongers have made things worse for us, by making European history mean American subservience to Britain's game."[28] Nevertheless, Barnes would remain a vocal and unrepentant opponent of what he would call "the New-Deal-war-mongering-globaloney gang."[29] His persistence was buttressed by his refusal to experiment with any relativism and to adhere to the old-line Progressive history with an objective progress at its core.

When the Second World War brought about a diminution of Beard's public role, he had leisure to reassess his basic views on history. Progress, seen as a relentless process, remained at the heart of them, with the central "contention that the progressive realization of reason and good is *in* history, though not the sum of history" (emphasis in original). As one of the futile attempts to give an absolute (and deterministic) explanation of history, the interpretation of history in terms of the conflict of economic interests was losing much of its fascination for him. In his introduction to the 1935 edition of *An Economic Interpretation of the Constitution of the United States,* Beard had already pronounced the book to have been merely an attempt to give the economic interpretation a hearing. Economic conflicts were no longer the primary forces for driving on progress, but they were part of a whole spectrum of conflicts produced in the course of the ever fuller realization of the idea of civilization. "This idea of civilization . . . embraces a conception of history as a struggle of human beings in the world for individual and social perfection—for the good, the true, the beautiful—against ignorance, disease, the harshness of physical nature, the forces of barbarism in individuals and society." In this process the United States acquired "unique features in origin, substance, and development."[30]

When Beard defined the "idea of civilization" as "respect for life, for human worth, for the utmost liberty compatible with the social principle, for equality of rights and opportunities, . . . for the rule of the universal participation in the work and benefits of society," he had no difficulty in linking America to it. Indeed, its advancement had been America's task for all of her history. This obligation Americans could fulfill only if the true American development were not diverted into wrong channels. It made it a central duty for Americans to resist all temptations to alter those values "inalienable to the civilization in the United States" or to hinder their full realization.[31] That meant to wage a valiant struggle against the temptation to become like other civilizations. Among the concepts foreign to American civilization was not only Marxism as an ideology, but also the Marxist modes of thought, which, so far, had evoked at least some sympathies in Beard. Now, all Marxist ideas were seen as Prussian in essence and rejected as "foreign in center of interest even when expounded by Americans."[32] Yet America's most dangerous temptation stemmed from the urge to lose herself in the world rather than keep at her true task, which was to realize fully her potential uniqueness. As of the 1940s, America's "convergence of national consensus" on the idea of civilization was still unfinished. For the first time, there was even a hint in Beard's view of history of America's possible ultimate failure.

Beard recovered the importance of the past for history when he found that "the idea of civilization predicates a partial determinism, such as an irreversible and irrevocable historical heritage, and a partially open and dynamic world in which creative intelligence can and does work." At the core of history was still "advancing civilization" furthered by human actions that made "the good, the true, and the beautiful prevail."[33] Only this time the guide was no flawless future democracy but the basic features of American civilization as they had emerged through a consensus on basic ideas and ideals. The latter, shaped by the experience of generations, provided the proper historical perspective. The institutions of the Republic were no longer seen as obstacles to progress. Beard avoided speaking of the Constitution as the bulwark of antidemocratic forces and of checks and balances as antimajoritarian devices. Instead, the Constitution emerged as a brilliant instrument against despotic power and the unstable judgments of majorities. By 1945, Beard, who had never left the confines of the American sense of history, had come close to fusing its traditional and Progressive versions. He did so by a balance between a new continuity, with reliance on the past, and the openness of the future to innovation within limits. The exclusive focus on America would prove to be a severe impediment to an integration of American history into a universal progressive development. This came at a time when the interdependence of the world grew steadily. Much like Becker's, Beard's last interpretation of history would remain at a clear distance from a New History with universal applications.

When, during wartime, Beard could only criticize the projections for the future and not the realities of the present, he championed continentalism by speaking out against the schemes being devised for the postwar order. Measured on the requirements of American civilization, a false conception of the universality of progress was undergirding the policies of the United States. These policies would fail because the new internationalists (the "world imagists" or "world savers") had a wrong understanding of history. They considered feasible a radically different world on the basis of "common bonds of humanity, of the natural rights all human beings enjoy, of the similarities among nations and peoples."[34] Overlooked was the staying power in all nations of broad basic attitudes and traditions. The talk by the "world planners" about a world federation, built on principles of the American civilization, was an egregious result of such thinking. American civilization could not be exported. Indeed, none of the peoples or nations would behave much differently after the war. Beard repeated Jefferson's assessment of Europe and, by implication, of all of the world's nations. "Their mutual jealousies, their balance of power, their complicated alliances, their forms and principles of government, are all foreign to us. They are nations of eternal war."[35] Unfortunately, the internationalists' illusions about changing the world and about a permanent universal peace provided ever new reasons for American interventions abroad. The hope of the "world planners" for permanent peace through a world federation was nonsensical, because the struggle of nations and groups for power would continue within such a federation. In that spirit Beard ridiculed Roosevelt's conviction that "after the Axis powers have been destroyed a new world order guaranteeing permanent peace and the four freedoms to all peoples will be established."[36] Such illusions gave strength to those forces that did not understand the essence of American civilization, which prescribed the genuinely American policy of continentalism.

After Becker's death in 1945, Beard was the only one of the founders' generation left to cope with the world, which years ago had started to develop in a wrong direction. Before he took up the role of postwar Cassandra, Beard had one last opportunity to speak out on historiography. It came when a group of historians endeavored to produce "a little handbook which we hope will clarify thought about the nature of historical interpretations."[37] In 1942, a paper on research in American history, sponsored by the Social Science Research Council, was discussed at a follow-up conference.[38] The aim was to bring the historians' theoretical considerations up to the (at least perceived) more rigorous level of the social scientists. As a member of the subsequent Committee on Historiography, Beard undertook the writing of portions of the committee's bulletin, specifically the chapter titled "Grounds for a Reconsideration of Historiography" and those propositions (chapter 5) that, it was thought, were "accepted by persons competent in such fields as valid themselves and for applications."[39]

Not a trace showed of the stormy development in Progressive history's concepts of historical truth finding as Beard focused on the aspect of theory he was most comfortable with: history's usefulness in the public arena. He pleaded that what he called "the fundamentals of historiography in relation to practical affairs of the gravest import" deserved equal or even more reconsideration than the "love of knowledge in itself or the advancement of learning for its own sake." Indeed, Beard blamed the historians' insufficient attention to history's practical dimensions for the fact that "the Western world has long been at a crisis in thought and learning, as well as in practice—the most widespread and tumultuous crisis of the kind since the beginning of recorded history." The overcoming of the crisis demanded that historians avoid in their thinking about history getting lost in abstractions, lest they be captured by the concept of a "natural course" of history from which developments might deviate but to which they will always return: a history full of repetitions and sameness.[40] Such approaches failed to find the truth and led to wrong choices that impeded proper public policy. While the concept of an objective progress was not openly at the center of Beard's argument, it was very much at the heart of it. However, Beard bequeathed a theoretical void to subsequent historians on the crucial question that the bulletin aimed to address. He defined it as the clarification of the relationship between written history and history-as-actuality and of the assumptions, processes, and results used to connect the two.

In the end, the bulletin shed little new light on the theory of history and had a modest influence on the practice of historiography. That did not surprise Beard, who suspected his fellow historians to be immune to appeals for change. Illusions were far from the mind of a weary man who now suffered recurrently from pulmonary illness and soon would be besieged by harsh criticisms of his postwar works. Although, as Beard claimed, he continued with "a lot of reading in Historiography— my true major interest: what, how much, history can we know and what methods are best for inquiry and exposition in the interest of increasing our knowledge," historiography was not really his burning concern.[41] His central concern was the recent course of history, which ran counter to his expectations.

The young Beard would have welcomed the postwar world with its dense interconnections between nations, the spread of industrialization across the globe, and the concomitant promise of universal progress. Only his aversion to imperialism would have tempered somewhat his praise for the new situation. For the older Beard, the continentalist, the growing interdependence of the world was still an inevitable, though not always welcome, development, but America's new status in it could not be condoned, since it was the result of a decisively wrong turn in her development. As far as he was concerned, the year 1945 had brought the belated triumph of a rampant Wilsonianism. The "world imagists" and "world savers" had won, although they had not achieved the world federation their radical wing had sought. The world in which the United States had assumed a great-power role remained one of nation-states, and thus full of the old power antagonisms—just as he had predicted well before 1945. These conflicts would keep the attention of America fixed on the outside world and away from her great domestic task—a fact doubly regrettable because the peaceful world, the one feature that could have been a consolation for America's erroneous ways, also failed to arrive. Competition with the Soviet Union would prevent the realization of American dreams about a new world order. American ideals and moral leadership would find the limits to their application in the scope of America's power. It would show that "undoubtedly the United States is a great power *in* the world and has obligations as such. But the range of its *effective* power supportable by armed forces and economic resources is limited" (emphasis in original). As for "the duty of the United States to assume and maintain 'the moral leadership of the world,'" the idea was repulsive and would only awaken resentment in the world rather than assure peace.[42] Fearful of the diversion of energies and resources to foreign countries, Beard opposed the Marshall Plan and the general expansion of American power, especially as defined in the Truman Doctrine, as a waste of national resources. Whenever appropriate, he reiterated his now long-standing position that imperialism and internationalism retarded the urgent reform of American society. No temporary prosperity could compensate for the harm caused by the delay of fundamental solutions. New postwar conflicts and the possibility of yet another war exerted further pressure on Beard.

The indefinite postponement, perhaps even abandonment, of the building of the Good Society oppressed Beard, who, seventy years old and with his strength sapped by the long struggle, saw his chances of changing things dwindling. He also felt deserted. "Most of my old friends are either dead or busy with projects and battles with fog giants that seem nonsensical to my poor befuddled mind."[43] Nevertheless, pitting hope against experience, he set out for the last time to demonstrate how America had missed the call of history by pursuing a completely wrong course in foreign policy. Aside from a number of articles on the matter, *American Foreign Policy in the Making, 1932–1940* (1946) and *President Roosevelt and the Coming of the War 1941: A Study in Appearances and Realities* (1948) were Beard's last grand statements on the American republic he loved with a passion and criticized for not living up to the mandate of history. Now, in direct contradiction to his own warning against blaming individuals for major historical developments, especially for wars, Beard vented his bitterness and anger at President Roosevelt's role in prewar diplomacy and in the debacle of Pearl Harbor. The sense of grievance gave the books a passionate, even fiery quality.

In the first of the two works, Beard saw in Roosevelt's leadership more than an opportunistic deception. The president's separation of rhetoric from actual policies had deprived the people of their right to participate in the making of policy decisions. The people and the members of Congress had been duped and the democratic process corrupted. In 1937, Beard had warned that, if the United States participated in another European war, "that participation will mark the end of democratic institutions in the United States."[44] Now, with the decline of domestic leadership, Beard sensed that "although not exactly in the form that Madison foresaw, the test is here, now—with no divinity hedging our Republic against Caesar."[45] In the end, it was not so much a matter of conspiracy, but a blind and unscrupulous pursuit of policies formulated without regard for or even understanding of the course prescribed by the needs of American civilization. The widely praised war, with its constitutionally suspect origin, had enhanced sinister developments. Many readers did not reach that understanding. Scholars of a different liberal persuasion took the book as a purely ad hominem attack that sought to create the impression of a "gigantic fraud" and a "super-Machiavellian effort" by the president.[46]

The second work dealt with the war guilt question as far as America and Japan were concerned. Pearl Harbor, as the trigger of the war, had raised in Beard the grave suspicion of possible foreknowledge and willful unpreparedness. In 1947, George Morgenstern published *Pearl Harbor: The Story of the Secret War,* a book that conformed basically to Beard's thoughts on the matter, although Morgenstern was a man of the "right," a member of the *Chicago Daily Tribune* circle. Both men saw the catastrophe of Pearl Harbor as exactly what Roosevelt had wanted to occur in order to propel America into the war. It was suggested that American policies toward Japan were either ignorantly or deliberately so harsh that Japan had to fire the first shot. Despite this, Beard did not argue for a plot but against the pursuit of wrong policies. Although, in both books, his arguments came close to those of the old political history, stressing the actions of a few individuals as causes, Beard's real issues remained the exclusion of the people from the decision-making process and the danger for the Republic that resulted from the war and its outcome. The "internationalists" could not even claim that the end justified the means, since the end was wrong.

Not surprisingly, those who saw the American present and future differently rendered harsh judgments on Beard's efforts. Most were not as philosophical as Perry Miller, who expressed the hope "that I may not grow old and embittered and end by projecting my personal rancor into the tendency of history. If history does not fulfill the hope, no matter how intense the grief, may I not let vindictiveness take the place of divination."[47] Yet against the background of Beard's work, the charge of vindictiveness seems inappropriate. As a man who, once more, was sure of the course of history the American republic must follow, he thought he had reasons to condemn the American foreign policies pursued between 1935 and 1945. His passion, even bitterness, became too narrowly focused, but was not primarily rooted in personal rancor. Beard revealed both the black mood from which his judgments arose and the faint glow of hope for change that sustained him when he spoke of his vision for the future:

I do not see any signs of a reversal in the headlong trend in the direction of war and national collapse. But I suspect that we do not see very deeply into the underlying dynamics of history. Mighty trends in history have been broken as the overthrow and breakdowns of great empires and dynasties indicate. Some at their very climax falter and begin a decline into dust. Some crash or death which we do not foresee or even divine may come tomorrow and alter the face of things.[48]

In his typical manner, Beard could not quite leave his bitterness unalleviated by some vague hope that somewhere and sometime the proper course of history would prevail.

On September 3, 1948, the voice of criticism and prophecy was stilled. Beard, who had always loved Shelley's "Prometheus Unbound" with its message of "empire o'er the disentangled doom" and of "Life, Empire, and Victory" after darkness and suffering, must have died feeling like Prometheus chained to a rock, unable to influence the course of things.

18

Heritage and Assessment

The end of the Second World War coincided with the end of Progressive history as a coherent attempt to modernize American historiography. The group of "congenial gropers," as Robinson once modestly called the innovators, was vanishing.[1] Robinson had died in 1936; Becker's death came in April 1945; and Beard had then only a little over three years to live. Beard made the most of his remaining years, although he found the condition of the world abominable, and his health became increasingly frail. He confessed that "at 71 I must work against time and hence try to limit my scope to things I can manage, . . . leaving larger problems to others.[2] Clearly, the time was approaching when, as Hofstadter put it, the Progressive historians "ceased to be the leading interpreters of our past and became simply a part of it."[3]

The grand experiment in the modernization of American historiography that had been so prominent in the 1920s and '30s now became a heritage from which elements were taken for the construction of new historical accounts at a greater or lesser distance from the intent of Progressive historians. But, although such reflective overall assessments were surprisingly few, it also was scrutinized as to its role in American historiography. All of this occurred in an America that was substantially changing, particularly with respect to its position in an increasingly global world. While the integration of America into that world had begun around the turn of the century, it now accelerated. As a result, American culture began to experience a much greater influence from other cultures, even though, until the late 1960s, America's newly dominant political, economic, and military position kept the cultural gradient pointing away from rather than toward America. In particular, the American sense of history remained intact until many of its features were challenged in the social upheavals of the 1960s. Even afterwards, the American faith in history as the ever-closer approximation of the "is" to the "ought" remained strong and, although not yet sufficiently modernized for some, a sturdy frame of reference. Only in the late 1970s did the American intellectual world show a truly significant impact of historical theories and interpretations that differed radically from the American sense of history.

The intellectual climate of the immediate postwar years favored a continuation through adaptations of the concepts and views typical of Progressive history during its formative and mature phases from 1907 to the late 1920s. The last two phases—the experiment with relativism and its subsequent reassessment—were largely ignored, because they were outside the perimeter of need and perception. Barnes alone maintained virtually unchanged the original version of Progressive history, in which historical truth rested solidly on a presumed scientific basis, history was a simple dualistic struggle, and historians spoke confidently of a known and better future in the context of an objective progress. In 1937, his last major work, *A History of Historical Writing,* had shown no trace of the relativistic climate of opinion and the increase of irrational worldviews around it. Now, Barnes still proclaimed that historical reality moved from a world of ignorance and superstition to one of intrinsic harmony between rationality, science, technology, industrialization, and democratization. History was the story of the advance of "social intelligence" and its only value lay in its "potential aid in enabling us better to understand, control and redirect our own civilization."[4] The lack of any further creative development, and Barnes's brash demeanor, made for his negligible influence in the postwar period, apart from some prominence in the textbook field.

By far the most typical continuation of Progressive history came from historians who, while retaining its core elements, innovated within the perimeter set during Progressive history's early periods. Thus, Arthur Schlesinger, Jr.'s book, *The Age of Jackson* (1945) kept intact the basic dualism of business and people, but emphasized (against Turner rather than the Progressive historians) the role of the urban industrial classes of the East. Many historians modified precisely that grand dualism by making visible the complex motivations and interests involved in social and political conflicts. While accepting the economic basis for many such conflicts, C. Vann Woodward produced analyses of Southern history that contradicted Beard's widely accepted concept of a Second American Revolution. What had been held to be a monolithic agrarian South turned out to have been, at least after the Civil War, a society pervaded by struggles between agrarian and industrial interests—the past struggling against the future. For the postwar years, Merle Curti's book *The Growth of American Thought* (1943) provided a comprehensive intellectual history in the Progressive vein of instrumentalism and environmentalism with a far greater scope and sophistication than Parrington's. The price was a much diminished declamatory quality, in line with Curti's reticence to engage in brash pronouncements. More important, in his work the ambiguities in Progressive thought on the status of ideas became more clearly visible—those ideas central to Progressive history took on the status of universally valid structural entities, well beyond being pragmatic instruments. These works and many others amounted to Progressive history's late harvest, brought in by the immediate successor generation.

Yet, after 1945, Progressive history, and especially its central theme of progress through conflict, experienced a decisive downgrading by other historians. A victorious America that saw her status elevated to that of a global superpower, and in which large parts of the population experienced an increasing prosperity, had little use for a history based on social conflict. The sense of commonality seemed a better foundation. For the Consensus historians, conflicts were not expressions of profound structural rearrangements but rather adjustments within a fairly stable American society. Their interpretations were anchored in a slowly changing collective experiential core. Welded together over long years and manifested in a common outlook on life, the core carried the marks of a nation that used the continent to create abundance and was able to do so insulated from outside interference.

No connections seemed to lead from such a view to Progressive history as long as Becker's and Beard's post-1936 reassessments were ignored. But after 1936, the two historians suggested just such an experiential collective core as the basis for the certainty and authority of their final version of Progressive history. Life gave neither of the two men sufficient time to develop that version fully. Nevertheless, it was clear that American history had regained the essential elements for historical certainty and continuity. In Becker's case they were American traditional values and rights that derived their enduring validity and strength not from their presumed timeless and universal quality but from being embedded in the habits and institutions of self-government. Beard found the new sturdy basis for rebuilding Progressive history in the ideas and institutions of American civilization, with their special affinity to the idea of civilization itself. These anchors of certainty and continuity, rather than being features of the scientific culture, scholarly constructs, or useful myths, were part and parcel of the American context. Put differently, the values and habits of American public life and of American civilization were "givens" whose usefulness and truth had been tested in life. Thus, Becker's and Beard's last understanding of history accented the American context, affirmed experiential verities, suspended universal progress and an ideal future, and ended radical doubt at the border of experiential truth. In it, basic features of the American tradition, far from being obstacles to a truly modern future, gave certainty and continuity to history.

Becker's and Beard's last version of Progressive history paralleled Consensus history's reliance on an experiential basis of certainty. In Consensus history, the common core, whether defined as Daniel Boorstin's "unrepeatable combination of circumstances," David Potter's experience of Abundance, or Louis Hartz's pervasive liberal climate of thought, created America's uniqueness. That uniqueness provided an interesting link to Beard's continentalism and Becker's quiet acquiescence in it, since according to the Consensus historians, American society could not to any significant extent be copied by other people. Therefore, America's mission to the world would have clear limits, not in order to foster the great internal reform at home but because efforts exceeding these limits made little sense. All of that does not argue for a direct influence operating between the two groups of scholars, but only against the observations that Becker's and Beard's last insights were the products of old and disillusioned reformers and that the Consensus historians were ad hoc advocates of a self-satisfied age. The congruence of ideas among such different groups of scholars came from the stipulation of elements in American historiography that transcended scholarly invention.

Consensus history's exclusive emphasis on certain features of history soon evoked a strong critical reaction. As early as 1959, John Higham complained of "a massive grading operation to smooth over America's social convulsions."[5] In Hofstadter's terms, the "pendulum" soon swung back, when Progressive history's first phase experienced a revival in a heavily modified form. Under the impact of the social and political conflicts of the 1960s and early 1970s, the New Left or Radical historians shifted the emphasis back to the concept of conflict. It and other concepts of Progressive history were now lifted out of the reassuring context of a progress through gradual enlightenment and radicalized. In this continuation, with conflict's edge no longer dulled, the dualistic contest of forces in society changed from a process amenable to gradual amelioration into a harsh struggle between oppressors and oppressed. Progress would come from a basic, even revolutionary, institutional reconstruction, and not from the gradual enlightenment of the people or from institutional adjustments. The Progressive historians had invested their hope in the emancipated people; the New Left historians narrowed the emancipation to that of the oppressed. This had the beneficial effect of giving the racial problem the authenticity it had lacked in Progressive history. Much intellectual activity, including Progressive history in its orthodox form, now was seen as producing rationalizations for and by powerful groups seeking to preserve their dominant positions. On this ground, the New Left and Radical historians denied even the validity of Progressive history's versions of objectivity and rationality. That history was seen as an American understanding of history limited to the insights of middle class intellectuals. After having rejected a continuity based on the realization of rights in the traditional and Progressive versions of the American understanding of history, New Left historians nevertheless expected the class struggle and oppression to end in a cooperative society. They, unlike the Progressive historians, did not see the pragmatic matching of means to ends as essential. Beard's continentalism was left intact. New Left historians (supported by Barnes) would condemn the neglect of domestic reform stemming from America's deep involvement in foreign affairs as the "Great Evasion" of the country's historical responsibility. As motive for that involvement, these historians suggested a deliberate distraction (Beard), naïveté (William Appleton Williams), and, less often, a wrong understanding of the situation (Walter LaFeber). Yet, despite their partially effective criticism, the New Left historians did not create a coherent historical interpretation from the reshaped elements of Progressive history.

Other scholars were more intent on assessing Progressive history's role in the development of American historiography than on continuing its interpretation of history in a revised form. A first group emphasized Progressive history's part in the comprehensive revolution in American thought during the early 1900s. In his *Social Thought in America: The Revolt Against Formalism* (1949; rev. 1957), Morton White considered Beard and Robinson, the representatives of the "new history," to have been key figures in the revolt against formalism—a revolt that pitted pragmatism, instrumentalism, institutionalism, economic determinism, and legal realism against outdated American thought in terms of essences, eternal verities, and fixed traditions. Cushing Strout's book *The Pragmatic Revolt in American History: Carl Becker and Charles Beard* (1958) offered a more focused account of Progressive history's importance in the American intellectual revolution since 1900. It was the attempt to protect the certainties of liberalism—progress, democracy, and the beneficent nature of science—from the corrosion of the modern crisis. Strout also pointed beyond the purely American context when, with his strong emphasis on intellectual history, he traced American pragmatism's links to Europe, and he struck a profoundly philosophical note in acknowledging historiography's intimate connections with the general structure of life beyond its social dimension. That perspective also led him to deal with the relativistic phase in more than a cursory manner. But since Strout saw in Becker's and Beard's failure to proceed to a radical pragmatism a major reason for the fading of Progressive history, he did not see in the period of reassessment a major development.

Robert A. Skotheim's account of Progressive history in the context of his *American Intellectual Histories and Historians* (1966) also stressed the character of Progressive history as a coherent set of ideas with more than an instrumental status, although its connection to the American social and intellectual climate of the period was sufficiently acknowledged.

Yet already at that point, in the late 1960s, a second way of assessing Progressive history was becoming dominant. Reflecting in part the social conflicts of the 1960s and 1970s, this view would emphasize Progressive history's links to American reform movements since the 1880s. Even Charles Crowe's assessment of Progressive history, which still had a strong intellectual history component, was influenced by this approach.[6] Then, in three chapters of his *History: Professional Scholarship in America,* John Higham offered a systematic account that portrayed Progressive history as a historiographical revolution accentuating its social reform dimension. As would become typical, the rise and fall of that historical interpretation was linked closely to the changing fortunes of American reform movements.

The best-known assessment of Progressive history is also a quintessentially American one. Hofstadter's book, despite its title *The Progressive Historians: Turner, Beard, Parrington* (1968), was really a collection of analyses of a few important works, with its scope enlarged by introductory and concluding chapters. This format, together with the questionable inclusion of Turner and exclusion of Becker and Robinson, gave the book stringent limits. Its main parts offered less of a coherent account than Strout's book or even Skotheim's and Higham's chapters. With little dynamic of its own, Progressive history emerged as an enterprise that supplied "a historical rationale" to progressive reform movements and "memory and myth" or the "philosophical nerve" to American liberalism. Hofstadter, who by that time had overcome his attachment to Progressive history, gave that history credit for raising the proper questions, highlighting the economic interpretation of history, focusing on conflict, helping displace the Brahmins of the historical profession, seeing the need for a new American history, and offering a usable past. But he criticized Progressive historians for their insularity, nostalgia, simple faith in the American virtues, and a technological definition of modernity. In lieu of a systematic treatment of Progressive history, the book delivered brilliant analyses of selected works, sharpened by Hofstadter's disenchantment with his former idols. His book also gave a quasi finality to the assessment of Progressive history. The Progressive historians had indeed been analyzed and assessed sufficiently if the frame of reference remained restricted to turn-of-the-century America and its reform movements, their epistemology was not seen to pose any problems, and the second half of Becker's and Beard's work received little or no attention.

At this point, developments made themselves felt that would gradually affect all of American historiography and bring about a third type of assessment. The emergence of a powerful Europe and East Asia as well as the creation of many independent Third World nations raised important questions about a number of components of the American sense of history—traditional or Progressive.[7] Most affected would be the idea of a new order of human affairs in which reformed American economic, social, and political institutions would also set the pattern for a future universal order. Such an interpretation made Progressive history for one new group of scholars not the trail blazer of a modern interpretation of history but rather the last phase of America's age of innocence. In his *Historians against History* (1965) and, later, *The End of American History* (1985), David Noble has seen American history as dominated by various transformations of the Puritan myth of the exodus from the Old World to a totally new and potentially perfect New World. To these metamorphoses of the Puritan vision of a covenant with God into secular versions, Turner and the Progressive historians supplied the conclusion. Progressive history was the last major attempt to maintain an interpretation of American history as a jeremiad (a lament over the perennial failure to reach perfection) and hence was an anachronism in the modern world.[8] In Gene Wise's *American Historical Explanations* (1980) that decisive development appeared simply as an inevitable paradigm change. The emergence of Consensus history signaled the change from the Progressive to the counter-Progressive paradigm. Unfortunately, Wise relied too heavily on Turner's works and views for the construction of the Progressive paradigm.

Another assessment, cognizant of the new diversity in American historiography, arrived at a more positive judgment of Progressive history. Fascinated by the problem of truth-finding, one group of historians brought modernity's radical questioning of all certainties to bear on American epistemological arrangements and faith in progress. All claims of one culture to universal validity for its ideas and institutions were rejected in favor of cultural relativism, understood as a pluralism with only functional and structural commonalities. Scholars of this group have harbored much sympathy for Progressive history's relativistic phase. Becker's and Beard's talk of myths and acts of faith appealed to them as an explicit American rejection of all remnants of positivism. Thus, despite the brevity of the relativistic phase, the two historians have emerged as pioneers of the true modernization of historiography. In this assessment, Beard's and Becker's ringing pronouncements on historical theory of the early 1930s obliterated their earlier views and drowned out their subsequent statements. Taken from its original matrix, Progressive history's relativistic period found new continuity in the development of a truly modern (relativistic) American historiography (Peter Novick), or a new role in the transformation of American thought on social matters into a properly modern mode (Dorothy Ross). Proponents of this new assessment of Progressive history have received some support from historians who saw in the relativistic interpretation of history an epistemological justification for the view that the writing of history was a weapon in power struggles, or for the rejection of "dominant" or "authoritative" accounts. Credit for that accomplishment of the relativistic phase has offered to Progressive historians a faint and partial redemption from the generally negative judgments of more recent critics.

This volume has assessed Progressive history by dealing with it as a coherent experiment in the modernization of historiography. The attention given to all phases of Progressive history and the theoretical issues raised in them demonstrate that Progressive history developed in a dialogue with American life. The dialogue made apparent that this experiment in the modernization of historiography, predicated on seeing modernity as a radical break in human history, was forced nevertheless to cope with problems that have been perennial features of historiography. This put into doubt the notion of Progressive historians that modernization was a transformation *sui generis*. As a result the story of Progressive history became a journey of discovery in the complexity of the theory of history rather than a march of triumph.

When the Progressive historians tried to modernize the American sense of history they undertook the age-old task of understanding and explaining the unique contexts of life in ways general enough for universal validity. The vigor, confidence, and enthusiasm of Progressive historians during their experiment's first two phases were generated by the conviction that this fundamental historiographical problem had been reduced to a purely technical one. Their task was to align the American sense of history and through it American life with the perceived basic elements of modernity—science, technology, and the advance of rationality—that were assumed to be universal by nature. The revised American sense of history would then not be a framework for the understanding of America's past alone but all of history. In such an interpretation of history modernity would supply both the forces shaping life and the knowledge necessary to master them.

At first the course of American life seemed to confirm the views of the Progressive historians, who in turn became part of contemporary reform movements. Up to the late 1920s, Progressive historians scored successes with their view of history that pronounced the forces of modernity to be intrinsically good. The problems delaying the full realization of the envisaged beneficent world were diagnosed as results of the ignorance of the masses and the malevolence of a few. The whole experiment, including the central concepts of progress and conflict, was colored by this and other simplified views on the human condition and, with it, on historiography. The corrections came with the disappointing course of American life, the failure of attempts at a rational global order, the collapse of the turn-of-the-century concept of the natural sciences, and a strong influx of divergent European influences. While the role of facts in historiography supplied the focus of the ensuing debate, much more was at stake. Not only did a sharp break occur in Progressive history's development, but many American historians began to be more keenly aware of the problems in the theory of historiography.

Beard and Becker first tried to find certainty without a new link between facts and interpretation. But neither Beard's heroic "act of faith" (an affirmative relativism) nor Becker's resigned acceptance of historical interpretations as useful myths (a bittersweet historicism) proved to be a viable solution. The two historians came to realize that the absence of standards for certainty in historical truth-finding destroyed the authority of their own historical interpretations. Their relativistic stance in epistemology negated their easy equation of modernity with science or the upward march of rationality, destroyed the rationale for subordinating the role of the past in life and historiography to that of the projected future, and made untenable the simplified view of the human condition on which the scientific, technological, and rationalist concept of progress rested. The comfortable bridge leading from a revised American sense of history to a universal understanding of history had collapsed. The American sense of history—revised or not—represented no more than one possible historical interpretation among many.

The attempt at freedom from the need to validate one's historical interpretation proved short-lived. Life in the midst of ideological struggles and global upheavals taught the two historians about another perennial feature of historiography: the link between a historical interpretation's nature and degree of authority and its usefulness in the praxis of life. That praxis included the wish of scholars for intellectual certainty as well as that of groups for clarity about their identity and destiny.

The intent to be directly useful to Americans of the 1930s and 1940s,

spurred Beard's and Becker's search for a new certainty about and continuity in history. Beard found these in the unique thrust and substance of
American civilization and Becker in a set of basic American ideas,
values, and habits. In doing so, they stressed that in the process of historical truth-finding the context in which historians worked was not just a
source of distortion but had a more constructive role. In particular, elements of the American tradition, seen as the result of long years of collective actions and reflection, could be the source of a certainty
substantiated by collective experience. The sought-after juncture of the
actual past with its record—the point at which in historiography con-
textual and universal validity were reconciled—could be found in the
basic propositions not of science but of American collective experience.

Beard and Becker never had an opportunity to test their regained certainty in the reconstruction of Progressive history. However, some of its
features were clearly visible. The revised Progressive history would have
shown a better balance between the past, the present, and expectations
for the future because the past had regained a substantial role. Progress
would still have supplied the dynamics of history. American values were
in need of ever greater fulfillment either by more appropriate institutional expressions for enduring values (Becker's social democracy) or by
pushing American civilization to its fullest congruence with the essence
of human civilization (Beard). In both versions the pragmatic usefulness
of history would have been preserved.

On the other hand, the two historians would have experienced formidable obstacles in explaining how their new approach to certainty and
interpretation, so firmly grounded in American tradition, could claim
authority beyond the American context. Becker and Beard had long ago
burnt the bridges between the unique and the general offered by those
philosophical and theological concepts that transcended positivist and
pragmatic approaches to life. The comparative approach increasingly
important in the quest for a New History would not have been useful
because its inherent historicism shed doubt on the new certainty gained
from specific cultural contexts. The difficulty remained invisible because, at the time, neither Beard nor Becker were interested in the international (or, as we would say now, cross-cultural) aspects of their last
historical views.

Postwar historians, becoming less sure about which understanding of
history was appropriate to America in a scientific culture and global
world, have been more concerned with that issue. In their discussions,
often conducted as a criticism of an American "exceptionalism," Progressive history was figured as an outmoded modernism or a remnant of

"prehistoricism."[9] Although such a judgment has always been based on the early phase of Progressive history, by implication it also held true for the last one.

Progressive history's inconclusive ending highlights the complexity of its experiment in modernization, one not fully reflected in assessments of failure or of contributions. In particular, the irony of its last turn points beyond them. Progressive historians tried to accomplish what Lucien Febvre described as an important goal of the New History: to lift the heavy weight of tradition from modern people. They understood this task as depriving the past of any significant role in the shaping of the present and the future. Instead, their experiment ended with the acceptance of features of the American tradition as core elements of a New History. This turn is too easily understood as a retreat into the security of the known from what at one point was an audacious thrust at a truly modern historiographical understanding of the world and its progress. Actually, it was only one of the adjustments that characterized the development of Progressive history. All of that history's original contributions to the quest for a New History experienced corrections. That included the Progressive historians's versions of the drive for an encompassing history, the modernization of historical methods and interpretations, and the striving for a global grasp. The realities of human life negated Progressive history's key assumption that modernity meant the fulfillment of the aspirations for a radical break with the order of the past. When a new intellectual climate eroded belief in objective progress and the human condition retained much of the old order, Progressive history, designed as an instrument for and reflection of the future proper order of human affairs, underwent revisions. The last and fragmentary effort to stabilize Progressive history through the inclusion of elements of a critically sifted American tradition recognized Progressive history's predicament.

In the end, Progressive history created neither the modern version of the American understanding of history nor the model for a modern historiography. Without a triumphant ending, the story of Progressive history stands as a reminder of a once vibrant endeavor, offers a source of insights, and conveys a note of caution for those engaged in the quest for a New History.

Notes

1. The American Sense of History

1. The name "White City" stemmed from the decision to whitewash the buildings of the artificial city (the core of the fair), in lieu of a complicated color scheme.

2. *The Education of Henry Adams*, with an introduction by James Truslow Adams (New York, 1931), 339.

3. George Bancroft, *History of the United States of America: From the Discovery of the Continent*, the author's last revision (New York, 1882), 6:5–6.

4. Hugo Münsterberg, *The Americans*, trans. Edwin B. Holt (New York, 1907), 5.

5. For the phrase, see *Farmers' Alliance*, 12 June 1889, 1; Nebraska State Historical Society, Lincoln.

6. The denial of an "exceptional protection" by Divine Providence and assertion of America's subjection to "the same rigorous laws that have shaped the destinies of nations on the other side of the Atlantic" had been voiced earlier by Charles Kendall Adams, *A Manual of Historical Literature* (New York, 1882), 17–18.

7. *Education of Henry Adams*, 343.

8. Agnes Sinclair Holbrook, "Map Notes and Comments," in *Hull-House Maps and Papers*, by residents of Hull-House (1895; reprint, New York, 1970), 5.

9. For the phrase, see *Farmers' Alliance*, 8 Nov. 1890, 2.

10. The Congress of Evolution was one of the scholarly conferences held within the framework of the World's Fair Auxiliary.

11. For a discussion of the ancient ideas of the Four Empires, see Ernst Breisach, *Historiography: Ancient, Medieval, Modern* (Chicago, 1983), entry "Empire Schemes," 482. For the idea of a Fifth Empire, see George Berkeley, "Verses on America," in *The Works of George Berkeley*, ed. A. A. Luce and T. E. Jessop (London, 1955), 7:370.

12. James A. Skilton, as quoted in Maurice Neufeld, "The Contribution of the World's Columbian Exposition of 1893 to the Idea of a Planned Society in the United States" (Ph.D. diss., University of Wisconsin, 1935), 271.

13. Frederick J. Turner, *The Frontier in American History* (New York, 1920), 38.

14. For contemporary doubts about the progressive vision in the vein of a technological and efficient mastery of life, see T. J. Jackson Lears, *No Place of Grace: Antimodernism and the Transformation of American Culture, 1880–1920* (New York, 1981).

2. Scientific History

1. John Dewey, *The Later Works, 1925–1953*, ed. Jo Ann Boydston, textual ed. Patricia Baysinger, with an introduction by David Sidorsky (Carbondale, Ill., 1984), 3:307.

2. William M. Sloane, "The Science of History in the Nineteenth Century," in *Congress of Arts and Science: Universal Exposition, St. Louis, 1904*, ed. Howard J. Rogers (Boston, 1906), 2:24–25.

3. Henri Berr, *La synthèse en histoire: Essai critique et théoretique* (Paris, 1911), vi; my translation.

4. Henry Adams, "The Tendency of History," in *Annual Report of the American Historical Association for the Year 1894* (Washington, D.C., 1895), 17–18.

5. *Historical Scholarship in the United States, 1876–1901: As Revealed in the Correspondence of Herbert B. Adams*, ed. W. Stull Holt (Baltimore, 1938), 69, n. 1.

6. That feature was stressed by John Higham when he spoke of the "conservative evolutionism" of early history professors in his *History: Professional Scholarship in America* (1965; reprint, Baltimore, Md., 1983), pt. 3, chap. 2, and by Richard Hofstadter, who criticized the "stark conservatism" of late-nineteenth-century historians in his book *The Progressive Historians: Turner, Beard, Parrington* (New York, 1968), 27.

7. Similar European attempts at collective synthesis were *The Cambridge Modern History*, planned by the late Lord Acton, ed. A. W. Ward, G. H. Prothero, and Stanley Leathes, 13 vols. (Cambridge, England, 1902–12), and Ernest Lavisse's *Histoire de France illustrée depuis les origines jusqu'à la Révolution*, 9 vols. (1911).

8. For example, the writing of Edward Channing's *History of the United States* took from 1905 to 1925.

9. James Bryce, *The American Commonwealth* (London, 1888), 3:570.

10. Walter Lippmann, *Drift and Mastery: An Attempt to Diagnose the Current Unrest*, with an introduction and notes by William E. Leuchtenburg (Englewood Cliffs, N.J., 1961), 151.

11. Henry Adams, "The Tendency of History," 19.

12. William M. Sloane, "History and Democracy," *American Historical Review* 1 (October 1895): 1–23 (hereafter cited as *AHR*).

3. Turner's Quest for a New History

1. For a discussion of Henri Berr's article in *La nouvelle revue* (1890): 517–23, see Martin Siegel, "Henri Berr's *Revue de synthèse historique*," *History and Theory* 9 (1970): 322–23.

2. Karl Lamprecht, *Deutsche Geschichte*, 12 vols. (Berlin, 1891–1909) and *Ergänzungsbände*, 1. und 2. Aufl., 2 vols. (Freiburg im Breisgau, 1905–6).

3. In August 1890, Turner spoke to a gathering of the Southwest Wisconsin Teacher's Association at Madison. The abbreviated reprinting of the address in *The Varieties of History*, ed. Fritz Stern (New York, 1956), 198–208, has res-

cued it from obscurity. An earlier complete printing in *The Early Writings of Frederick Jackson Turner,* comp. Everett E. Edwards, with an introduction by Fulmer Mood (Madison, Wis., 1938), 43–68, had had much less impact.

4. *Early Writings of Frederick Jackson Turner,* 65. He paraphrased here a key passage from Johann Gustav Droysen's *Outline of the Principles of History (Grundriss der Historik),* trans. E. Benjamin Andrews (New York, 1967), 44 (74): "History is the 'Know Thyself' of Humanity, its consciousness."

5. Frederick J. Turner's article "The Significance of History" was published first in the *Wisconsin Journal of Education* 21 (October 1891): 230–34 and (November 1891): 253–56. The rather simplistic nature of Turner's presentation (it was developed from a talk to teachers) has contributed to the unwarranted neglect of the article up to this day.

6. Berr, *Synthèse en histoire,* viii.

7. Frederick J. Turner, "Problems in American History," *Aegis* (University of Wisconsin, Madison) 7 (4 November 1892): 48–52, reprinted in *Early Writings of Frederick Jackson Turner,* 71–83; "The Significance of the Frontier in American History," reprinted in Frederick J. Turner, *The Frontier in American History* (New York, 1920), 1–38.

8. Karl Lamprecht to J. Franklin Jameson, 4 August 1906, Jameson Papers, Box 101 (944), Manuscript Division, Library of Congress (hereafter cited as Jameson Papers); my translation. Interestingly, Lamprecht crossed out the word *Ansiedlungsgeschichte* and substituted *Entwicklungsgeschichte* for it.

9. Friedrich Ratzel, *Die Vereinigten Staaten von Nord-Amerika,* vol. 2, *Culturgeographie der Vereinigten Staaten von Nord-Amerika unter besonderer Berücksichtigung der wirtschaftlichen Verhältnisse* (Munich, 1880), 16; my translation.

10. Postcard, Karl Lamprecht to Frederick Jackson Turner, 28 April 1895, Turner Papers, Box 2 (10), Manuscript Collection, Huntington Library (hereafter cited as Turner Papers). The offprint had been sent to Lamprecht, who gave it to his colleague Ratzel.

11. Friedrich Ratzel, *Anthropogeographie,* 2 vols. (Stuttgart, 1882–91). For Turner's testimony on the matter, see his letter to Merle Curti, 15 August 1928, in Ray Allen Billington, *Genesis of the Frontier Thesis* (San Marino, Calif., 1971), 272. Paul Vidal de la Blache's *Tableau de la géographie de la France* appeared only in 1911 as the first part of volume 1 of Lavisse's *Histoire de France,* and his *Principes de géographie humaine* in 1922. The earlier article "De divisions fondamentales du sol français" appeared in the *Bulletin littéraire* 2 (1888–89), 1–7 and 49–57, well out of Turner's reach.

12. Reasons range from space offering a seemingly natural and scientific framework for unifying the study of human life to its being propelled into the center of discussions because talk about *Lebensraum,* colonies, and Manifest Destiny—all of them spatial concepts—increased at the turn of the century, when Western civilization's expansionary period had just about ended.

13. *Early Writings of Frederick Jackson Turner,* 72.

14. Ibid., 71.

15. Turner learned about the stages (a product of the German historical

school of economics) through Richard T. Ely, Francis Amasa Walker, and various census bulletins. In any case, the stages were widely known.

16. See Achille Loria, *Analisi della proprietà capitalista* (Turin, 1889), 2:15; my translation. The English translation quoted by Turner in his *Frontier in American History*, 11, interestingly renders the word *mistero* not as "mystery," but as "course."

17. Allen's enthusiasm for the role of expansion in history showed in his last work, *A Short History of the Roman People* (Boston, 1890).

18. Turner, *Frontier in American History*, 38.

19. An important line leads to August Meitzen, Loria's teacher. Meitzen was a professor at the University of Berlin and also among Lamprecht's teachers. He was one of the foremost contemporary scholars of agricultural and settlement history, who, in 1871, became a pioneer of maps denoting population densities in different colors.

20. Loria, *Analisi* 2:416; my translation.

21. *Early Writings of Frederick Jackson Turner*, 47–48. While in proposing other changes Turner had dutifully cited his mostly European authorities, in this case he did not. He would have had to give as his source his populist spirit, rooted in a deep love of the common people of the Midwest and already manifest in his undergraduate years. Indeed, for this part of the essay Turner lifted many phrases and sentences from his prize-winning student orations. See "The Poet of the Future," Adelphia Society, Portage, Wis., 1883, and Prize Oration, "Architecture through Oppression," given at his own commencement, 1884, Turner Papers, Box 54 (1 and 3).

22. In none of that did the native people, then still called American Indians, figure, since all judgments of "free land" were made from an evolutionary and a more intensive land-use standpoint, without thought about the rights and the fate of Native Americans.

23. *Frontier and Section: Selected Essays of Frederick Jackson Turner*, with an introduction by Ray Allen Billington (Englewood Cliffs, N.J., 1961), 72, 90.

4. The Prelude to Progressive History

1. For a recent study that concentrates on Scientific history's limitations and stresses the elements of power and social class in the historical profession, see Peter Novick, *That Noble Dream: The "Objectivity Question" and the American Historical Profession* (New York, 1988).

2. Earle W. Dow, "Features of the New History: Apropos of Lamprecht's 'Deutsche Geschichte,'" *AHR* 3 (April 1898): 441.

3. Ibid., 431.

4. Edward Eggleston, "The New History," in *Annual Report of the American Historical Association for the Year 1900* (Washington, D.C., 1901), 37–47.

5. William E. Dodd, "Karl Lamprecht and *Kulturgeschichte*," *Popular Sci-*

ence Monthly 63 (September 1903): 418. Dodd was in contact with Lamprecht for years, although the latter was not his *Doktorvater.*

6. Ibid., 424.

7. As early as July 1902, in a review of Lamprecht's first supplementary volume to the *Deutsche Geschichte,* titled *Zur jüngsten deutschen Vergangenheit* (Freiburg im Breisgau, 1902) in *AHR* 7 (April 1902): 791, Dodd had urged that, with French and Russian editions available, an English translation should not be far behind. For the doomed attempts to interest American publishers in Lamprecht's *Deutsche Geschichte,* see William E. Dodd's correspondence with Karl Lamprecht during the years 1905 and 1906, William E. Dodd Papers, Box 4, Manuscript Division, Library of Congress, Washington, D.C. The reason for the failure was well put: "The difficulties which have confronted the translator are appalling." See Asa Currier Tilton's review of Karl Lamprecht's *Moderne Geschichtswissenschaft: Fünf Vorträge* (Freiburg im Breisgau, 1905) and *What Is History: Five Lectures on the Modern Science of History,* trans. from the German by E. A. Andrews (New York, 1905), *AHR* 11 (October 1905): 119.

8. Fred Morrow Fling, "Historical Synthesis," *AHR* 9 (October 1903): 1–22.

9. See Luther V. Hendricks, *James Harvey Robinson: Teacher of History* (New York, 1946), 4–18.

10. Hugo Münsterberg, "The Scientific Plan of the Congress," in *Congress of Arts and Science: Universal Exhibition, St. Louis, 1904,* ed. Howard J. Rogers (Boston, 1905), 1:89. Actually, Münsterberg had argued for an emphasis on the progress in thought, a more theory-oriented stance, while Albion Small wished for an "equally comprehensive review of the great public questions unresolved in human progress." Small won the argument. See report to Nicholas Murray Butler by the Committee on the Plan and Scope for the International Congress of Arts and Science, 19 January 1903, Hugo Münsterberg Papers, Mss. Acc. 2476, Manuscript Department, Boston Public Library, Boston, Mass.

11. Woodrow Wilson, "The Variety and Unity of History," in *Congress of Arts and Science: Universal Exposition, St. Louis, 1904,* ed. Howard J. Rogers (Boston, 1906), 2:3.

12. Ibid., 14.

13. Woodrow Wilson had suggested that solution already in 1895. See "On the Writing of History," in *The Papers of Woodrow Wilson,* ed. Arthur S. Link and others (Princeton, N.J., 1970), 9:293–305.

14. Sloane, "Science of History," 28.

15. Karl Lamprecht, "Historical Development and Present Character of the Science of History," in *Congress of Arts and Science: Universal Exposition, St. Louis, 1904,* ed. Howard J. Rogers (Boston, 1906), 2:111.

16. John B. Bury, "The Place of Modern History in the Perspective of Knowledge," in *Congress of Arts and Science: Universal Exposition, St. Louis, 1904,* ed. Howard J. Rogers (Boston, 1906), 2:149.

17. Ibid., 145–46.

18. The paper also showed clear signs of Turner's work on his *Rise of the New West, 1819–1829* (New York, 1907), which was then fully under way and may well have contributed further to his general unwillingness to address substantial theoretical issues, preferring rather to make another "appeal."

19. Frederick Jackson Turner to his wife, Mae Turner, 25 September 1904, Turner Papers, Box F (50).

20. Henri Berr, "About Our Program," introduction to the first issue of *Revue de synthèse historique*, trans. Deborah H. Roberts, printed in Stern, *Varieties of History*, 254.

21. See President Seth Low's address at the dedication of the university's new Morningside Heights site, in *Columbia University: Dedication to the New Site, Morningside Heights* (New York, 1896).

22. Charles A. Beard, "Ruskin Hall and Temperance Reform," *Young Oxford* 2 (March 1901): 221.

23. Münsterberg, "Scientific Plan of Congress," 89.

5. Putting a Progressive Accent on Encompassing History

1. James H. Robinson and Charles A. Beard, *The Development of Modern Europe: An Introduction to the Study of Current History*, 2 vols. (New York, 1907–8).

2. A phrase used by Henri Berr in *Synthèse en histoire*, viii.

3. Karl Lamprecht's Columbia lectures were published as *What Is History? Five Lectures on the Modern Science of History*, trans. from the German by E. A. Andrews (New York, 1905).

4. Turner's teacher, William F. Allen, had already reviewed books for the *Revue historique*. Turner related that the Johns Hopkins seminar was used "to aid Herbert B. Adams in furnishing American reviews for the *Revue historique*." See Turner's notes, no date, Turner Papers, Box 1 (14). J. Franklin Jameson, who met Lamprecht and some French innovators at the International Congress of History in Paris (July 1900), remained unaffected by the reform activities.

5. *Early Writings of Frederick Jackson Turner*, 52, 57.

6. Wilson, "Variety and Unity of History," 5.

7. Edwin R. A. Seligman, *The Economic Interpretation of History*, 2d ed., rev. (New York, 1907), 2.

8. Albert B. Hart's introduction to the series he edited, The American Nation: A History, vol. 1, Edward P. Cheyney, *European Background of American History: 1300–1600* (New York, 1904), xvii.

9. Charles A. Beard, *Politics* (New York, 1912), 6; a lecture delivered at Columbia University in the Series on Science, Philosophy and Art, February 12, 1908.

10. James H. Robinson, *The New History: Essays Illustrating the Modern Historical Outlook* (New York, 1912), 2–5.

11. "Historical Theories," review of *The New History*, by James Harvey Robinson, *New York Times*, 28 April 1912, p. 253.

12. William A. Dunning, "A Generation of American Historiography," in

Truth in History and Other Essays by William A. Dunning, with an introduction by J. G. de Roulhac Hamilton (New York, 1937), 159.

13. See "History for the Common Man," in Robinson, *New History,* 132–53.

14. Charles A. Beard, "Lessons from Science," *Young Oxford* 2 (June 1901): 340.

15. Robinson, *New History,* 106.

16. Robinson and Beard, *The Development of Modern Europe* 1:53, 52, 278.

17. Wilson, "Variety and Unity of History," 4.

18. Robinson, *New History,* 203–4. In "The Tennis Court Oath," in *Annual Report of the American Historical Association for the Year 1894* (Washington, D.C., 1895), 541, he spoke of "a picturesque incident" that he wished "to assign . . . its proper place in the great and irresistible current of advance."

19. Robinson, *New History,* 204.

20. James H. Robinson, *An Introduction to the History of Western Europe* (Boston, 1902), 233.

6. The Redefinition of History's Truth and Usefulness

1. William A. Dunning, "Truth in History," *AHR* 19 (January 1914): 219.

2. Sloane, "The Science of History," 24.

3. See discussion in Paul Lacombe, *De l'histoire considérée comme science* (Paris, 1894), x–xi.

4. James H. Robinson, "The Conception and Methods of History," in *Congress of Arts and Science: Universal Exposition, St. Louis, 1904,* ed. Howard J. Rogers (Boston, 1906), 2:48.

5. Woodrow Wilson, "The Variety and Unity of History," 7.

6. Sloane, "Science of History," 29.

7. Andrew D. White, "On Studies in General History and the History of Civilization," in *Papers of the American Historical Association* 1:2 (New York, 1885): 6.

8. Dunning, "Truth in History," 219.

9. George Burton Adams, "History and the Philosophy of History," *AHR* 14 (January 1909): 236.

10. Lacombe, *Histoire considérée comme science,* x; my translation.

11. Cited in Dodd, review of *Zur jüngsten deutschen Vergangenheit,* 789.

12. Carl L. Becker, "Detachment and the Writing of History," *Atlantic Monthly* 106 (October 1910): 526, 527.

13. Ibid., 528.

14. One may suspect that Fling's 1903 article "Historical Synthesis" had some influence on Becker, but no evidence for it exists.

15. Charles Homer Haskins to Carl Lotus Becker, 18 October 1910, and Fred Morrow Fling to Carl Lotus Becker, 4 October 1910, Carl L. Becker Papers, Box 7, Department of Manuscripts and University Archives, Cornell University (hereafter cited as Becker Papers).

16. William B. Yeats, *Essays and Introductions* (New York, 1961), 253.

17. Wilhelm Dilthey, *Gesammelte Schriften,* vol. 7, *Der Aufbau der ge-schichtlichen Welt in den Geisteswissenschaften,* 2d ed. (Stuttgart, 1958), 290; my translation. At that point, the passage signaled to the Progressive historians a typical German *Kulturpessimismus* with its attendant conservatism, aiming in the short run at preserving the status quo. Historicism, a term given many meanings, refers here to an interpretation of history that knows a sequence of unique phenomena with some commonalities but no overriding order or development.

18. In his book *That Noble Dream,* Novick presented an extensive account of the objectivity question in modern American historiography. He emphasized the connection between objectivity and the established historians' status and power as the reason for the lack of an epistemological debate. Novick stipulated a nearly automatic link between traditional objectivity and conservative politics. In the area of epistemology he discerned a sharp dichotomy between objectivity (claim to complete certainty) and relativism (decision to live with provisional and perspectival certainties).

19. Charles Francis Adams, "The Sifted Grain and the Grain Sifters," *AHR* 6 (January 1901): 199.

20. See Henry Adams, "The Tendency of History," 19.

21. Dow, "Features of the New History," 448.

22. The phrase *internal forum* is adapted here from the Cartesian *forum internum,* as discussed in Richard Rorty, *Philosophy and the Mirror of Nature* (Princeton, N.J., 1979), 50. In the Cartesian sense it referred to an inner space in which sensations and mental phenomena were scrutinized.

23. Russell B. Nye, *George Bancroft: Brahmin Rebel* (New York, 1944), 199.

24. Carl L. Becker, "Some Aspects of the Influence of Social Problems and Ideas upon the Study and Writing of History," *American Journal of Sociology* 18 (March 1913): 660.

25. Becker, "Detachment and the Writing of History," 526; he quoted from Ernest Renan, *Les apôtres* (Paris, 1866), liii. Renan actually wrote: "Ces oeuvres doivent être exécutées avec une suprême indifférence, comme si l'on écrivait pour une planète déserté."

26. Becker, "Some Aspects of the Influence of Social Problems and Ideas," 642.

27. Becker, "Detachment and the Writing of History," 529, 534.

28. "The Meeting of the American Historical Association of Chicago [1904]," *AHR* 10 (April 1905): 497.

29. James H. Robinson, *The New History,* 127–28.

30. Ibid., 36.

31. H. G. Wells, *The Discovery of the Future* (London, 1902), 8–9, 70.

32. Robinson and Beard, *Development of Modern Europe* 1:iii.

33. Lippmann, *Drift and Mastery,* 163.

34. Robinson, *New History,* 24.

35. In their various textbooks Progressive historians were much more bal-

anced in their views on the value of the past because of the politics of educational publishing.

36. For the idea of the two histories, see John Dewey, "Instrument or Frankenstein," *Saturday Review of Literature* 8 (12 March 1932): 581.

37. Robinson, *Development of Modern Europe* 1:2.

38. Carl L. Becker, "What Are Historical Facts?" in *Detachment and the Writing of History: Essays and Letters of Carl L. Becker*, ed. Phil Snyder (Ithaca, N.Y., 1958), 43.

39. *Early Writings of Frederick Jackson Turner*, 53.

40. Ray A. Billington, *Frederick Jackson Turner: Historian, Scholar, Teacher* (New York, 1973), 478.

41. Beard, "Ruskin Hall and Temperance Reform," 221.

42. Carl Lotus Becker to Wendell Phillips Garrison, 1 July 1906, Becker Papers, Box 7; and Becker, "Some Aspects of the Influence of Social Problems and Ideas," 642.

43. Charles A. Beard, *The Economic Basis of Politics* (New York, 1922), 9; a collection of four lectures given at Amherst College in 1916.

7. The Fragile Alliance with the Social Sciences

1. For the importance of the increased interdependence of modern life for the intellectual history of the period, see Thomas L. Haskell, *The Emergence of Professional Social Science: The American Social Science Association and the Nineteenth-Century Crisis of Authority* (Urbana, Ill., 1977).

2. Frederick Jackson Turner to Carl Lotus Becker, 3 July 1896, Turner Papers, Box 2 (28).

3. George Burton Adams, "History and the Philosophy of History," 232.

4. Robinson, "Conception and Methods of History," 41–42.

5. Ibid., 50.

6. William Archibald Dunning to Carl Lotus Becker, 11 March 1911, Becker Papers, Box 8.

7. Henry Adams to J. Franklin Jameson, 22 March 1911, Jameson Papers, Box 46 (16).

8. For the most recent treatment of the topic, see Dorothy Ross, *The Origins of the American Social Science* (New York, 1991).

9. Albion W. Small, "The Present Outlook of Social Science," in *Papers and Proceedings of the American Sociological Society* 7 (June 1912): 34.

10. For an extensive account of this transition see Haskell, *Emergence of Professional Science.*

11. Carl L. Becker, "Wild Thoughts Notebook II," 16 November 1894, Becker Papers, Box 7.

12. George Burton Adams, "The Present Problems of Medieval History," in *Congress of Arts and Science: Universal Exhibition, St. Louis, 1904,* ed. Howard J. Rogers (Boston, 1906), 2:137.

13. George Burton Adams, "History and the Philosophy of History," 224.

14. Ibid., 229.

15. Frederick J. Turner, "Social Forces in American History," *AHR* 16 (January 1911): 232.

16. Émile Durkheim, "Cours de science sociale, leçon d'ouverture," *Revue internationale de l'enseignement* 15 (1888): 46; my translation.

17. The occasion was an address at the annual meeting of the American Sociological Society in 1912, published later as "Some Aspects of the Influence of Social Problems and Ideas upon the Study and Writing of History."

18. Frederick Teggart, "The Circumstance or the Substance of History," *AHR* 15 (July 1910): 710.

19. Robinson, *New History,* 100. Curiously, Robinson made little of sociology—perhaps because neither William Graham Sumner's laissez-faire approach nor Lester F. Ward's and Franklin Henry Giddings's belief in rigid social laws fit a supporting role.

20. Ibid., 90.

21. Robinson cited influences on him by William Graham Sumner's *Folkways: A Study of the Sociological Importance of Usages, Manners, Customs, Mores, and Morals* (1906), F. C. Conybeare's *Myth, Magic, and Morals: A Study of Christian Origins* (1909), George H. Mead's ego psychology, Edward L. Thorndike's psychology of association, and Salomon Reinach's *Orpheus: A General History of Religions* (1909).

22. Robinson, "Conception and Methods of History," 51.

23. Robinson, *New History,* 25.

24. Mrs. Potter Palmer, "Address to the Opening Session," 12 June 1893, in International Congress of Charities, Correction and Philanthropy (1893: Chicago), *Report of the Proceedings: General Exercises* (Baltimore, Md., 1894), 32.

25. Robinson, "Conception and Methods of History," 48.

26. Lacombe, *De l'histoire considérée comme science,* 52; my translation.

27. Karl Lamprecht, "Historical Development and the Present Character of the Science of History," 121. The cumbersome and misleading translation of *Geisteswissenschaften* as "mental science" was common. The term *humanities* in its widest sense is by far a better translation.

28. For sketches of personalities and analyses of human motivations see his "Wild Thoughts Notebook" for the year 1895, Becker Papers, Box 7.

29. Robinson, *New History,* 53.

30. Charles H. Haskins's report on George Lincoln Burr's remarks on the nature of history at the American Historical Association meeting in 1903; see *Annual Report of the American Historical Association for the Year 1903* (Washington, D.C., 1904), 1:36.

31. Beard, *Politics,* 32.

32. Robinson, *New History,* 53.

33. Fling, "Historical Synthesis," 9; quoting, in translation, from Alexandre Xénopol's review of *Die Grenzen der naturwissenschaftlichen Begriffsbildung,* by Heinrich Rickert, *Revue de synthèse historique* (June 1902): 292.

34. Robinson, "Conception and Methods of History," 48.

35. Becker, "Some Aspects of the Influence of Social Problems and Ideas," 663.

8. Sorting Out History's Grand Forces

1. Turner, *Frontier in American History,* 2.

2. Ibid., 293.

3. See Charles A. Beard, *An Economic Interpretation of the Constitution of the United States* (1913; with new introduction, New York, 1935), 2–3.

4. For Turner's oral review (never published by him) of Hermann von Holst's *Constitutional and Political History of the United States,* trans. John J. Lalor and others (Chicago, 1876–92), before the University of Wisconsin's Historical and Political Science Association, 23 January 1894, see Billington, *Frederick Jackson Turner,* 149 and nn. 34, 35.

5. Turner, "Social Forces in American History," 230.

6. *Early Writings of Frederick Jackson Turner,* 71–72.

7. Charles A. Beard, "A Living Empire I," *Young Oxford,* 3 October 1901, 25.

8. Turner, *Frontier and Section,* 126.

9. From Josiah Royce's address "Provincialism," given at the State University of Iowa in 1902, Turner Papers, File Drawer L2 (0501).

10. Turner, *Rise of the New West,* 67, 71.

11. Ibid., 107.

12. Hans Vaihinger's *Die Philosophie des Als Ob* (1911), once translated into English in 1924 as *The Philosophy of 'As If,'* would influence both Beard and Becker.

13. Carl L. Becker, *The History of Political Parties in the Province of New York, 1760–1776* (Madison, Wis., 1909), no. 286 of the University of Wisconsin History Series, vol. 2, no. 1.

9. Beard's Economic Interpretation of History

1. George Burton Adams, "History and the Philosophy of History," 226.

2. *Early Writings of Frederick Jackson Turner,* 48.

3. Turner, "Social Forces in American History," 227.

4. Beard, *Economic Interpretation of the Constitution of the United States,* 5.

5. Charles A. Beard, "Cooperation and the New Century," *Young Oxford* 2 (December 1900): 96.

6. Charles A. Beard, *The Supreme Court and the Constitution* (1912; reprint, New York, 1938), 75.

7. Beard, *Economic Interpretation of the Constitution,* 9.

8. *Early Writings of Frederick Jackson Turner,* 64.

9. Beard, *Economic Interpretation of the Constitution,* 13–14. He cited the German legal scholar Rudolf von Ihering as main source for that view. The ac-

cess to Ihering came most likely through Arthur F. Bentley's works, particularly *The Process of Government: A Study in Social Pressures* (Bloomington, Ind., 1908).

10. Beard, *Politics*, 21.

11. Beard, *Economic Interpretation of the Constitution*, 324.

12. The Amherst lectures were published as *The Economic Basis of Politics* (New York, 1922).

13. Charles A. Beard, "Some Economic Origins of Jeffersonian Democracy," *AHR* 19 (January 1914): 298. The article contained the essential ideas and arguments of *The Economic Origins of Jeffersonian Democracy* (New York, 1915).

14. Beard, *Economic Basis of Politics*, 89.

15. Ibid., 79.

16. William E. Dodd, review of *An Economic Interpretation of the Constitution of the United States*, by Charles A. Beard, *AHR* 19 (October 1913): 162.

17. Beard, *Economic Interpretation of the Constitution*, 19.

18. Ibid., 14.

19. James Madison, "The Federalist. No. 10," in Alexander Hamilton, J. Jay, and J. Madison, *The Federalist: Or, The New Constitution* (London, 1911), 42.

20. Seligman, *Economic Interpretation of History*, 101. See also Seligman's footnote on the same page regarding the discussion in contemporary Marxism on that point.

21. Robinson, *New History*, 50–51.

22. Charles A. Beard, *An Introduction to the English Historians* (1906; reprint, New York, 1968), 608.

23. Beard, *Economic Interpretation of the Constitution*, 10.

24. Beard, "Some Economic Origins of Jeffersonian Democracy," 298.

25. Beard, *Economic Interpretation of the Constitution*, 24.

26. The concept can be called pivotal if it is kept in mind that in Progressive history conflict is auxiliary to progress and not a force important in and by itself.

27. Beard could have grasped the latter point when, in his *Economic Origins of Jeffersonian Democracy*, 464–67, he came to realize how, in the end, the hopes he had placed in Jefferson had been disappointed by Jefferson's deviation from true democratic ideals.

10. A Sense of Triumph

1. Turner, Prize Oration, "The Poet of the Future."

2. Turner, "Social Forces in American History," 217.

3. George Burton Adams, "History and the Philosophy of History," 235.

4. Carl L. Becker, "An Interview with the Muse of History," review of *Clio, a Muse, and Other Essays, Literary and Pedestrian,* by George Macaulay Trevelyan, *Dial* 56 (16 April 1914): 338.

5. Carl L. Becker, "Wild Thoughts Notebook I," 6 March 1894, Becker Papers, Box 7.

6. Carl L. Becker, "The New History," review of *The New History: Essays Illustrating the Modern Historical Outlook*, by James Harvey Robinson, *Dial* 53 (1 July 1912): 21.

7. Beard, *Politics*, 26.

8. Charles A. Beard, *The Industrial Revolution* (London, 1901), 104.

9. Turner, *Frontier in American History*, 207.

10. Ibid., 320.

11. Ibid., 309.

12. In this connection Hofstadter rightfully pointed out the lasting influence of John Ruskin's *Unto This Last: Four Essays on the First Principles of Political Economy* (New York, 1901), a collection of four essays in the *Cornhill Magazine*, first published as a volume in 1862. At the core of the essays stands an appeal for the reintroduction of ethics into laissez-faire economics. Beard's Oxford period produced many references to Ruskin, including the naming of Ruskin Hall.

13. H. G. Wells, *First and Last Things: A Confession of Faith and Rule of Life* (London, 1908), 67.

14. Most influential for the concept of social control was Edward R. Ross's *Social Control: A Survey of the Foundation of the Social Order* (New York, 1901).

15. Of importance for forming Beard's view of administration's role in public life were Arthur F. Bentley's book *The Process of Government* and his own work in the New York Bureau of Municipal Research and National Municipal League.

16. Robinson, *New History*, 265.

17. "Home and Field Notes," *Young Oxford* 2 (February 1901): 193.

18. Becker, "Detachment and the Writing of History," 526.

19. Becker, "Some Aspects of the Influence of Social Problems and Ideas," 665.

20. James H. Robinson, *An Introduction to the History of Western Europe*, completely rev. and enl. ed. (Boston, 1924–26), 1:5. Robinson and Beard softened their revisionism in the textbooks they wrote for obvious commercial reasons, particularly the statements in prefaces—hence in this case the greater appreciation of the past. For the inertia of routine life, see also Robinson's article "The Tennis Court Oath," 541–47.

21. Walter Lippmann, *A Preface to Politics* (1913; reprint, New York, 1933), 298.

22. Henry Adams, "The Tendency of History," 21.

23. Robinson, *New History*, 126.

24. Becker, "The Dilemma of Diderot," in *Everyman His Own Historian: Essays on History and Politics* (New York, 1935), 273.

25. Carl L. Becker, "A New Philosophy of History," review of *The Interpretation of History*, by L. Cecil Jane, *Dial* 59 (2 September 1915): 148.

26. Wells, *Discovery of the Future*, 94–95.

11. A Defiant Reaffirmation

1. George Creel, *How We Advertised America* (New York, 1920), 4.

2. James H. Robinson, "The Newer Ways of Historians," *AHR* 35 (January 1930): 252.

3. His resignation in October 1917 was Beard's protest against the dismissal of two professors (James E. Catell and Henry W. L. Dana) for opposing conscription. Beard had been persona non grata with many administrators and trustees of Columbia University for some years.

4. James H. Robinson, "The Threatened Eclipse of Free Speech," *Atlantic Monthly* 120 (December 1917): 818.

5. Carl Lotus Becker to William Edward Dodd, 17 June 1920, Becker Papers, Box 7. That long and crucial letter is printed in *"What Is the Good of History?": Selected Letters of Carl L. Becker, 1900–1945*, ed. Michael Kammen (Ithaca, N.Y., 1973), 71–74; the specific citation is on pp. 73–74.

6. Ibid., 71.

7. Ibid., 72.

8. Frederick Jackson Turner to Dorothy Kinsley Turner, 18 February 1921, Turner Papers, Box 1 (63).

9. Dunning, "A Generation of American Historiography," 160.

10. Charles A. Beard, "The Frontier in American History," review of *The Frontier in American History,* by Frederick Jackson Turner, *New Republic* 25 (16 February 1921): 349.

11. Arthur Meier Schlesinger, Sr., to Harry Elmer Barnes, 4 May 1923, Harry Elmer Barnes Papers, Box 11, American Heritage Center, University of Wyoming, Laramie (hereafter cited as Barnes Papers). Schlesinger introduced a pioneering course in social and cultural history of the United States at the University of Iowa in 1922–23.

12. Arthur M. Schlesinger, Sr., *In Retrospect: The History of a Historian* (New York, 1963), 200.

13. Arthur Meier Schlesinger, Sr., to Harry Elmer Barnes, 4 May 1923, Harry Elmer Barnes Papers, Box 11.

14. Arthur Meier Schlesinger, Sr., to Harry Elmer Barnes, 10 May 1923, Barnes Papers, Box 11.

15. He eventually promised to write the preceding volume, *The Quest for Social Justice*, although he still suspected that the editors were weary of his authorship of the concluding volume, Schlesinger's assurance to the contrary. Arthur Meier Schlesinger, Sr., to Harry Elmer Barnes, 21 May 1923, Barnes Papers, Box 11.

16. In reality, the distance of the series from Progressive history was much less. With its wish to show the multifaceted reality of American society, it developed a varied social history akin to the Progressive spirit. Many of its volumes went well beyond description and took up themes of equity and justice (such as the very volume on the Progressive Era by Harold U. Faulkner, *The Quest for Social Justice, 1898–1914* [1931]). Progressive themes were also manifest in its volumes on immigration, cities, and labor.

17. Lucien Febvre, *A New Kind of History and Other Essays,* ed. Peter Burke, trans. K. Folca (New York, 1973), 11.

18. See especially his essay "A Contribution towards a Comparative History of European Societies," in Marc Bloch, *Land and Work in Mediaeval Europe: Selected Papers,* trans. J. E. Anderson (Berkeley, Calif., 1967), 44–81.

19. Carl L. Becker, *The Eve of the Revolution: A Chronicle of the Breach with England* (New Haven, Conn., 1918), vii, viii.

20. Graham Wallas, *The Great Society: A Psychological Analysis* (New York, 1914). The book was dedicated to Walter Lippmann.

21. James H. Robinson, *The Mind in the Making: The Relation of Intelligence to Social Problems* (New York, 1921), 228.

22. Ferdinand Schevill, "Professor Barnes on War Guilt," review of *The Genesis of the World War,* by Harry Elmer Barnes, *Christian Century* 43 (17 June 1926): 77.

23. An elaborate course syllabus had been published as James H. Robinson, *An Outline of the History of the Intellectual Class in Western Europe* (New York, 1911).

24. Lynn Thorndike to Harry Elmer Barnes, 28 February 1920, Barnes Papers, Box 9.

25. James H. Robinson, *The Humanizing of Knowledge* (New York, 1923).

26. James Harvey Robinson to Harry Elmer Barnes, 16 July 1928, Barnes Papers, Box 17.

27. James Harvey Robinson to Harry Elmer Barnes, 9 May 1927, Barnes Papers, Box 16.

28. James Harvey Robinson to Harry Elmer Barnes, 15 November 1926, Barnes Papers, Box 15, and 16 July 1928, Barnes Papers, Box 17.

29. Robinson, "New Ways of Historians," 245–55.

30. William R. Shepherd to Harry Elmer Barnes, 24 September 1925, Barnes Papers, Box 13.

31. Henry L. Mencken to Harry Elmer Barnes, 11 February 1925, Barnes Papers, Box 8. In the collected papers there exist numerous examples of editors protesting Barnes's lack of writing discipline.

32. Preserved Smith to Harry Elmer Barnes, 11 September 1935, Barnes Papers, Box 22.

33. J. Franklin Jameson to Harry Elmer Barnes, 13 February 1926, Barnes Papers, Box 14.

34. Merle Curti to Harry Elmer Barnes, 8 November 1925, Barnes Papers, Box 13.

35. Vernon L. Parrington, *Main Currents of American Thought* (New York, vols. 1 and 2, 1927; vol. 3, 1930), 3:xx.

36. Becker, "The New History," 21.

37. Their model was the English Workers' Education Association. The Workers Bookshelf never fulfilled the expectations of its planners and financial sponsors. Only four new works were created (including Robinson's). Mary R. Beard supplied her previously published *A Short History of the American Labor Movement* (New York, 1920).

12. The Quasi Alliance with the Social Sciences

1. Barnes had been recommended for the job to write a history of the New Jersey criminal law and correctional institutions by Croly and James T. Shotwell (professor of history at Columbia University) to Dwight Morrow, the chairman of the New Jersey Prison Inquiry Committee. The 654-page report was then accepted in lieu of Barnes's doctoral dissertation, for which he lacked the money to get it printed. Barnes did have an interest in sociology as early as his undergraduate years at Syracuse University.

2. Harry E. Barnes, ed., *The History and Prospects of the Social Sciences* (New York, 1925), xiii.

3. Robinson, *Mind in the Making,* 122.

4. Ibid., 12.

5. John Dewey, "Pragmatic America," *New Republic* 30 (12 April 1922): 186.

6. Robinson, *Humanizing of Knowledge,* 104.

7. Becker, *Everyman His Own Historian,* 139.

8. Harry E. Barnes, *The History and Social Intelligence* (New York, 1926), 55.

9. Ibid., 55 and 56.

10. Ibid., 324.

11. Harry E. Barnes, "The Essentials of the New History," *Historical Outlook* 18 (May 1927): 209.

12. Harry E. Barnes, ed., *History and Prospects of the Social Sciences* (New York, 1925), 34.

13. Barnes, "The Essentials of the New History," 209.

14. Robinson, *Humanizing of Knowledge,* 87. The novel referred to is *Fielding Sargent* (New York, 1922).

15. Barnes had a more extensive exposure to psychoanalytical thought. His contact with Dr. L. Clark began in October 1916 and continued for many years. Clark pointed him to Ernest Jones as the best guide to Freud's work and approved of Barnes's reading Freud and "Young" (Jung?). Clark subsequently wrote psychoanalytical biographies of Napoleon and Alexander the Great. L. Pierce Clark to Harry Elmer Barnes, 30 October 1916, Barnes Papers, Box 8.

16. Barnes, *History and Prospects of the Social Sciences,* 35.

17. Harry E. Barnes, "Psychology and History: Some Reasons for Predicting Their More Active Co-operation in the Future," *American Journal of Psychology* 30 (October 1919): 362.

18. Barnes, *New History and the Social Studies,* 232.

19. Becker, *Everyman His Own Historian,* 299. The specific reference is to the memoirs and the letters of Madame Roland.

20. Barnes, "The Essentials of the New History," 203.

21. The accent is here on "direct," since both Febvre and Bloch considered their research part of a badly needed modernization of France in the scientific spirit. They were ardent French patriots who viewed their work at the University of Strasbourg (regained in 1918 from Germany) as important to France.

13. The Battle for Progress

1. Charles A. Beard and Mary R. Beard, *The Rise of American Civilization* (New York, 1927), 2:746.

2. Charles A. Beard, "Time, Technology, and the Creative Spirit in Political Science," *American Political Science Review* 21 (February 1927): 5.

3. John Dewey, *Characters and Events: Popular Essays in Social and Political Philosophy*, ed. Joseph Ratner (New York, 1929), 2:755–56.

4. Beard, "Time, Technology, and the Creative Spirit in Political Science," 9–10.

5. Barnes, *History and Social Intelligence*, 2. He, like Robinson, put much stock in Wilfred Trotter's book *Instincts of the Herd in Peace and War* (New York, 1916).

6. Robinson, *Mind in the Making*, 127, 81.

7. Barnes, *History and Social Intelligence*, 277.

8. John Dewey, *Characters and Events* 2:49, quoting Thomas Jefferson.

9. Robinson, *Mind in the Making*, 80.

10. Robinson, *An Introduction to the History of Western Europe* 2:586.

11. Barnes, *History and Social Intelligence*, vii, viii.

12. James H. Robinson, *The Ordeal of Civilization: A Sketch of the Development of World-Wide Diffusion of Our Present-Day Institutions and Ideas* (New York, 1926), 736.

13. Ibid., 749.

14. Robinson, *Mind in the Making*, 79.

15. Barnes, *History and Social Intelligence*, vii.

16. Robinson, *Ordeal of Civilization*, 737.

17. Robinson, *Mind in The Making*, 173 and title of chapter 14.

18. Parrington, *Main Currents* 3:xxv.

19. Charles A. Beard and Mary R. Beard, *Rise of American Civilization* 2:744.

20. Carl Lotus Becker to William Edward Dodd, 17 June 1920, Becker Papers, Box 7.

21. Robinson, *Mind in the Making*, 220.

22. See William C. Bagley, *Educative Process* (New York, 1905), 58–65. He teamed up with Charles A. Beard to produce *The History of the American People* (New York, 1918) and *Our World Background* (New York, 1922) for use in schools.

23. Charles Austin Beard to Nicholas Murray Butler, president of Columbia University, 8 October 1917, as included in report "Quits Columbia; Assails Trustees," *New York Times*, 9 October 1917, p. 1.

24. Charles A. Beard, "Making the Fascist State," review of *Making the Fascist State*, by Herbert W. Schneider, *New Republic* 57 (23 January 1929): 278.

25. Charles A. Beard, *Cross Currents in Europe To-Day* (Boston, 1922), 163.

26. Dewey, *Characters and Events* 1:380.

27. Beard, *Cross Currents in Europe To-Day*, 166.

28. Dewey, *Characters and Events* 1:380.

29. Robinson, *Mind in the Making*, 167; Barnes, *History and Social Intelligence*, 18.

30. The phrase is Dewey's in *Characters and Events* 2:621.

31. See Carl L. Becker, "Tender and Tough Minded Historians," review of *France, England and European Democracy: 1215–1915. A Historical Survey of the Principles Underlying the Entente Cordiale*, by Charles Cestre, and of *America among the Powers*, by H. H. Powers, *Dial* 65 (15 August 1918): 106–9; "The League of Nations," review of nineteen books on the League of Nations, *Nation* 109 (16 August 1919): 225–27.

32. See Charles A. Beard and George Radin, *The Balkan Pivot* (New York, 1929).

33. Charles Austin Beard to Merle Curti, 29 January 1947, Merle Curti Papers, Box 4, State Historical Society of Wisconsin, Madison (hereafter cited as Curti Papers).

34. Carl Lotus Becker to Harry Elmer Barnes, 1 November 1927, Barnes Papers, Box 16.

35. Carl Lotus Becker to William Edward Dodd, 17 June 1920, Becker Papers, Box 7.

36. Beard, *Cross Currents in Europe To-Day*, 270.

37. Charles A. Beard, "Prospects for Peace," *Harper's Magazine* 158 (February 1929): 330.

38. Ibid., 320.

39. Beard, *Cross Currents in Europe To-Day*, 270.

40. Ibid.

14. The Twilight of Certainty

1. Robinson, "Newer Ways of Historians," 251, 252.

2. Barnes, *History and Social Intelligence*, 123; Barnes cited here a passage from Robert Shafer, *Progress and Science: Essays in Criticism* (New Haven, Conn., 1922).

3. Regarding the important links of Barnes to Alfred von Wegerer, director of the *Zentralstelle für Erforschung der Kriegsursachen*, and to ex-Emperor William II, which extended to 1940, see Barnes Papers, Boxes 20–26.

4. Robinson, *Mind in the Making*, 224.

5. Ibid., 13.

6. Carl L. Becker, "The Foundations of the Nineteenth Century," review of *The Foundations of the Nineteenth Century*, by Houston Stewart Chamberlain, *Dial* 50 (16 May 1911): 388.

7. Carl L. Becker, "Mr. Wells and the New History," in *Everyman His Own Historian*, 177.

8. An authorized translation, published in 1921 in New York, of Benedetto Croce's *Teoria e storia della storiografia* (Bari, Italy, 1917).

9. Carl L. Becker, "History as the Intellectual Adventure of Mankind," re-

view of *History: Its Theory and Practice,* by Benedetto Croce, *New Republic* 30 (5 April 1922): 174.

10. Carl Lotus Becker to the editor of the *New Republic,* autumn 1938, printed in "Books that Changed Our Minds," *New Republic* 97 (7 December 1938): 135.

11. Becker, *Detachment and the Writing of History,* 48, 49.

12. Ibid., 47, 59, 62.

13. Even in 1936, Barnes still urged Becker to publish it. See the exchange of letters: Harry Elmer Barnes to Carl Lotus Becker, 26 February 1936, Becker Papers, Box 11; Carl Lotus Becker to Harry Elmer Barnes, 29 February 1936, Barnes Papers, Box 22; Harry Elmer Barnes to Carl Lotus Becker, 25 April 1936, Becker Papers, Box 11. Posthumously, the article was published as "What Are Historical Facts?" in *Western Political Quarterly* 8 (September 1955): 327–40 and reprinted in *Detachment and the Writing of History,* 41–64. In a review of the latter, Barnes suggested that the reluctance to publish the paper was due to the fact that "the very implications of Becker's paper even seemed to frighten him"; Barnes Papers, Box 1.

14. Carl L. Becker, review of *The Art of History: A Study of Four Great Historians of the Eighteenth Century,* by J. B. Black, *AHR* 32 (January 1927): 295.

15. Robinson, *Mind in the Making,* 201.

16. Carl Stephenson, "Facts in History," *Historical Outlook* 19 (November 1928): 316, 317.

17. Charles A. Beard, *Whither Mankind: A Panorama of Modern Civilization* (New York, 1928), v.

18. See Charles A. Beard's presidential address to the American Political Science Association in St. Louis, Mo., 29 December 1926, "Time, Technology, and the Creative Spirit in Political Science," 1–11.

19. Burleigh T. Wilkins, *Carl Becker: A Biographical Study in American Intellectual History* (Cambridge, Mass., 1961), 149; a quote from the letter, Charles Austin Beard to Felix Frankfurter, Ithaca, 2 June 1927.

15. Collapse in a Triumphant Mode

1. Barnes used the term "highbrow editor" in a letter to G. B. Parker, Esq., 26 September 1929, Barnes Papers, Box 18, in which he also mentioned that Walter Lippmann had been the first choice; his column carried the caption "Liberal Viewpoint."

2. Becker, *Everyman His Own Historian,* 233.

3. Ibid., 235.

4. Ibid., 244, 245.

5. Ibid., 245.

6. Ibid., 249.

7. Carl L. Becker, *The Heavenly City of the Eighteenth-Century Philosophers* (New Haven, Conn., 1932), 2; based on the four Storrs lectures delivered at Yale University, April 1931.

8. The more recent concept of *mentalité* includes that understanding, but also emphasizes the limits such a collective climate of thought puts on all intellectual, artistic, and other modes of expression.

9. Becker, *Everyman His Own Historian*, 247.

10. Ibid., 252. 247.

11. Charles A. Beard, "Written History as an Act of Faith," *AHR* 39 (January 1934): 219.

12. Charles A. Beard, *The Republic: Conversations on Fundamentals* (New York, 1943), 328. In a way, this was Beard's answer to later critics who have pointed out the discrepancies between his simultaneous assertion of the power of science, economic determinism, and extreme contingency. Ellen Nore tried to demonstrate a more systematic quality in Beard's relativism in "Charles A. Beard's Act of Faith: Context and Content," *Journal of American History* 66 (March 1980): 850–66.

13. Beard, "Written History," 221.

14. Charles A. Beard, "That Noble Dream," *AHR* 41 (October 1935): 87.

15. Beard, "Written History," 219–20.

16. Ibid., 225.

17. Charles A. Beard, *Discussion of Human Affairs* (New York, 1936), 28–29.

18. In his book *The Pragmatic Revolt in American History: Carl Becker and Charles Beard* (New Haven, 1958), Cushing Strout saw in this holding on to an overall interpretation of history a central reason for Progressive history's failure.

19. Beard, "Written History," 226.

20. Charles A. Beard, *A Charter for the Social Sciences in the Schools*, American Historical Association, Report of the Commission on the Social Studies, pt. 1 (New York, 1932), 5, 18–19. Beard can be listed as the author, although, technically, he only drafted the report. There is no evidence that his draft was changed substantially by the Commission on the Social Studies in the Schools, for which the draft was prepared.

21. Beard, *Discussion of Human Affairs*, 11.

22. Beard, *Charter for the Social Sciences*, 11.

23. Ibid., 109. Beard here used phrasing from his introduction to the American edition of John B. Bury's book *The Idea of Progress: An Inquiry into Its Origin and Growth* (New York, 1932).

24. Charles A. Beard, ed., *A Century of Progress* (Chicago, 1933), 3, 4. A publication in conjunction with the Century of Progress exposition in Chicago.

25. Beard, *Century of Progress*, 3, 6.

26. Ibid., 6.

27. Charles A. Beard and George H. E. Smith, *The Open Door at Home: A Trial Philosophy of National Interest* (New York, 1934), 19, 20.

28. Beard, *Discussion of Human Affairs*, 11, 35.

29. See Beard and Smith, *Open Door at Home*, 13–14.

30. Beard, *Discussion of Human Affairs*, 15.

31. Beard, *Charter for the Social Sciences*, 2–3.

32. Beard, "Written History," 228–29.

33. Beard, "That Noble Dream," 87.

34. Theodore C. Smith, "The Writing of History in America, from 1884 to 1934," *AHR* 40 (April 1935): 447.

35. Ibid., 448.

36. See Carl L. Becker, review of Maurice Mandelbaum's *The Problem of Historical Knowledge: An Answer to Relativism,* in *Philosophical Review* 49 (April 1940): 361–64; and Beard's review of the same book in *AHR* 44 (April 1939): 571–72, cited passage on p. 572.

16. Becker's Struggle for Usefulness

1. Carl L. Becker, *New Liberties for Old* (New Haven, Conn., 1941), xiv.

2. Becker, *Everyman His Own Historian,* 255.

3. George Santayana, *The Life of Reason; or, The Phases of Human Progress* (New York, 1906), 5:68.

4. Becker, *Heavenly City,* 12.

5. Becker, *Everyman His Own Historian,* 92. The passage is from an article characteristically titled "Liberalism—A Way Station," published in 1932.

6. Becker, *New Liberties for Old,* 28–29, 42.

7. In 1935 and again in 1940 his textbooks triggered charges of Communist sympathies that came to nothing. Becker issued a rejoinder that was published as "Becker Denies Leanings to Communism in Reply to Attacks on Textbook," *Ithaca Journal,* 27 November 1935. In it he clearly rejected communism as a social philosophy.

8. Becker, *New Liberties for Old,* 43, xvi.

9. Ibid., 121.

10. Carl L. Becker, *How New Will the Better World Be? A Discussion of Post-War Reconstruction* (New York, 1944), 245. For the quote from Edmund Burke, see his *Reflections on the Revolution in France,* ed. and with an introduction by Conor Cruise O'Brien (1790; Harmondsworth, England, 1968), 194–95.

11. Carl L. Becker, *Progress and Power: Three Lectures Delivered at Stanford University, on the Raymond Fred West Memorial Foundation, April 1935* (Palo Alto, Calif., 1936), ix.

12. Becker, *New Liberties for Old,* 32.

13. Ibid., xvi.

14. Carl L. Becker, "What Is Still Living in the Political Philosophy of Thomas Jefferson," *AHR* 48 (July 1943): 702; the Penrose lecture, delivered before the American Philosophical Society in Philadelphia in 1943.

15. Ibid., 691, 704, 693, 705.

16. Becker, *New Liberties for Old,* 119.

17. Becker, *How New Will the Better World Be?* 136.

18. Carl L. Becker, *Freedom and Responsibility in the American Way of Life,* with an introduction by George H. Sabine (New York, 1945), 106.

19. Becker, *How New Will the Better World Be?* 134.

20. Becker, *New Liberties for Old,* 45.

21. Carl L. Becker, "Why Europe Fights," *Cornell Alumni News* 42 (1939): 33, as cited in Strout, *Pragmatic Revolt in American History,* 152.

22. Carl Lotus Becker to Mrs. M. M. Kesterson, 16 February 1945 (typed copy), Barnes Papers, Box 31.

23. Becker, *Progress and Power,* 13, 14.

24. Carl L. Becker, review of *The Idea of Progress: An Inquiry into Its Origin and Growth,* by John B. Bury, *AHR* 38 (January 1933): 305, 306.

25. Becker, *Progress and Power,* 101.

17. Beard and Post-1935 Reality

1. Charles A. Beard, "We're Blundering into War," *American Mercury* 46 (April 1939): 388–99.

2. Ibid., 395.

3. For the term *old isolationist* see Beard's *Republic,* 302.

4. Barnes was in contact with some anti-Fascist associations, which opposed the entrance into the war, and with the National Speakers Bureau of the America First Committee. His close connection with Charles Lindbergh (through him indirectly also with Robert E. Wood) came only later, in the early 1940s.

5. Charles A. Beard, "Peace for America. I: The Devil Theory of History and War," *New Republic* 86 (4 March 1936): 102. His book titled *The Devil Theory of War* was published in the same year.

6. Charles A. Beard and Mary R. Beard, *The American Spirit: A Study of the Idea of Civilization in the United States* (New York, 1942), 216.

7. Beard was impressed by the flood of communications from people and attributed Roosevelt's subsequent hesitancy to repeat openly the idea of America's intervention to the president's recognition of the people's strong and sound traditionalism.

8. Charles A. Beard and Mary R. Beard, *American Spirit,* 213.

9. Charles A. Beard and Mary R. Beard, *A Basic History of the United States* (New York, 1944), 366.

10. Charles A. Beard, *A Foreign Policy for America* (New York, 1940), 13.

11. Ibid., 13, 14.

12. Charles A. Beard and George H. E. Smith, *The Old Deal and the New* (New York, 1940), 249. The dating of the change is Beard's. The book was a sequel to *The Future Comes: A Study of the New Deal* (New York, 1933).

13. Beard, *Foreign Policy,* 149.

14. Some suggestions on the connection between foreign policy, domestic politics, naval policies, and internal reforms came from a book that caused great controversy in Germany, Eckart Kehr's *Schlachtflottenbau und Partei-Politik, 1894–1901* (Berlin, 1930). The book soon made Kehr persona non grata in Germany, and in 1933 he died in exile in the United States.

15. Beard, *Foreign Policy,* 89.

16. Beard acknowledged the connection in *America in Midpassage* (New York, 1939), 1:453 (written with Mary R. Beard).

17. Charles A. Beard and Mary R. Beard, *Basic History*, 455.

18. Charles A. Beard, *Giddy Minds and Foreign Quarrels: An Estimate of American Foreign Policy* (New York, 1939).

19. Henry R. Luce, "The American Century," *Life* 10 (17 February 1941): 65; Charles A. Beard and Mary R. Beard, *American Spirit*, 575–76, partly a paraphrase of Luce's text in the cited article.

20. Beard, *Century of Progress*, 12, 14, 15. As a foil for his arguments and his description of the future American society, Beard chose passages from *Amiel's Journal: The Journal Intime of Henri-Frédéric Amiel*, trans. with an introduction and notes by Mrs. Humphry (Mary A.) Ward (New York, 1907), especially 2:227–28 and 279.

21. Henry A. Wallace, "Beard: The Planner," review of *The Open Door at Home*, by Charles A. Beard and George H. E. Smith, *New Republic* 81 (2 January 1935): 226, 227.

22. Raymond Leslie Buell, *Isolated America* (New York, 1940).

23. Charles A. Beard, *The Economic Basis of Politics*, 3d rev. ed. (New York, 1945), 89–90. See the cited pages for Beard's critical remarks on Friedrich A. Hayek's book *The Road to Serfdom* (Chicago, 1944).

24. Lewis Mumford, "The Corruption of Liberalism," *New Republic* 102 (29 April 1940): 573. The reference is to two prominent Nazi ideologists, Alfred Rosenberg and Gottfried Feder.

25. Ibid., 568, 572.

26. Ibid., 568–71.

27. These points were made by Barnes in a column titled "No. 1 Problem for America" in *World Telegram*, 1 August 1939. See criticism of it in the letter from Cyril Lee Ellison to Harry Elmer Barnes, 2 August 1939, Barnes Papers, Box 24.

28. Charles Austin Beard to Harry Elmer Barnes, 18 February 1941, Barnes Papers, Box 27.

29. Harry Elmer Barnes to Bruce Barton, 28 July 1944, Barnes Papers, Box 30.

30. Charles A. Beard and Mary R. Beard, *American Spirit*, 672.

31. Ibid., 673, 647.

32. Ibid., 526.

33. Ibid., 674.

34. Beard, *Republic*, 251.

35. Beard, *Foreign Policy*, 16.

36. Beard, *Republic*, 303. He referred to a statement after the attack on Pearl Harbor.

37. Merle Curti to Harry Elmer Barnes, 18 April 1944, Barnes Papers, Box 30.

38. The initial paper was written by Professor Roy F. Nichols on "Current Research in American History." The conference was held on November 8, 1942, at the office of the Social Science Research Council in New York. From the original, larger group came the Committee on Historiography of the Social Science

Research Council. Chaired by Merle Curti, it had eight members—among them Beard and his son-in-law, Alfred Vagts.

39. *Theory and Practice in Historical Study: A Report of the Committee on Historiography,* Social Science Research Council Bulletin no. 54 (New York, 1946), viii.

40. Ibid., 5, 6.

41. Charles Austin Beard to Merle Curti, 29 January 1947, Curti Papers, Box 4.

42. Charles A. Beard, *President Roosevelt and the Coming of the War 1941: A Study in Appearances and Realities* (New Haven, Conn., 1948), 592, 595.

43. Charles Austin Beard to Merle Curti, 4 April [1948?], Curti Papers, Box 4.

44. Charles A. Beard, "The Future of Democracy in the United States," *Political Quarterly* 8 (October 1937): 505.

45. Beard, *President Roosevelt,* 598.

46. Perry Miller, "Censure of History," review of *President Roosevelt and the Coming of the War 1941: A Study in Appearances and Realities,* by Charles A. Beard, Nation 166 (12 June 1948): 666.

47. Ibid.

48. Charles Austin Beard to Merle Curti, 4 April [1948?], Curti Papers, Box 4.

18. Heritage and Assessment

1. Robinson used the phrase in his letter to Harry Elmer Barnes, 16 July 1928, Barnes Papers, Box 17.

2. Charles Austin Beard to Harry Elmer Barnes, 15 September 1945, Barnes Papers, Box 31.

3. Richard Hofstadter, *The Progressive Historians: Turner, Beard, Parrington* (New York, 1968), xv.

4. Harry E. Barnes, *A History of Historical Writing* (Norman, Okla., 1937), 377.

5. John Higham, "The Cult of the 'American Consensus,'" *Commentary* 27 (February 1959): 94.

6. Charles Crowe, "The Emergence of Progressive History," *Journal of the History of Ideas* 27 (January–March 1966): 109–24.

7. One of the earliest and clearest calls for the recognition of inevitable changes in American historiography came in C. Vann Woodward, "The Age of Reinterpretation," *AHR* 66 (October 1960): 1–19, also issued, with revisions, as the American Historical Association's Service Center for Teachers of History Publication, no. 35 (Washington, D.C.: 1961).

8. Noble was influenced by discussions on the topic by American scholars of literature and political theory. Of special influence were Sacvan Bercovitch, *The American Jeremiad* (Madison, 1978), and J. G. A. Pocock, *The Machiavellian Moment: Florentine Political Thought and the Atlantic Republican Tradition* (Princeton, N.J., 1975).

9. For a recent example of a discussion on the topic (in which Progressive history however did not figure directly) see the contributions to an *AHR* Forum by Ian Tyrell, "American Exceptionalism in an Age of International History"; Michael McGerr, "The Price of the 'New Transnational History'"; and "Ian Tyrell Responds," in *AHR* 96 (October 1991): 1031–55, 1056–67, 1068–72.

Bibliographic Note

A comprehensive bibliography of sources and publications relating to Turner and the Progressive historians would require a separate volume. For example, Charles Beard was involved in the creation of approximately 170 books either as author, coauthor (with Mary Ritter Beard and others), editor, or contributor. In addition, he published approximately 330 articles and 340 book reviews. A comprehensive bibliography is also not necessary, because bibliographic access to the field of Progressive history can be gained with relative ease through printed material and electronic means. This note, therefore, offers readers guidance to major collections of source materials and to especially informative publications about Turner and the Progressive historians. Works already cited in the text or notes are generally not included. Within the segments of this note, publications are listed either chronologically or alphabetically by author—whichever seemed more appropriate.

Primary Sources

The papers of Turner are mainly in the Manuscript Collection of the Huntington Library, San Marino, California, and in the Archives of the Wisconsin State Historical Society in Madison. Those of Becker are in the Department of Manuscripts and University Archives, Cornell University, Ithaca, New York. Robinson and Beard's papers are not preserved in great numbers and the holdings are scattered widely. Some Beard papers are deposited in the DePauw University Archives, Greencastle, Indiana. Only few of Parrington's papers are available, some of them in the University Archives, University of Washington, Seattle. The bulk of the Barnes papers is accessible at the American Heritage Center, University of Wyoming, Laramie, and that of Merle Curti at the Archives of the Wisconsin State Historical Society. The papers of J. Franklin Jameson and William E. Dodd can be found in the Manuscript Division, Library of Congress, Washington, D.C., and those of Hugo Münsterberg, with information on the St. Louis Congress of Arts and Science of 1904, in the Manuscript Department, Boston Public Library, Boston, Massachusetts.

Helpful printed collections are: *"Dear Lady": The Letters of Frederick Jackson Turner and Alice Forbes Perkins Hooper, 1910–1932*, ed. Ray A. Billington, with the collaboration of Walter Muir Whitehill (San Marino, Calif.: Huntington Library, 1970); Wilbur R. Jacobs, *The Historical World of Frederick Jackson Turner, With Selections From His Correspondence* (New Haven, Conn.: Yale University Press, 1968); and *"What is the Good of History?": Selected Letters of Carl L. Becker, 1900–1945*, ed. Michael Kammen (Ithaca, N.Y.: Cornell University Press, 1973). Material on Charles Beard's most important co-worker, Mary Ritter Beard, can be found in *A Woman Making*

History: Mary Ritter Beard through Her Letters, ed. and with an introduction by Nancy F. Cott (New Haven, Conn.: Yale University Press, 1991); and in *Mary Ritter Beard: A Sourcebook,* ed. Ann J. Lane (New York: Schocken Books, 1977).

Key Publications on Turner, Beard, Becker, Robinson, Parrington, and Barnes

Much information on Turner, Beard, and Parrington can be gained from Richard Hofstadter's book *The Progressive Historians: Turner, Beard, Parrington* (New York: Alfred A. Knopf, 1968), and from the essays on Turner (by Howard R. Lamar, pp. 74–109), Beard (by Forrest McDonald, pp. 110–41), and Parrington (by Ralph H. Gabriel, pp. 142–66), in *Pastmasters: Some Essays on American Historians,* ed. Marcus Cunliffe and Robin W. Winks (1969; reprint, Westport, Conn.: Greenwood Press, 1979). Other publications offering information on specific historians include the following.

ON TURNER: Carl L. Becker, "Frederick Jackson Turner," pp. 273–318 in *American Masters of Social Science,* ed. Howard W. Odum (New York: Henry Holt & Co., 1924); and Ray A. Billington, *Frederick Jackson Turner: Historian, Scholar, Teacher* (New York: Oxford University Press, 1973).

ON BEARD: Ellen Nore, *Charles A. Beard: An Intellectual Biography* (Carbondale: Southern Illinois University Press, 1983).

ON BECKER: Burleigh T. Wilkins, *Carl Becker: A Biographical Study in American Intellectual History* (Cambridge, Mass.: M.I.T. Press and Harvard University Press, 1961).

ON ROBINSON: Luther V. Hendricks, *James Harvey Robinson, Teacher of History* (New York: King's Crown Press, 1946); and Harry E. Barnes, "James Harvey Robinson," pp. 321–408 in *American Masters of Social Science,* ed. Howard W. Odum (New York: Henry Holt & Co., 1924).

ON BARNES: "Harry Elmer Barnes: A Personalized Profile," autobiographical article written by Harry E. Barnes for the *Hartwick Review* (published by Hartwick College), Fall 1968, n.p.

ON PARRINGTON: William T. Utter, "Vernon Louis Parrington," pp. 394–408 in *The Marcus W. Jernegan Essays in American Historiography,* ed. William T. Hutchinson (Chicago: University of Chicago Press, 1937).

Works with Substantial Information and Bibliographies on Turner and the Progressive Historians

ON TURNER: *The Early Writings of Frederick Jackson Turner,* comp. Everett E. Edwards, with an introduction by Fulmer Mood (Madison: University of Wisconsin Press, 1938); Lee Benson, *Turner and Beard: American Historical Writing Reconsidered* (Glencoe, Ill.: Free Press, 1960); Vernon E. Mattson and William E. Marion, *Frederick Jackson Turner: A Reference Guide* (Boston: G. K. Hall and Co., 1985).

ON BEARD: Howard K. Beale, ed., *Charles A. Beard: An Appraisal* (Lexington: University of Kentucky Press, 1954); Bernard C. Borning, *The Political and Social Thought of Charles A. Beard* (Seattle: University of Washington Press, 1962); Robert E. Brown, *Charles Beard and the Constitution: A Critical Analysis of "An Economic Interpretation of the Constitution"* (Princeton, N.J.: Princeton University Press, 1956); Whitaker T. Deininger, "The Skepticism and Historical Faith of Charles A. Beard," *Journal of the History of Ideas* 15 (October 1954): 573–88; John P. Diggins, "Power and Authority in American History: The Case of Charles A. Beard and His Critics," *American Historical Review* 86 (October 1981): 701–30; Thomas C. Kennedy, *Charles A. Beard and American Foreign Policy* (Gainsville: University Presses of Florida, 1975); David W. Marcell, *Progress and Pragmatism: James, Dewey, Beard, and the American Idea of Progress* (Westport, Conn.: Greenwood Press, 1974); Harry J. Marks, "Ground under Our Feet: Beard's Relativism," *Journal of the History of Ideas* 14 (October 1953): 628–33; Jack W. Meiland, "The Historical Relativism of Charles A. Beard," *History and Theory* 12 (1973): 405–13; Gerald D. Nash, "Self-education in Historiography: The Case of Charles A. Beard," *Pacific Northwest Quarterly* 52 (1961): 108–15; Hugh I. Rodgers, "Charles A. Beard, the 'New Physics,' and Historical Relativity," *The Historian* 30 (August 1968): 545–60; Lloyd R. Sorenson, "Charles A. Beard and German Historiographical Thought," *Mississippi Valley Historical Review* 42 (September 1955): 274–87; William A. Williams, "A Note on Charles Austin Beard's Search for a General Theory of Causation," *American Historical Review* 62 (October 1956): 59–80.

ON BECKER: Robert E. Brown, *Carl Becker on History and the American Revolution* (East Lansing, Mich.: Spartan Press, 1970); David W. Noble, "Carl Becker: Science, Relativism, and the Dilemma of Diderot," *Ethics: An International Journal of Social, Political, and Legal Philosophy* 67 (July 1957): 233–48; Charlotte W. Smith, *Carl Becker: On History and the Climate of Opinion* (Ithaca, N.Y.: Cornell University Press, 1956). Perez Zagorin, "Professor Becker's Two Histories: A Skeptical Fallacy," *American Historical Review* 62 (October 1956): 1–11.

ON ROBINSON: *Essays in Intellectual History: Dedicated to James Harvey Robinson by His Former Seminar Students* (1929; reprint, Freeport, N.Y.: Books for Libraries Press, 1968).

ON SCHOLARS RELATED TO PROGRESSIVE HISTORY: Robert Dallek, *Democrat and Diplomat: The Life of William E. Dodd* (New York: Oxford University Press, 1968); Joseph Dorfman, *Thorstein Veblen and His America* (New York: Viking Press, 1934); George Dykhuizen, *The Life and Mind of John Dewey* (Carbondale: Southern Illinois University Press, 1973); David W. Levy, *David Croly of the New Republic: The Life and Thought of an American Progressive* (Princeton, N.J.: Princeton University Press, 1985); Morey D. Rothberg, "'To Set a Standard of Workmanship and Compel Others to Conform to It': John Franklin Jameson as the Editor of the *American Historical Review*," *American Historical Review* 89 (October 1984): 957–75; Arthur M.

Schlesinger, *In Retrospect: The History of a Historian* (New York: Harcourt, Brace and World, 1963); Ronald Steel, *Walter Lippmann and the American Century* (Boston: Little, Brown, 1980).

Assessments of Progressive History

Of the relatively few works that have assessed Progressive history, the following have done so in terms of American reform movements and intellectual history: Morton G. White, *Social Thought in America: The Revolt Against Formalism* (New York: Viking Press, 1949); Cushing Strout, *The Pragmatic Revolt in American History: Carl Becker and Charles Beard* (New Haven, Conn.: Yale University Press, 1958); John Higham, *History: Professional Scholarship in America* (1965; reprint, Baltimore, Md.: Johns Hopkins University Press, 1983); David W. Noble, *Historians against History: The Frontier Thesis and the National Covenant in American Historical Writing since 1830* (Minneapolis: University of Minnesota Press, 1965); Charles Crowe, "The Emergence of Progressive History," *Journal of the History of Ideas* 27 (January–March, 1966): 109–24; Robert A. Skotheim, *American Intellectual Histories and Historians* (Princeton, N.J.: Princeton University Press, 1966); Richard Hofstadter, *The Progressive Historians: Turner, Beard, Parrington* (New York: Alfred A. Knopf, 1968).

From about 1980 on, assessments have been linked to the increasingly theory-conscious discussions on American history: Gene Wise, *American Historical Explanations: A Strategy for Grounded Inquiry,* 2d rev. ed. (Minneapolis: University of Minnesota Press, 1980); David W. Noble, *The End of American History: Democracy, Capitalism, and the Metaphor of Two Worlds in Anglo-American Historical Writing, 1880–1980* (Minneapolis: University of Minnesota Press, 1985); Peter Novick, *That Noble Dream: The "Objectivity Question" and the American Historical Profession* (New York: Cambridge University Press, 1988); and Dorothy Ross, *The Origins of American Social Science* (New York: Cambridge University Press, 1991).

A brief assessment can be found in Michael Kraus and Davis D. Joyce, *The Writing of American History,* rev. ed. (Norman: University of Oklahoma Press, 1985).

Publications on the Cultural Context of Progressive History

Of the few contemporary works, five are of special relevance: George B. Adams, "History and the Philosophy of History," *American Historical Review* 14 (January 1909): 221–36; Herbert B. Adams, "Special Methods of Historical Study" in *Methods of Teaching History,* by A. D. White et al., 2d ed. (Boston: Ginn, Heath and Co., 1885), 1:113–47; American Historical Association, Committee of Seven, "The Study of History in Schools," pp. 427–564 in *Annual Report of the American Historical Association for the Year 1898* (Washington D.C.: Government Printing Office, 1899); Karl Pearson, *The Grammar of Sci-*

ence (New York: Charles Scribner's Sons, 1892); Frederick J. Teggart, *Prolegomena to History: The Relation to Literature, Philosophy, Science* (Berkeley: University of California Press, 1916).

Of the more numerous retrospective works, the following are especially helpful: Richard J. Bernstein, *The Restructuring of Social and Political Theory* (New York: Harcourt, Brace, Jovanovich, 1976); Chester M. Destler, "Some Observations on Contemporary Historical Theory," *American Historical Review* 55 (April 1950): 503–29; David Glassberg, "History and the Public: Legacies of the Progressive Era," *Journal of American History* 73 (March 1987): 957–80; Eric F. Goldman, *Rendezvous with Destiny: A History of Modern American Reform* (New York: Alfred A. Knopf, 1952); David A. Hollinger, *In the American Province: Studies in the History and Historiography of Ideas* (Bloomington: Indiana University Press, 1985); James T. Kloppenberg, *Uncertain Victory: Social Democracy and Progressivism in European and American Thought, 1870–1920* (New York: Oxford University Press, 1986); Leo Marx, *The Machine in the Garden: Technology and the Pastoral Ideal in America* (New York: Oxford University Press, 1964); Jan Romein, *The Watershed of Two Eras: Europe in 1900*, trans. Arnold Pomerans (Middletown, Conn.: Wesleyan University Press, 1978).

Works Offering Access to French and German Developments

Assistance for further explorations of the links and parallels to French and German developments is offered by the following works.

ON BOTH DEVELOPMENTS: H. Stuart Hughes, *Consciousness and Society: The Reconstruction of European Social Thought, 1890–1930* (New York: Alfred A. Knopf, 1958); and Georg G. Iggers, *New Directions in European Historiography* (Middletown, Conn.: Wesleyan University Press, 1975).

ON FRENCH DEVELOPMENTS: Peter Burke, *The French Historical Revolution: The 'Annales' School 1929–89* (Stanford, Calif.: Stanford University Press, 1990); William R. Keylor, *Academy and Community: The Foundation of the French Historical Profession* (Cambridge, Mass.: Harvard University Press, 1975); Hans-Dieter Mann, *Lucien Febvre: La pensée vivante d'un historien* (Paris: Armand Colin, 1971); Traian Stoianovich, *French Historical Method: The 'Annales' Paradigm* (Ithaca, N.Y.: Cornell University Press, 1976).

ON GERMAN DEVELOPMENTS: Horst W. Blanke, *Historiographiegeschichte als Historik* (Stuttgart-Bad Cannstatt: Froomann-Holzboog, 1991); for access to Wilhelm Dilthey's thought see the publications by Ilse N. Bulhof, Michael Ermarth, Rudolf R. Makkreel, Theodore Plantinga, and H. P. Rickman; Georg G. Iggers, *The German Conception of History: The National Tradition of Historical Thought from Herder to the Present* (Middletown, Conn.: Wesleyan University Press, 1968); Fritz K. Ringer, *The Decline of the Mandarins: The German Academic Community, 1890–1933* (Cambridge, Mass.: Harvard University Press, 1969); Guenther Roth and Wolfgang Schluchter, *Max Weber's Vision of History: Ethics and Methods* (Berkeley and

Los Angeles: University of California Press, 1979); Luise Schorn-Schütte, *Karl Lamprecht: Kulturgeschichtsschreibung zwischen Wissenschaft und Politik* (Göttingen: Vandenhoeck and Ruprecht, 1984).

Selected Works with a General Relevance to Progressive History

Adler, Selig. *The Isolationist Impulse: Its Twentieth-Century Reaction.* New York: Abelard-Schuman, 1957.

Baker, Keith M. *Condorcet: From Natural Philosophy to Social Mathematics.* Chicago: Chicago University Press, 1975.

Bentley, Arthur F. *The Process of Government: A Study of Social Pressures.* Bloomington, Ind.: Principia Press, 1908.

Buell, Raymond, L. *Isolated America.* New York: Alfred A. Knopf, 1940.

Bury, John B. *The Idea of Progress: An Inquiry into Its Origin and Growth.* New York: Macmillan, 1932.

Chamberlain, John. *Farewell to Reform: Being a History of the Rise, Life, and Decay of the Progressive Mind in America.* New York: Liveright, 1932.

Cole, Charles W. "The Relativity of History." *Political Science Quarterly* 48 (June 1933): 161–71.

Croly, Herbert D. *The Promise of American Life.* New York: Macmillan, 1909.
———. *Progressive Democracy.* New York: Macmillan, 1914.

Crunden, Robert M. *Ministers of Reform: The Progressives' Achievement in American Civilization, 1890–1920.* New York: Basic Books, 1982.

Forcey, Charles. *The Crossroads of Liberalism: Croly, Weyl, Lippmann, and the Progressive Era, 1900–1925.* New York: Oxford University Press, 1961.

Goodnow, Frank J. *Social Reform and the Constitution.* New York: Macmillan, 1911.

Hofstadter, Richard. *The Age of Reform: From Bryan to F.D.R.* New York: Alfred A. Knopf, 1955.

Holt, W. Stull. *Historical Scholarship in the United States and Other Essays.* Seattle: University of Washington Press, 1967.

Jonas, Manfred. *Isolationism in America, 1935–1941.* Ithaca, N.Y.: Cornell University Press, 1966.

Lasch, Christopher. *American Liberals and the Russian Revolution.* New York: Columbia University Press, 1962.

Maeterlinck, Maurice. *The Measure of the Hours.* Trans. Alexander Teixeira de Mattos. New York: Dodd, Mead, 1907.

Mandelbaum, Maurice. *History, Man, & Reason: A Study in Nineteenth-Century Thought.* Baltimore, Md.: Johns Hopkins Press, 1971.

Minus, Paul M. *Walter Rauschenbusch: American Reformer.* New York: Macmillan, 1988.

Ross, Dorothy. "Historical Consciousness in Nineteenth-Century America." *American Historical Review* 89 (October 1984): 909–28.

Smith, David C. *H. G. Wells: Desparately Mortal: A Biography.* New Haven, Conn.: Yale University Press, 1986.

Trachtenberg, Alan. *The Incorporation of America: Culture and Society in the Gilded Age.* New York: Hill and Wang, 1982.

Wagar, W. Warren. *Good Tidings: The Belief in Progress from Darwin to Marcuse.* Bloomington: Indiana University Press, 1972.

Weinstein, James and David W. Eakins, eds. *For a New America: Essays in History and Politics from Studies on the Left, 1959–1967.* New York: Random House, 1970.

Index

Activism for reform, 45, 62–64, 68, 72–73, 124–25, 128–29, 132, 185; by Barnes, 122, 124, 125, 141–42, 197; by Beard, 37, 46, 63–64, 72, 76, 106, 124–26, 152, 171–72, 175, 200; and Beard's relativism, 171, 172, 174–76, 189; by Becker, 63, 64, 72, 101–2, 113, 133, 150, 187–88; by Parrington, 125, 128; by Robinson, 64, 72, 124–25, 128, 129, 132–33, 156; by Turner, 63

Acton, Sir John Emmerich Dahlberg, 34, 216n.7

Adams, Brooks, 9, 32–33; *The Law of Civilization and Decay,* 9

Adams, Charles Kendall, 215n.6

Adams, Georg Burton, 34, 52, 69

Adams, Henry, 7, 9, 10, 20, 57, 67, 110–11, 141

Adams, Herbert Baxter, 220n.4

Adams, John, 143

Allen, William Francis, 26, 218n.17, 220n.4

American Historical Association, 29, 36, 69; meetings of, 11, 20, 159; presidential addresses, 30, 126, 132, 154, 160, 171

American Nation Series, 19, 42

American Revolution, 98–99, 186, 193

American sense of history, defined, 3–4, 8–9; criticism of, 210, 215n.6, 238nn. 8, 9; future-centeredness of, 8–9; modernization of, 3, 4, 12–15, 18–19, 20, 23, 29, 31, 33, 36, 38, 43, 94, 181, 189–90, 198–99, 204; and Progressive history, 53, 85, 101, 120–23, 141, 150, 181, 198–99; and relativism, 179, 186, 211, 212; traditional form of, 8–9, 18, 19, 20, 28, 33, 44, 64–65, 106, 111, 132, 145, 150, 165, 176, 185; accent on uniqueness in, 49, 111, 199, 213–14; and Turner, 24, 25, 81, 83

American Social Science Association, 69

American Sociological Society, 69, 109, 224n.17

Annales d'histoire économique et sociale, 139

Annales school, 83, 123, 139, 156

Anthropology, 68, 133–34

Aristotle, 69, 70, 131

Bacon, Roger, 46, 125, 130

Bancroft, George, 7, 13, 17–18, 19, 57, 58, 67, 83, 96, 133

Barnes, Harry Elmer: and American policies, 197, 208n.15; on epistemology, 123, 127, 130, 131, 156; as historian, 2, 205, 228n.15; in journalism, 166, 229n.31, 233n.1; life, 122, 126–27, 197, 230n.1; and progress, 137, 149, 154; and psychology, 136–37, 138–39, 230n.15; and relativism, 127, 130, 161, 162, 165–66, 192, 233n.13; and social sciences, 130, 131, 133, 134; and war, 127, 155, 191, 192, 232n.3, 236n.4

—Works: *The Genesis of the World War,* 126; *A History of Historical Writing,* 205; *History and Social Intelligence,* 127; *History: Its Rise and Development,* 122; *New History and Social Studies,* 126; *Psychology and History,* 126; *Social History of the Western World,* 122; *The Twilight of Christianity,* 127, 143; *World Politics and the Expansion of Western Civilization,* 122. *See also under* Activism for reform; People

Beard, Charles Austin: and American civilization, 191, 198–99, 202, 206, 213; and American domestic policy and its primacy, 112, 189–90, 193–94, 198, 201; on epistemology, 55, 56, 132, 161, 170, 175, 200–201; and American foreign policy, 189–90, 202–3; as historian, 1, 2, 3, 37, 180; and ideologies, 148, 179, 189; and in-